Very Little . . . Almost Nothing

'A wonderfully lucid and readable account of the issues that, despite the modesty of Simon Critchley's title, are of infinite concern and urgency to thought today. His book deserves to be debated at length not only by those who have an interest in philosophy, but by everyone – whether their involvement is in literary criticism, literary theory, or simply in reading itself – who has a care for the possibilities and the demands of tomorrow.'

Leslie Hill, *University of Warwick*

This book is haunted by an image: that of death. If we are to understand where philosophy begins, we must understand the significance of death or finitude for philosophy. Beginning with a consideration of the first use of the concept of nihilism in philosophy, *Very Little . . . Almost Nothing* moves through the work of Nietzsche and Heidegger before considering Blanchot, Levinas, Cavell and Beckett. The contribution of these writers to the question of death or finitude is considered, which in turn allows us to view the relation between philosophy and literature anew.

The focus of the book is religious disappointment and the consequent problems this creates for meaning. The task of philosophical modernity may be a thinking through of the death of God, but as Simon Critchley argues, this leaves us with an atheistic philosophy which offers little comfort in the face of an uncertain world. The possibilities that literature has to offer are thus called upon not to restore meaning to life, but precisely by viewing the meaninglessness of life as an achievement, the achievement of the ordinary or the everyday.

Very Little . . . Almost Nothing opens up new means of understanding important contemporary issues such as the death of man, the end of history or the end of philosophy and will fascinate those interested in philosophy, literature and cultural theory.

Simon Critchley is Reader in Philosophy at the University of Essex. He is the author of *The Ethics of Deconstruction*, and co-editor of *Re-Reading Levinas, Deconstructive Subjectivities, Emmanuel Levinas: Basic Philosophical Writings* and *A Companion to Continental Philosophy*.

Warwick Studies in European Philosophy

Edited by Andrew Benjamin
Professor of Philosophy, University of Warwick

This series presents the best and most original work being done within the European philosophical tradition. The books included in the series seek not merely to reflect what is taking place within European philosophy, rather they will contribute to the growth and development of that plural tradition. Work written in the English language as well as translations into English are to be included, engaging the tradition at all levels – whether by introductions that show the contemporary philosophical force of certain works, or in collections that explore an important thinker or topic, as well as in significant contributions that call for their own critical evaluation.

Very Little . . . Almost Nothing

Death, Philosophy, Literature

Simon Critchley

London and New York

First published 1997
by Routledge
11 New Fetter Lane, London EC4P 4EE

Simultaneously published in the USA and Canada
by Routledge
29 West 35th Street, New York, NY 10001

Reprinted 2000

Routledge is an imprint of the Taylor & Francis Group

© 1997 Simon Critchley

Typeset in Perpetua by Routledge
Printed and bound in Great Britain by
TJ International Ltd, Padstow, Cornwall

British Library Cataloguing in Publication Data
A catalogue record for this book is available from the British Library

Library of Congress Cataloguing in Publication Data
Critchley, Simon, 1960–
Very little–almost nothing : death, philosophy, literature /
Simon Critchley.
p. cm. – (Warwick studies in European philosophy)
Includes bibliographical references and index.
1. Philosophy, Modern. 2. Literature, Modern–History and criticism.
3. Nihilism. 4. Death. I. Title. II. Series.
B791.C75 1997
149'.8–dc21
96–39076
CIP

ISBN 0–415–12821–8 (hbk)
ISBN 0–415–12822–6 (pbk)

In memory of William James Critchley
Born 10th February 1929
Died 28th December 1994

Contents

Contents

Abbreviations

AE   Emmanuel Levinas, *Autrement qu'être ou au-delà de l'essence* (Martinus Nijhoff, The Hague, 1974).

AF   Friedrich Schlegel, 'Athenäum Fragments' in *Philosophical Fragments*, trans. P. Firchow (University of Minnesota Press, Minneapolis, 1991), pp. 18–93.

AL   Philippe Lacoue-Labarthe and Jean-Luc Nancy, *L'absolu littéraire* (Seuil, Paris, 1978).

AST   Theodor Adorno, *Aesthetic Theory*, trans. C. Lenhardt (Routledge & Kegan Paul, London, 1984).

AT   Theodor Adorno, *Ästhetische Theorie, Gesammelte Schriften Bd. 7* (Suhrkamp, Frankfurt am Main, 1970).

BF   Friedrich Heinrich Jacobi, 'Brief an Fichte' in *Appelation an das Publikum. Dokumente zum Atheismusstreit Jena 1798/99* (Reclam, Leipzig, 1987), pp. 153–67.

CF   Friedrich Schlegel, 'Critical Fragments' in *Philosophical Fragments*, trans. P. Firchow (University of Minnesota Press, Minneapolis, 1991), pp. 1–16.

CP   Wallace Stevens, *Collected Poems* (Faber, London, 1955).

CPP   Emmanuel Levinas, *Collected Philosophical Papers*, trans. A. Lingis (Kluwer, Dordrecht, 1987).

CR   Stanley Cavell, *The Claim of Reason* (Oxford University Press, Oxford, 1979).

DEE   Emmanuel Levinas, *De l'existence à l'existent,* 3rd edition (Vrin, Paris, 1986).

DQVI   Emmanuel Levinas, *De Dieu qui vient à l'idée*, 2nd edition (Vrin, Paris, 1986).

ED   Maurice Blanchot, *L'écriture du désastre* (Gallimard, Paris, 1980).

EE   Emmanuel Levinas, *Existence and Existents*, trans. A. Lingis (Martinus Nijhoff, The Hague, 1978).

EeI   Emmanuel Levinas, *Ethique et infini* (Fayard/France Culture, Paris, 1982).

EI   Maurice Blanchot, *L'entretien infini* (Gallimard, Paris, 1969).

EL   Maurice Blanchot, *L'espace littéraire* (Gallimard, Paris, 1955 (Collection Idées, 1968)).

FP   Maurice Blanchot, *Faux pas* (Gallimard, Paris, 1943).

GO   Maurice Blanchot, *The Gaze of Orpheus*, ed. P. Adams Sitney, trans. Lydia Davis (Station Hill, New York, 1981).

HAH   Emmanuel Levinas, *Humanisme de l'autre homme* (Fata Morgana, Montpellier, 1972 (livre de poche edition)).

HO   Martin Heidegger, *Holzwege*, 6th edition (Klostermann, Frankfurt am Main, 1980).

IC   Maurice Blanchot, *The Infinite Conversation*, trans. Susan Hanson (University of Minnesota Press, Minneapolis, 1993).

ID   Friedrich Schlegel, 'Ideas' in *Philosophical Fragments*, trans. P. Firchow (University of Minnesota Press, Minneapolis, 1991), pp. 94–109.

IQO   Stanley Cavell, *In Quest of the Ordinary* (University of Chicago Press, Chicago, 1988).

KA   *Kritische Friedrich Schlegel Ausgabe*, Vol. II, ed. H. Eichner (Ferdinand Schöningh, Munich, 1967).

LA   Philippe Lacoue-Labarthe and Jean-Luc Nancy, *The Literary Absolute*, trans. P. Barnard and C. Lester (State University of New York Press, Albany, 1988).

LF   Friedrich Heinrich Jacobi, 'Open Letter to Fichte', trans. D. I. Behler in *Philosophy of German Idealism*, ed. E. Behler (Continuum, New York, 1987).

LV   Maurice Blanchot, *Le livre à venir* (Gallimard, Paris, 1959 (livre de poche edition)).

MWM   Stanley Cavell, *Must We Mean What We Say?* (Cambridge University Press, Cambridge, 1976).

NA   Wallace Stevens, *The Necessary Angel* (Faber, London, 1960).

ND   Theodor Adorno, *Negative Dialektik* (Suhrkamp, Frankfurt am Main, 1966).

NDS   Theodor Adorno, *Negative Dialectics*, trans. E. B. Ashton (Continuum, New York, 1973).

NL   Theodor Adorno, *Noten zur Literatur* (Suhrkamp Taschenbuch, Frankfurt am Main, 1981).

NTL   Theodor Adorno, *Notes to Literature*, Vol. 1, trans. S. Weber Nicholsen (Columbia University Press, New York, 1991).

NTL2   Theodor Adorno, *Notes to Literature*, Vol. 2, trans. S. W. Nicholsen (Columbia University Press, New York, 1992).

NYUA   Stanley Cavell, *This New Yet Unapproachable America* (Living Batch, Albuquerque, 1989).

OB   Emmanuel Levinas, *Otherwise than Being or Beyond Essence*, trans. A. Lingis (Martinus Nijhoff, The Hague, 1981).

PF   Maurice Blanchot, *La part du feu* (Gallimard, Paris, 1949).

QB   Martin Heidegger, *The Question of Being*, trans. W. Kluback and J.T. Wilde (Twayne, New York, 1958).

QT   Martin Heidegger, *The Question Concerning Technology*, trans. W. Lovitt (Garland, New York, 1977).

RP   Hilary Putnam, *Renewing Philosophy* (Harvard University Press, Cambridge MA, 1992).

SL   Maurice Blanchot, *The Space of Literature*, trans. Ann Smock (University of Nebraska Press, Lincoln, 1982).

T   *The Beckett Trilogy: Molloy, Malone Dies, The Unnameable* (Picador, London, 1979).

TA   Emmanuel Levinas, *Le temps et l'autre* (Presses Universitaires de France, Paris, 1989).

TeI   Emmanuel Levinas, *Totalité et infini* (Martinus Nijhoff, The Hague, 1961).

TI   Emmanuel Levinas, *Totality and Infinity*, trans. A. Lingis (Duquesne University Press, Pittsburgh, 1969).

TO   Emmanuel Levinas, *Time and the Other*, trans. R. Cohen (Duquesne University Press, Pittsburgh, 1987).

WE   Martin Heidegger, *Wegmarken*, 2nd edition (Klostermann, Frankfurt am Main, 1978).

WM   Friedrich Nietzsche, *Der Wille zur Macht* (Kröner, Leipzig, 1930).

WP   Friedrich Nietzsche, *The Will to Power*, trans. W. Kaufmann and R. J. Hollingdale (Vintage, New York, 1968).

Images by Shizuka Yokomizo

Preamble

Travels in Nihilon

Under a vast grey sky, on a vast and dusty plain without paths, without grass, without a nettle or a thistle, I met several men bent double as they walked.

Each one of them carried on his back an enormous Chimera as heavy as a sack of flour or coal or the paraphernalia of a Roman infantryman.

But the monstrous beast was no inanimate weight; on the contrary, it enveloped and oppressed the man with its elastic and powerful muscles; it clutched at the breast of its mount with two vast claws; and its fabulous head overhung the man's forehead like one of those horrible helmets with which ancient warriors hoped to add to the terror of their enemy.

I questioned one of these men and asked him where they were going like that. He replied that he did not know and that none of them knew, but that they were evidently going somewhere since they were driven by an invincible need to go on.

A curious thing to note: none of these travelers seemed irritated by the ferocious beast hanging around his neck and glued to his back; one might have said that they considered it part of themselves. All these tired and serious faces showed not the least sign of despair; under the spleenful dome of the sky, their feet deep in the dust of the earth as desolate as the sky, *they continued along with the resigned physiognomy of those who are condemned to hope forever* [SC's emphasis].

And the cortège passed by me and disappeared in the atmosphere of the horizon, where the rounded surface of the planet is concealed from the curiosity of the human gaze.

1

And for a few moments I persisted in trying to comprehend this mystery; but soon irresistible Indifference descended upon me and I was more heavily overwhelmed than they were by their crushing Chimeras.

(Baudelaire, 'Chacun sa chimère', *Le spleen de Paris*, Armand Colin, Paris, 1958: 10–11)

(a)
Philosophy begins in disappointment

Where does philosophy begin? It begins, I believe, in an experience of *disappointment*, that is both *religious* and *political*. That is to say, philosophy might be said to begin with two problems: (i) religious disappointment provokes the problem of *meaning*, namely, what is the meaning of life in the absence of religious belief?; and (ii) political disappointment provokes the problem of *justice*, namely, 'what is justice' and how might justice become effective in a violently unjust world? In most of my previous work, I have sought to address, more or less directly, the problem of political disappointment in terms of an ethical injunction that might at least permit one to face critically the experience of injustice and domination.[1] However, the focus of this book is religious disappointment, the problem of meaning, which will nonetheless continually broach ethical and political issues, but in a more oblique way.

Religious disappointment is born from the realization that religion is no longer (presuming it ever was) capable of providing a meaning for human life. The great metaphysical comfort of religion, its existential balm, surely resides in its claim that the meaning of human life lies outside of life and outside humanity and, even if this outside is beyond our limited cognitive powers, we can still turn our faith in this direction. For me, philosophizing begins from the recognition of the literal incredibility of this claim, that the possibility of a belief in God or some God-equivalent, whether vindicable through faith or reason, has decisively broken down.

Of course, the proper name for this breakdown is *modernity*, and the task of *philosophical* modernity, at least in its peak experiences – Hegel, Nietzsche, Heidegger – is a thinking through of the death of God in terms of the problem of finitude. Such a thinking through does not only entail the death of the God of the Judaeo–Christian tradition, but also the death of all those ideals, norms, principles, rules, ends and values that are set above humanity in order to provide human beings with a meaning to life. Such is the twilight of the idols. As

2

Heidegger notes in a striking remark from 1925, thinking of Nietzsche, 'Philosophical research is and remains atheism, which is why philosophy can allow itself "the arrogance of thinking" '.[2] Philosophy is nothing if not arrogant, and furthermore it *should* be arrogant, a continual arrogation of the human voice.[3] But the source of philosophical arrogance, its undoubted hubris, is a disappointment that flows from the dissolution of meaning, the frailty that accompanies the recognition of the all-too-human character of the human. So, in my view, philosophy – at least under modern conditions – is atheism, and to have an experience of faith would mean stopping doing philosophy. . . stopping immediately. . . right away.

If atheism produced contentment, then philosophy would be at an end. Contented atheists have no reason to bother themselves with philosophy, other than as a cultural distraction or a technical means of sharpening their common sense. However, in my view, atheism does not provide contentment, but rather unease. It is from this mood of unease that philosophy begins its anxious and aporetic dialectics, its tail-biting paradoxes, '*Not* to esteem what we know, and not to be *allowed* to esteem the lies we should like to tell ourselves' (WM 11/ WP 10). Those familiar with the landscape of philosophical modernity will recognize this situation as a description of the problem of nihilism, and it is to this problem that I would like to turn in detail as a way of framing the argument of the following lectures.

(b)
Pre-Nietzschean nihilism

What is nihilism? Although the pre-Nietzschean history of the concept of nihilism is an area of much contestation, the first *philosophical* employment of the concept occurs in Jacobi's 1799 'Letter to Fichte'.[4] For Jacobi, Fichtean idealism is nihilism. What he means by this must be understood with reference to the deflationary effects of the Kantian critique of metaphysics, which not only denies human beings cognitive access to the speculative objects of classical metaphysics (God and the soul), but also removes the possibility of knowing both things-in-themselves and the ground of the self. Jacobi's basic thesis is that Fichte's reworking of Kantian transcendental idealism leads to an impoverished egoism which has no knowledge of objects or subjects in themselves. It is nihilistic because it allows the existence of nothing outside or apart from the ego and the ego is itself nothing but a product of the 'free power of imagination'. Jacobi protests, in an extraordinary passage:

> If the highest upon which I can reflect, what I can contemplate, is my empty and pure, naked and mere ego, with its autonomy and freedom: then rational self-contemplation, then rationality is for me a curse – I deplore my existence.
>
> (BF 164/LF 135)

Against what he sees as the monism of Fichtean idealism, which he calls 'an inverted Spinozism' (recalling the Pantheist-debate with Herder in the 1780s), Jacobi argues for a form of philosophical dualism, or more precisely what he calls his 'Unphilosophie', where beyond the philosophical or scientific preoccupation with truth (*die Wahrheit*) lies the sphere of the true (*das Wahre*), which is only accessible to faith or the heart. In many respects, Jacobi's critique of Fichte is strongly reminiscent of Pascal's critique of Descartes, where nihilism is the accusation levelled by a Christian world-view at a secularizing rationalism. Thus, the existential choice that faces us, which cannot be rationally proven but upon which we must wager, is between Fichtean idealism, which is nihilism because it offers knowledge of nothing outside of the ego's projections, and Jacobian dualism, which he describes self-mockingly as 'chimerism' because it claims that God is the essence of reason without being able to demonstrate this rationally. Jacobi concludes:

> But the human being has such a choice, this single one: Nothingness or a God. Choosing Nothingness, he makes himself into a God; that is, he makes an apparition into God because if there is no God, it is impossible that man and everything which surrounds him is not merely an apparition.
>
> I repeat: God is, and is outside of me, a living being, existing in itself, or I am God. There is no third.
>
> (BF 168/LF 138)

If nihilism is the accusation of philosophical egoism, where all that was solid in the pre-Kantian world-view melts into air, then one finds a bizarre confirmation of Jacobi's critique in the egoism of Max Stirner's *The Ego and Its Own* (1844). What is denigrated by Jacobi as nihilism is celebrated by Stirner as liberation. If I am nothing, Stirner argues, then 'I am not nothing in the sense of emptiness, but I am the creative nothing (*schöpferische Nichts*), the nothing out of which I myself as creator create everything'.[5] As the perverse

4

consequence of his attempt to show that Hegel's and Feuerbach's critiques of religion are still fatally entangled with religious modes of thinking, Stirner answers the question 'What is man?' by transforming the ego into a replica of the *causa sui* conception of God. To anticipate Sartre, this is perhaps why man is a useless passion.[6]

One finds an echo of Jacobi's Pascalian logic in Dostoevsky's depiction of Kirilov the nihilist in *The Devils* (1871):

> Everyone who desires supreme freedom must dare to kill himself. He who dares to kill himself has learnt the secret of the deception. Beyond that there is no freedom; that's all, and beyond it there is nothing. He who dares to kill himself is a god. Now every one can make it so that there shall be no God and there shall be nothing. But no one has done so yet.[7]

Such is the position that Dostoevsky describes as 'logical suicide'. That is, as he puts it in his Diaries, once human beings have lifted themselves above the level of cattle, then the 'basic', 'loftiest' and most 'sublime' idea of human existence becomes absolutely essential: belief in the immortality of the soul.[8] Once this belief breaks down, as Dostoevsky saw in the nihilism or indifferentism of the Russian educated classes of the 1860s, then suicide is the only logical conclusion. Hence, Kirilov who has lost belief in the immortality of the soul is trying to write a book investigating the reasons why people do not kill themselves.

Staying with the Russian context of what Nietzsche called 'nihilism à la Petersburg',[9] what distinguishes it from the German context is that in the latter nihilism is largely a metaphysical or epistemological issue, whereas in the former it has a more obviously socio-political range of meanings. Beginning with Chernyshevsky's attempt to 'nihilize' traditional aesthetic values by arguing that art is not the expression of some absolute conception of beauty but rather represents the interests of a certain class at a certain point in history, one could construct a trajectory of Russian nihilism that would include Bakunin's anarchistic critique of the state, Nechaev's Jacobinism and foreshadow Lenin's Promethean Bolshevism.[10]

In this sense, *nigilizm* is the expression of a radically sceptical, anti-aesthetic, utilitarian, and scientific world-view. Such a view is subjected to a genteel but devastating liberal critique in Turgenev's *Fathers and Sons* through the fate of the composite nihilist figure of Bazarov. The central dramatic conflict here is between two opposed world-views: the romanticism, liberalism, reformism and Europhilia of the fathers (Nickolai and Pavel) and the positivism, utilitarianism, radicalism and Russian nationalism of the sons (Arkady and Bazarov). In the central scene of the novel, amid vague intimations of nihilism as a force of violent insurrection, Bazarov sneers:

> 'We base our conduct on what we recognize as useful . . . In these days the most useful thing we can do is to repudiate – and so we repudiate.'
> 'Everything?'
> 'Everything.'
> 'What? Not only art, poetry . . . but also . . . I am afraid to say it . . .'
> 'Everything', Bazarov repeated with indescribable composure.[11]

The dramatic conflict between liberalism and nihilism is classically, if unconvincingly, resolved by Turgenev, where, after falling powerfully, irrationally and unrequitedly in love with Madame Odintsov – both an aristocrat and a romantic – Bazarov returns home to life as a country doctor like his father. In what amounts to an act of (logical) suicide, Bazarov contracts typhoid from the infected corpse of a peasant and confesses his love for Madame Odintsov on his deathbed. Thus, nihilism is overcome through the power of love and the novel ends with a Christian *apologia* for 'everlasting reconciliation and of life which has no end'.[12]

In its pre-Nietzschean phase and across these different contexts, we can perhaps already note a peculiar internal dialectic of nihilism. The Kantian critique of metaphysical dogmatism, a limitation of cognition that was intended to produce epistemological certainty and make room for the primacy of practical reason, seems instead to give rise to a Promethean egoism allied to positivism and moral indifferentism where the only criterion of social and political life is utility. This is why Bazarov can at once view himself as a Stirneresque egoist, a utilitarian in ethics and politics, a positivist in science and a philistine in art. Thus, there would seem to be some secret path from the 'nihilism' of the Kantian critique of metaphysics to the universalistic deployment of what Adorno and Horkheimer would call instrumental rationality. Such is perhaps the path from enlightenment to ideology.

(c)
Nietzschean nihilism

However, under the influence of Turgenev (read in French translation), Prosper Mérimée and Paul Bourget, nihilism receives its full philosophical statement and definitive articulation in Nietzsche's posthumously assembled miscellany *The Will to Power*. [13] For Nietzsche, nihilism means

> That the highest values devalue themselves [*dass die obersten Werte sich entwerten*]. The aim is lacking; 'why' finds no answer.
>
> (WM 10/WP 9)

Nihilism is the breakdown of the order of meaning, where all that was posited as a transcendent source of value becomes null and void, where there are no skyhooks upon which to hang a meaning for life. All transcendent claims for a meaning to life have been reduced to mere values and those values have become incredible, standing in need of what Nietzsche calls 'transvaluation' or 'revaluation'.

Beyond any influence exerted from the Russian and German contexts, what must be emphasized is the sheer audacity and originality of Nietzsche's concept of nihilism. For Nietzsche, the cause of nihilism cannot be explained socially, politically, epistemologically, or even physiologically (i.e. decline of the species), but is rather rooted in a specific interpretation of the world: *Christianity*. For Nietzsche, the 'Christian–Moral' interpretation of the world had the distinct advantage of being an antidote to nihilism by granting the world meaning, granting human beings value, and preventing despair (WM 10–11/WP 9–10). However, for Nietzsche – and this is decisive – there is an antinomy or antagonism within nihilism, namely that the Christian–Moral interpretation of the world is driven by a will to truthfulness, but that this very will to truth eventually turns against the Christian interpretation of the world by finding it untrue. That is to say, Christian metaphysics turns on the belief in a true world that is opposed to the false world of becoming that we inhabit here below. However, with the consciousness of the death of God, the true world is revealed to be a fable. Thus, and this is the antinomy, the will for a moral interpretation or valuation of the world now appears to be a will to untruth. Christianity, like ancient tragedy, does not so much die as commit suicide. [14] And yet – here's the rub – a belief in a world of truth is required simply in order to live because we cannot *endure* this world of becoming. Nietzsche writes:

> But as soon as man finds out how that world [of truth, SC] is fabricated solely from psychological needs, and how he has absolutely no right to it, the last form of nihilism comes into being: it includes disbelief in any metaphysical world and forbids itself any belief in a *true* world. Having

7

reached this standpoint, one grants the reality of becoming as the *only* reality, forbids oneself every kind of clandestine access to afterworlds and false divinities – but *cannot endure this world though one does not want to deny it.*

(WM 14–15/WP 13)

This explains the central antagonism of nihilism for Nietzsche, cited above, namely that we are not to esteem what we know, and we are not allowed to esteem the lies we should like to tell ourselves. We can no longer believe in a world of truth beyond this world of becoming and yet we cannot endure this world of becoming. Or, to put this in terms that recall Jacobi's critique of Fichte, 'everything egoistic has come to disgust us (even though we realize the impossibility of the unegoistic); what is necessary has come to disgust us' (WM 12/WP 11). This vicious antagonism results in what Nietzsche calls 'a process of dissolution'(WM 11/WP 10), namely that when we realize the shabby origin of our moral values and how the Christian–Moral interpretation of the world is driven by a will to untruth, our *reactive* response is to declare that existence is meaningless. It is this declaration of meaninglessness that Nietzsche identifies as nihilism and which he detects in various nascent forms: (i) Schopenhauerian pessimism or 'passive nihilism', that Nietzsche often identifies as European Buddhism; (ii) Russian anarchism or 'active nihilism', which is merely the 'expression of physiological decadence' (WM 30/WP 24); (iii) a general cultural mood of weariness, exhaustion and fatigue summarized in the memorable formula, 'Modern society. . . no longer has the strength to *excrete*' (WM 39/WP 32). The essential point to grasp here, against the entire pre-Nietzschean history sketched above, is that nihilism is not simply the negation of the Christian–Moral interpretation of the world, but is the *consequence* of that interpretation; that is to say, it is the consequence of moral valuation.

For Nietzsche, nihilism as a psychological state is attained when we realize that the categories by means of which we had tried to give meaning to the universe are meaningless. This does not at all mean that the universe is meaningless, but rather that 'the faith in the categories of reason is the cause of nihilism' (WM 15/WP 13). We therefore require new categories and new values that will permit us to endure the world of becoming. As I see it, this is the function of the seemingly enigmatic doctrine of eternal return, namely 'existence as it is, without meaning or aim, yet recurring inevitably without any finale of nothingness' (WM 44/WP 35). Nietzsche emphasizes that what is

8

being attempted with the thought of eternal return is an antithesis to pantheism; that is, if pantheism is the presence of God in all things, then eternal return is the attempt to think the universe consistently without God (WM 44/WP 36). What might this mean? Perhaps the following: recalling the theme of endurance discussed above, namely the knowledge that there is nothing beyond this world of becoming and the inability to endure this world, we might link this to a later fragment from *The Will to Power* where Nietzsche/Zarathustra speaks of the type of his disciples:

> To those human beings who are of any concern to me I wish suffering, desolation, sickness, ill-treatment, indignities – I wish that they should not remain unfamiliar with profound self-contempt, the torture of self-mistrust, the wretchedness of the vanquished: I have no pity for them, because I wish them the only thing that can prove today whether one is worth anything or not – *that one endures* [SC's emphasis].
>
> (WM 613/WP 481)

Might not the doctrine of eternal return be approached simply as that thought which enables one to endure the world of becoming without resenting it or seeking to construct some hinter-world? As I see it, and for reasons that will hopefully become obvious, this does not so much entail an overcoming of nihilism as an overcoming of the desire to overcome.

(d)
Responding to nihilism: five possibilities

To speak at a level of undoubted historical banality, we might say that modernity can be defined as a process of secularization or humanization which is post-religious or post-traditional, and where processes of societal and cultural rationalization and economic capitalization lead to an irreversible breakdown of traditional practices and the fragile web of the life-world. However, although modernity may be post-religious, it is not post-metaphysical, and it is witness to a series of attempts to secure a non-theological metaphysical basis for human activity through what Nietzsche calls '*the big words*' (WM 61/WP 50). That is to say, for example, the positing of a transcendent reason, the declaration of the libertarian and egalitarian values of republicanism, the codification of human rights, the belief in human happiness and its calculability, in social justice, in revolutionary love, or even a vision of positive annihilation.

9

The historical pathology of which nihilism is the diagnosis consists in the recognition of a double failure:

i   That the values of modernity or Enlightenment do not connect with the fabric of moral and social relations, with the stuff of everyday life, failing to produce a new mythic or rational totality, what the authors of the 'Earliest System-programme of German Idealism' in 1796 referred to as the need for a *mythology of reason*. The moral values of Enlightenment, and this is the core of Hegel's critique of Kant which is inherited by the young Marx (where Enlightenment values become bourgeois values), lack any effectivity, any connection to social praxis.

ii However, not only do the moral values of Enlightenment fail to connect with the fabric of moral and social relations, but – worse still – they lead instead to the progressive degradation of those relations through processes that we might call, with Weber, rationalization, with Marx, capitalization, with Adorno and Horkheimer, instrumental rationality, and with Heidegger, the oblivion of Being. Such is Enlightenment's fateful and paradoxical dialectic.

Thus, the problem of philosophical modernity, on this crude thumbnail sketch, is how to confront the problem of nihilism after one has seen how the values of Enlightenment not only fail to get a grip on everyday life, but lead instead to its progressive dissolution. Of course, the further difficulty here is that such a confrontation with nihilism cannot simply take place in philosophy, if it is granted – as it is by Nietzsche, Heidegger and Adorno in quite different registers – that philosophy has conspired with the very forces that produce nihilism. Philosophy is nihilistic: it is shot through, for Nietzsche, with the Christian–Moral interpretation of the world, for Heidegger, it wants to know nothing of the nothing at the heart of its principle of sufficient reason (*nihil est sine ratione*), and for Adorno, it is an ideological discourse of abstraction that conspires with the abstraction of reified, commodified society.

How, then, does one respond to nihilism? As I see it, four initial possibilities present themselves:

i   First, one can refuse to see the problem of nihilism at all and continue as a pre-nihilist metaphysician which may – if one has read some Kierkegaard – or may not have been forged in some dialogue with philosophical modernity. Such is the temptation of both religious fundamentalism – Christian, Judaic, Islamic, or whatever – and anti-metaphysical quietism that wants to delineate the limits of philosophy in order to clear a space of non-cognitive religious awaiting.[15]

ii Second, one can claim not to be bothered one way or the other, to have no metaphysical commitments and not to be concerned by not having them. This – very English – form of agnostic, hateful cheerfulness would refuse to see the problem of nihilism as an actual problem, but simply as a symptom of the malaise of the nineteenth-century central European liberal bourgeoisie. A more sophisticated analogue to this position would simply claim that the philosophy of history presupposed by nihilism gives a false and overly pessimistic picture of the modern world.

iii Third, one can react passively to nihilism, accepting it as a diagnosis of modernity, knowing the world to be absurd, but also knowing that nothing one can do will change matters: *don't worry, be happy*. Such an experience of spiritual recession and decline – what might be called 'Oblomovism' – is, as Raoul Vaneigem rightly points out, 'merely an overture to conformism'.[16]

iv Fourth, there is active nihilism, a violent force of destruction that Nietzsche associates with Russian anarchism and which imagines itself as the propaedeutic to a revolution of everyday life. Such a longing for total revolution can take many guises: the romantic and neo-romantic transformation of modernity through the production of a great work of art, Marxist revolution, fascist revolution, Ernst Jünger's total mobilization, apocalyptic Heideggerianism (there are other Heideggerianisms), the neo-Nietzschean obliteration of 'Man', or that unsubtle blend of Fichtean spontaneity and Fourieresque utopianism that one finds in the Situationist International and its various progeny: terrorism, angry brigades, punk and libidino-cyber revolution. This version of active nihilism is best expressed in Vaneigem's slogan: 'creativity plus a machine gun is an unstoppable combination'.[17]

The difficulty here is that if one rejects the first three responses to nihilism as either (i) refusing the problem through a return to religion, (ii) rejecting nihilism as a pseudo-problem with a fallacious philosophy of history, or (iii) failing to respond to the problem in passive acceptance, then the fourth response simply appears implausible (albeit wonderfully so). In our somewhat chastening contemporary circumstances, what I analyse in these lectures as our *dürtiger Zeit* (time of dearth), what might be referred to as the epoch of 'hurrah capitalism', I find the prospect of a revolution of everyday life or the achievement of theory in revolutionary praxis a little unlikely. Of course, such a revolution would also be

11

socially and politically disastrous for reasons I detail in Lecture 2 through a discussion of Hegel's and Carl Schmitt's critiques of romanticism. Paradoxically, there is something too *reactive* in Nietzsche's sense about the very activity of active nihilism, it is too negatively obsessed with what it seeks to oppose and risks failing to comprehend the phenomenon of nihilism in its manic desire to overcome it.

In this connection, and in order to consolidate a critique of active nihilism that does not passively fail to respond to the problem, I would like to try and delineate a *fifth* response to nihilism, that borrows heavily from the work of Heidegger and Adorno. With this fifth response, it is not a question of overcoming nihilism in an act of the will or joyful destruction, because such an act would only imprison us all the more firmly in the very nihilistic logic we are trying to leave behind. Rather than overcoming nihilism, it is a question of *delineating* it. What will be at stake is a liminal experience, a deconstructive experience of the limit – deconstruction *as* an experience of the limit – that separates the inside from the outside of nihilism and which forbids us both the gesture of transgression and restoration. On such a view, neither philosophy, nor art, nor politics alone can be relied upon to redeem the world, but the task of thinking consists in a historical confrontation with nihilism that does not give up on the *demand* that things might be otherwise. As we will see, such is the essential, but essentially disappointing, logic of redemption.

So, the question to which these lectures will be a minor contribution is the following: given the aporiae into which the problem of nihilism and its overcoming seems driven, what might count as a response to nihilism, given the pervasiveness of the experience of disappointment? What form(s) of imaginative resistance is (are) still possible, both philosophically, aesthetically and politically? Once one has accepted the disappointment that, in Adorno's words, 'philosophy... lives on because the moment to realize it was missed' (ND 13/NDS 3) – in 1848, 1871, 1917, or whenever – then how does one refuse the passive nihilist diagnosis of the end of philosophy one finds, say, in Rorty, where philosophy is reduced to the status of a private activity concerned with the cultivation of one's autonomy – should one be so disposed – but which has no public function? To put the question even more boldly, I am trying to formulate a response to the question: *How does one go on?* That is, how does one continue in thought?

12

(e)
Heidegger's transformation of Nietzschean nihilism

In order to understand the concept of nihilism in Heidegger, it is necessary to show how it arises in his long meditation on Nietzsche. Although Heidegger develops his interpretation of Nietzsche in a series of lecture courses given between 1936 and 1940, for brevity's sake I will look at his 1943 text, 'The Word of Nietzsche: "God is Dead" '. Although this text betrays a rigidity of reading and a hermeneutic violence that only emerges in the course of the Nietzsche Lectures, it offers an effective and brilliant *précis* of Heidegger's Nietzsche interpretation (HO 205–63/QT 53–112).[18]

How, then, does Heidegger understand Nietzsche's words 'God is Dead'? A number of steps in Heidegger's argument can be delineated:

1 Heidegger understands God metaphysically as the name for the supersensory realm of ideas and ideals, the 'true world' of Platonism.
2 Heidegger understands Nietzsche to have divested metaphysics of its essential possibility by showing how the supersensory world of metaphysics is a product of the sensory world; the true world has become a fable. Metaphysically understood, the declaration of the death of God is the acknowledgement that the supersensory no longer has any effective power.
3 If metaphysics is Platonism and Nietzsche understands his own thinking as the overturning of Platonism, then Nietzsche's thinking is a counter-movement to metaphysics.
4 However, and this is the core of Heidegger's critique of Nietzsche, this counter-movement to metaphysics is held fast to the essence of that which it opposes. According to Heidegger, Nietzsche believes that the overturning (*Umkehrung*) of Platonism is an overcoming (*Überwindung*) of metaphysics. However, every overturning of this kind is but a self-deluding entanglement within the logic of that which it opposes, and therefore the Nietzschean *Umkehrung* is simply a *Verkehrung*, a reversal. Thus, Nietzsche's thought remains internal to the very Platonist, metaphysical logic it seeks to oppose.
5 Thus, Nietzsche's thinking is a metaphysics. Heidegger writes:

Despite all his overturnings and revaluings of metaphysics, Nietzsche remains in the unbroken line of the metaphysical tradition when he calls

13

that which is established and made fast in the will to power for its own preservation purely and simply Being, or what is in being, or truth.

In his determination of the will to power as the Being of all beings, as that in which all entities participate, Nietzsche rejoins the metaphysical tradition, even if his work represents the final phase of that tradition.

(HO 235/QT 84)

The telling consequence of this argumentation is that if Nietzsche's thinking is grounded in the metaphysics of the will to power, then his interpretation of both nihilism and the counter-movement to nihilism (the devaluing and revaluing of values) is metaphysical. Although Heidegger acknowledges that, for Nietzsche, nihilism is ambiguous insofar as it is both negative (devaluing) and positive (revaluing), his essential claim is that *both the diagnosis of nihilism and the attempted overcoming of nihilism through the revaluation of values remain positions internal to metaphysics.* Towards the end of the essay, Heidegger asks:

What *is* now, in the age when the unconditional dominion of the will to power is openly dawning, and this openness and its public character are themselves becoming a function of this will?

(HO 253/QT 102)

Although the meditation on Nietzsche is inseparable from Heidegger's thinking of technology and his pathology of the modern world in terms of the unconditional dominion of the will-to-will and the devastation of the earth, the essential philosophical point here is that insofar as Nietzsche determines Being as will to power, he does not think Being (or the question of Being) as such, and thus the attempted overcoming of nihilism which considers itself an overturning of metaphysics remains metaphysical and nihilistic. Hence, the supposed overcoming (*Überwindung*) of metaphysics is merely its completion or fulfilment (*Vollendung*), and Nietzsche is the thinker who begins the final phase of metaphysics, a phase which, as Heidegger suggests in his more bleakly prophetic moments, might last longer than the previous history of metaphysics.[19]

Thus, on Heidegger's interpretation, Nietzsche's thinking remains in the oblivion of Being. But is this only true of Nietzsche's thinking? Not at all. Heidegger's more general historico-philosophical thesis is that '*Nowhere do we find such experiencing of Being itself*', not even amongst the pre-Socratics (HO 259/QT 108). The history of Being begins with the nihilation of Being, and metaphysics wants to know nothing of this nihilation, this nothing. For

14

Heidegger, then, the essence of nihilism lies in history, in the manner in which Being has fallen into nothing. However, if the hypothesis that the essence of nihilism lies in history can be sustained, then this enables Heidegger to draw a vast consequence. He writes, with a typical totalization of metaphysical categories downloaded directly into history:

> If the essence of nihilism lies in history... then metaphysics as the history of the truth of beings as such is, in its essence, nihilism. If, finally, metaphysics is the historical ground of the world history that is being determined by Europe and the West, then that world history is, in an entirely different sense, nihilistic.
>
> (HO 260/QT 109)

Thus, for Heidegger, nihilism thought in its essence is a history that runs its course with the history of Being, and this history is determinative for world history thought in terms of the planetary domination by technology. Nihilism is not only a history, it is a destiny.

(f)
Heidegger *contra* Jünger

However, if we now have a reasonably clear view of Heidegger's concept of nihilism, then what is much less clear is the precise nature of his *response* to nihilism. I think this response emerges most powerfully in Heidegger's 1955 contribution to a *Festschrift* for Ernst Jünger, 'Über "Die Linie" '.[20]

Let me try and briefly sketch the general structure of Heidegger's argumentation. In what appears to be an attempt to disguise a basic philosophical disagreement, Heidegger very politely chides and qualifies Jünger's active nihilism by making a distinction between the Nietzschean position of trying to think how to cross the line (*trans lineam*) separating nihilism from its overcoming, and suggests in its place a discussion (*de linea*), where it is not so much a question of overcoming as *delineating* nihilism. Teasing out the connotative differences in his and Jünger's titles, Heidegger distinguishes between *über* as *trans* or *meta* to describe Jünger's attempt to transcend nihilism, and *über* as *de* or *peri* which treats the line as such. For Heidegger, in a characteristic move, it is a question of thinking the essence of nihilism, which is nothing necessarily nihilistic (in fact, it is the opposite) and which is equiprimordial with thinking the essence of metaphysics. A thinking of the

15

essence of nihilism will lead us into the thinking of Being as that unthought ground of all metaphysical thinking. Thus, the question of an overcoming of nihilism must always be linked to a reappropriation of nihilism in its essence as the unthought essence of metaphysics, 'Worin beruht dann die Überwindung der Nihilismus? In der Verwindung der Metaphysik' (WE 408/QB 87).

Any discussion *de linea* of the essence of nihilism in terms of the forgetting of Being cannot hope to leave nihilism or metaphysics behind in an act of wilful overcoming. As we have already seen in Heidegger's reading of Nietzsche, this would be a reactive gesture of reversal that would leave us trapped within the very logic from which we are trying to twist free and behind which stands an uninterrogated metaphysics of the will. For Heidegger, any desire for a simple overcoming of nihilism must meditate the essence of nihilism, and with such a meditation the will to overcome becomes untenable (*'das Überwindenwollen hinfällig wird'* – WE 418/QB 105–7). For Heidegger, Jünger's aspiration to cross the line and overcome nihilism belongs to the domain of the forgetting of Being. This is why Jünger employs metaphysical concepts like *Gestalt*, *Wert* and *Transzendenz* (WE 415/QB 101).

This point can be made more strongly by considering the problematic of language that runs like a red thread through Heidegger's essay on Jünger. Heidegger asks: How can nihilism be overcome if our language remains the same, that is, remains the same metaphysical language of nihilism? Might not the very language of metaphysics be the barrier to any crossing of the line and hence the obstacle to any overcoming of nihilism? For Heidegger, a thinking of the essence of nihilism in non-metaphysical terms demands a transformation of language (*Verwandlung des Sagens*). Although it is not quite clear in what this transformation would consist, it clearly implies a dissatisfaction with propositional language and an attempt to articulate a pre-propositional vocabulary of basic words (*Grundworte* – WE 396/QB 67) that constitutes, as Heidegger already announced in *Being and Time*, 'the ultimate business of philosophy'.[21] However, as Heidegger was only too painfully aware, the language of his text on Jünger and his other texts remains propositional, and is therefore condemned to betray that which it was intended to express: *traduttore, traditore*. This betrayal extends to the very word *Sein* and Heidegger writes, 'A thoughtful forward glance into the realm of "Being" can only be written in the following way: ~~Being~~' (WE 404–5/QB 81). What this crossing out suggests is that, *contra* Jünger, the line separating nihilism from its overcoming is not something to be crossed, but rather the line should be

16

meditated in this crossing out, an attempt to render Being invisible that simply makes it more visible. Of course, what is being anticipated here is the logic of the *sous rature*, which Derrida initially formulates with explicit reference to Heidegger's text on Jünger.[22] For Derrida, the fact that Heidegger writes Being under erasure testifies to the fact that it is not simply a transcendental signified, but rather 'under its strokes the presence of a transcendental signified is effaced while still remaining legible'. This explains why, despite Heidegger's undoubted political and hermeneutic myopia, Derrida's meditation on the trace 'must therefore *go by way of* the question of being as it is directed by Heidegger and by him alone'.

Thus, in lieu of any attempt to cross the line and overcome nihilism in a Promethean act of will, an act that would only imprison us all the more securely in the very nihilistic logic we are trying to leave behind, Heidegger suggests a much more minimal task, which he describes with great caution, using his customary metaphorics:

> Thinking and poeticizing must in a certain way go back to where they have always already been and at the same time have still never built. However, we can only prepare such a dwelling in that place through building. Such a building may scarcely have in mind the erection of the house for the God or the dwelling places for the mortals. It must be content to build the *Way* that leads back into the place of the *Verwindung* of metaphysics and which in this way lets us wander through the destinal character of an overcoming of metaphysics.
>
> (WE 417/QB 103–5)

What is envisaged by Heidegger, as I see it, is a *delineation* of nihilism, a deconstructive experience of the line or limit that separates the inside from the outside of nihilism and which forbids us both the gesture of transgression and restoration. Such a *way* has in mind neither the building of the house of God, nor the erection of monuments to the false gods of active nihilism. In the final lines of the text on Jünger, Heidegger returns once more to the question of the essence of nihilism:

> The question has not become any easier for us. That's why it must limit itself to the preparatory: to reflect on old, venerable words, whose saying promises us the essential realm of nihilism and its *Verwindung*.
>
> (WE 419/QB 107–9)

17

He then adds, untranslatably:

Gibt es eine bemühtere Rettung des uns Geschickten und in Geschick Überlieferten als solches Andenken?

That is to say, is it only in a commemorative thinking of that which is destined to us and destinally handed down historically that the redemption we have striven for might take place? But what sort of redemption is implied here? If nihilism is not to be overcome but delineated, then how might one even speak of redemption? It is with these questions in mind that I would like to turn to Adorno.

(g)
Impossible redemption: Adorno on nihilism

In the much quoted and much misunderstood *finale* to *Minima Moralia*, Adorno writes:

The only philosophy which can be responsibly practised in face of despair is the attempt to contemplate all things as they would present themselves from the standpoint of redemption.[23]

After Auschwitz, philosophy must attempt (and the word *Versuch* should be emphasized here) to view things from the standpoint of redemption (*Erlösung* not *Rettung*). In this attempt, Adorno goes on, perspectives must be fashioned that reveal the world as it will appear in the messianic light, as needy and deformed, 'as indigent and distorted' (*'bedürftig und entstellt'*). The task of thought is to gain such messianic perspectives entirely from 'felt contact with objects', and to achieve this contact without capriciousness or violence.

So far, so good. However, Adorno then goes on to add two contradictory qualifications to this description of philosophy: 'It is the *simplest* of all things . . . but it is also the utterly *impossible* thing' (SC's emphasis). It is simple because, according to Adorno's broader social analysis, the historical situation out of which philosophy arises demands that we look at things from a messianic standpoint. Moreover, 'consummate negativity (*vollendete Negativität*), once squarely faced, delineates the mirror-image of its opposite'. That is to say, the sheer negativity of Adornian dialectic expresses its reflection of consummate positivity by refusing it direct expression. However simple philosophy might be, it is also impossible because it implies a redemptive standpoint, 'removed, even

18

though by a hair's breadth, from the scope of existence'. Why is this impossible? I take it that Adorno is making a simple logical point here – namely, that if philosophical knowledge is to be possible there has to be a correspondence between concepts and intuitions, otherwise it is either blind or empty. Thus, 'any possible knowledge must . . . be wrested from what is, if it shall hold good'. However, the problem here is that if the condition of possibility for philosophy is correspondence to that which is, then philosophy is always already going to be contaminated by the very 'distortion and indigence' of the world that the messianic perspective is seeking to escape. This is why Adorno writes:

> The more passionately thought denies its conditionality for the sake of the unconditional, the more unconsciously, and so calamitously, it is delivered up to the world.

There would seem to be only one possible conclusion to draw from Adorno's argumentation: if the only philosophy that can be responsibly practised is to contemplate things from the standpoint of redemption, then this standpoint is impossible and therefore philosophy cannot be responsibly practised. Yet, Adorno invites us to take one further step:

> Even its own impossibility it must at last comprehend for the sake of the possible. But beside the demand thus placed on thought, the question of the reality or unreality of redemption itself hardly matters.

Despite the strict impossibility of practising philosophy from the standpoint of redemption, what is essential for Adorno is the *demand* (*Forderung*) placed on thinking by imagining itself capable of assuming that standpoint. This is why the reality or unreality of redemption hardly matters. What is important is the messianic demand and not whether this demand is underwritten by some guarantee of redemption. I think this is why the impossibility of the redemptive standpoint must be comprehended 'for the sake of the possible'. In its very impossibility, the demand leaves open the horizon of the possible understood, I think, as the realm of future *action*.

But perhaps one can detect an even deeper logic at work in this passage. It might be asked: what if it *were* indeed possible to practise philosophy from the standpoint of redemption? What if we *could* fashion messianic perspectives entirely from felt contact with objects? What if we *had* some guarantee of salvation? I take it that even if the standpoint of redemption were possible, it would have to be refused because, at this historical point (I will come back to this), it would offer a false image of reconciliation. Even if redemption were possible, it would have to be denied in the name of a higher impossibility which takes place for the sake of the possible. As I see it, such a position is not a recipe for resignation and despair, but a preparation for action in the world, however minimal.

But what has this got to do with nihilism? Adorno is clearly suspicious of the entire post-Nietzschean problematic of nihilism because of its complicity with the reactionary modernism of Spengler, Jünger and the early Heidegger, and their anti-Marxist tendency to download metaphysical categories directly into social analysis. As such, nihilism is a key concept in 'the jargon of authenticity'. This jargon or 'German ideology' gives an ontological analysis of phenomena that would be better analysed in sociological and economic terms. Nonetheless, there is a powerful response to nihilism in Adorno, and it is at least arguable to view his work as a Marxist or, more properly, Weberian reworking of the problem of meaning.[24] This response emerges most clearly in a few pages from the final chapter of *Negative Dialectics*, 'Meditations on Metaphysics' (ND 367–72/NDS 376–81).[25]

After Auschwitz, the Kantian epistemological question 'How is metaphysics possible?' yields to a historical question 'Is it still possible to have a metaphysical experience?' (ND 362–63/NDS 372). For Adorno, this is because actual events – the Holocaust – have shattered the basis upon which metaphysical speculation might be reconciled with experience. He writes, in what might have been a motto for these lectures, 'Enlightenment leaves practically nothing of the metaphysical content of truth – *presque rien*' (ND 397/NDS 407). In this sense, metaphysics is only possible as what Adorno calls 'micrology', as a 'legible constellation of beings' (*'lesbare Konstellation von Seiendem'*). Only with this practice of micrology, this restless movement of dialectical analysis, does thinking find a haven from totality and a glimmer of hope, 'only for the sake of the hopeless are we given hope'.[26]

For Adorno, the categories of metaphysics live on in a secularized and vulgar form in the question of the meaning of life, the very question that propels the problem of nihilism and which he considers largely meaningless. If one has to ask the question of the meaning of life, then one has somehow missed the point. Adorno suspects that philosophy does not want to give up on the concept of nihilism, because it provides it with a straw man of meaninglessness that can easily be knocked down so that meaning can be restored. For good Hegelian reasons, the statement that 'everything is Nothing' is as meaningless as the concept of Being, and 'Faith in Nothing would be as insipid as would faith in Being' (ND 370/NDS 379). However, Adorno rightly suspects that the cultural indignation at nihilism is not a worry about some quasi-Buddhistic affirmation of the void, but is rather a concern about alleged moral decline and the refusal of the positivity and 'universal good cheer' of the Western heritage. In this regard, Adorno criticizes two features of what he calls 'the same subaltern language sphere': firstly, the talk about *Wertnihilismus* that desires a restoration of a Christian–Moral interpretation of the world; and secondly, the neo-Nietzschean talk of an *Überwinding* of nihilism that we have already examined in detail. With regard to this second feature, Adorno makes the oddly Burkean pronouncement:

> Acts of overcoming, even that of nihilism, together with the Nietzschean one that was otherwise intended but which still provided fascism with slogans, are always worse than what they overcome.
>
> (ND 371/NDS 380)

What Adorno is objecting to here (which Heidegger objected to in Jünger) is the active nihilist attempt to cross the line separating nihilism from its overcoming and to produce new values, new men and a new order. Such attempts at overcoming are symptomatic of a reactionary modernism whose ontologization of the social and facile positivity lead ineluctably to fascism. In this sense, the vocabulary of nothingness and despair becomes part of a masculinist philosophical jargon of resoluteness, decisiveness and hardness that ends up functioning as an *apologia* for immoral intolerance and political barbarism. By contrast, in an allusive swipe at Heidegger:

> Those to whom despair is not mere terminology may ask whether it would be better if there was nothing rather than something.
>
> (ND 371/NDS 380)

Thus, a victim of political intolerance, for example a person in a concentration camp, might legitimately apply the wisdom of Silenus and ask whether it would have been better not to be born. But if, as Adorno insinuates, the problem of nihilism and its overcoming conspires with the very intellectual and political forces that led to the death camps, then what might constitute a response to Auschwitz that takes account of the *presque rien* of our metaphysical faculties and how might matters then stand with the problem of nihilism? Adorno continues:

Beckett has given the only appropriate reaction to the situation of the concentration camp, that he never names, as if it lay under an image ban (*Bilderverbot*). What is, is like a concentration camp.

(ND 371/NDS 380)

At first sight this seems a paradoxical claim, for the most common and banal accusation levelled at Beckett's work is that it is apolitical and nihilistic because it lacks any of the critical social content evident, say, in the theatre of Brecht or Sartre. Yet, Adorno shockingly suggests that Beckett's work is the *only* appropriate response to the Holocaust, more so than direct witness accounts, precisely because it is not part of the manifest content of Beckett's work, as if it were subject to a *Bilderverbot*. What is being alluded to here – and this will be discussed in more critical detail in Lecture 3 – is Adorno's belief that the best modernist artworks, like Beckett's, in their aesthetic autonomy and their refusal of meaning (hence the superficial accusation of nihilism) function as determinate negations of contemporary society and can give the formal semblance of a society free from domination. Beckett's work successfully negotiates the dialectic between the necessary autonomy of modernist art and the function of social criticism *not* by raising its voice against society or protesting against the obvious injustice of the Holocaust, but rather *by elevating social criticism to the level of form*. This means that Beckett's work, in its steadfast refusal to mean something – a refusal of meaning that is still achieved by way of dramatic or novelistic form – exhibits an autonomy that, far from conspiring with apolitical decadence or 'nihilism', gives an indication of the transformative political praxis from which it abstains, namely 'the production of a right or just life' (*'die Herstellung rightigen Lebens'* – NL 429/NTL2 93). Thus, it is because Beckett's *Endgame* refuses any claim to meaning or positivity, because he balks at 'squeezing any kind of sense, however bleached, out of the victim's fate', that it constitutes the only appropriate response to Auschwitz (ND 352/NDS 361).

Such is the necessarily weak messianic power of Beckett's work, a weakness necessitated by the strictures placed above on the concept of redemption. Adorno sees this weak power at work in Beckett's use of language and its 'fissure of inconsistency'. He writes:

Once he speaks of a lifelong death penalty. The only dawning hope is that nothing more will be. This also he rejects.

(ND 371/NDS 380)

22

As we will see in Lecture 3, Beckett's language is an endlessly proliferating series of *non sequiturs*, of planned inconsistencies and contradictory sayings and unsayings, a *syntax of weakness*. For example:

I shall have to speak of things, of which I cannot speak, but also, which is even more interesting, but also that I, which is if possible even more interesting, that I shall have to, I forget, no matter.

(T 267)

Beckett's sentences are a series of *weak intensities*, sequences of antithetical inabilities: unable to go on, unable not to go on. And yet, as Adorno astutely points out, what seems like Stoicism on Beckett's part ('I can't go on, I'll go on') is 'a legacy of action' that 'silently screams that things should be otherwise. Such nihilism implies the opposite of an identification with the Nothing' (ND 371–72/NDS 381). Thus, Beckett's 'nihilism' is not an affirmation of the Nothing, for there is no affirmation in his work. Rather this 'nihilism' is redemptive in the specific sense discussed above – namely, the only philosophy that can be responsibly practised after Auschwitz is the attempt to view things from the standpoint of redemption, which is impossible, and yet this impossibility must be comprehended for the sake of the possible.

Adorno finds an analogue to Beckett in the Gnostic belief in the radical evil of the created world, or in the vocabulary of *Minima Moralia*, the world as 'indigent and distorted'. However, the Gnostic negation of this world would be 'the possibility of another world, not yet in being' (ND 372/NDS 381). It is precisely this negation that Adorno finds at work in Beckett, which means that his work takes the impossible standpoint of redemption, impossible because it is removed – 'by a hair's breadth' – from the standpoint of existence. Therefore, 'for so long as the world is as it is', and we have *absolutely* no reason to expect that it might change on Adorno's account, 'all images of reconciliation, peace and quiet resemble death'. To offer a picture of a reconciled and peaceful world at this point in history would be to offer something that can simply be recuperated by the culture industry and reproduced as ideology. That is to say, it would conspire with the very forces that resulted in the death camps. This is why Adorno insists that the real nihilists are not writers like Beckett, but are those active nihilists

Who oppose nihilism with their more and more faded positivities, and through this conspire with all extant meanness and finally with the destructive principle.

(ND 372/NDS 381)

Thus, the very worst nihilism would be to offer a positive vision of a reconciled future world that would follow the overcoming of nihilism. This is why acts of overcoming are always worse than what they overcome. This is also why authentic artworks must 'efface any memory-trace of reconciliation – in the interest of reconciliation' (AT 348/AST 333). In order to preserve the impossible possibility of the messianic perspective, the demand that we view the world from the standpoint of how things might be otherwise, it is not a question of an *Überwinding* of nihilism but of getting consciousness to wrest or extricate (*entwinden*) from nihilism what is lost sight of in the desire for overcoming. This is why Adorno concludes by saying that 'Thought has its honour by defending what is condemned as nihilism'.

Although the Enlightenment project might have left us with *presque rien*, Adorno does not leave us with nothing. On the contrary, the task of thinking is to keep open the slightest difference between things as they are and things as they might otherwise be, an otherwise that is persistently but obliquely offered by Beckett. It is only with this contradictory imperative that we look at things from the standpoint of redemption together with the knowledge that it is because such a standpoint is impossible that we are permitted the possibility of hope. Hope against hope. Austere messianism. Very little.

(h)
Learning how to die – the argument

Having now outlined a fifth response to nihilism through discussions of Heidegger and Adorno, thinkers who maintain philosophical proximities despite their deep political antipathies, I would like to take a broad sideways step before beginning Lecture 1.

To accept the diagnosis of modernity in terms of nihilism is to accept the ubiquity of the finite. That is, if God is bracketed out as the possible source of a response to the question of the meaning of life, then the response to that question must be sought within life, conceived as a finite temporal stretch between birth and death. So, under the nihilistic conditions of modernity, the question of the meaning of life becomes a matter of finding a meaning to human finitude. In this way, we rejoin Cicero's question, restated by Montaigne, 'That to Philosophie is to Learne How to Die'.[27] Our difference with antiquity, for good or ill, is that there is little sense of philosophy as a calmative or consoling influence that prepares the individual stoically for his passage on to either nothingness or eternal bliss. Beckett's Murphy strapped into his chair has replaced the Garden of Epicurus as an image of the philosopher in late modernity. To philosophize in the time of nihilism is to learn how to die *this* death, *my* death, knowing that there is nothing else after this death − *chacun sa chimère*.

Now, if (and this is a vast qualification) death is not just going to have the character of a brute fact, then one's mortality is something in which one has to find a meaning. In the vocabulary of *Being and Time*, death is something that one has to project freely in a resolute decision. The acceptance of the ubiquity of the finite is not simply expressed in the fact that human beings are mortal, rather the human being must *become* mortal − '*werde was du bist*'! For the early Heidegger, death is something to be achieved, it is the fundamental possibility which permits us to get the totality of existence, and hence authenticity, into our grasp − the possibility of impossibility. The human being is death in the process of becoming. A possible active response to nihilism, which I will describe and criticize in Lecture 1, and which stalks Heidegger up to the period of his National Socialist political commitment, is to see the collapse of theological and metaphysical certainty as the occasion for an explosion of creative energy where death becomes my work and nihilism is overcome in an affirmation of finitude.[28] In the face of a God-less world, individual authenticity produces itself through acts of self-invention and self-creation, where death becomes my work and suicide becomes the ultimate possibility − *ergo* the logical suicide of Kirilov. Perhaps this goes some way to explaining why the soil of the nineteenth and twentieth centuries is so scattered with the bodies of young writers and artists, from Kleist to Kurt Cobain.

However, if the response to nihilism in philosophical modernity centres on the question of finding a meaning to human finitude and making sense of the brute facticity of death, then − and this is the key to Lectures 1 and 3 − is life something for which one can and should find a meaning? Can I assume my finitude affirmatively as a source of meaning in the absence of God? Is death possible? *Can* I die? Can I say 'I can' with respect to death? Can I? The response given in the following lectures is that 'I cannot'.

A personal anecdote might shed light on matters here. Throughout the writing of these lectures, I have been haunted by an image: it is a death's head, or rather the head of a dying man, mumbling incessantly, gradually disappearing into a mute dullness. His hand scribbles almost noiselessly in a child's exercise book, his eyes stare blankly out of the window onto a featureless cityscape. I am obviously thinking of the figure who calls himself Malone in Beckett's *Trilogy*, but most of all of my father dying of cancer, rambling obliquely under his oxygen mask, his pain masked by morphine. What this composite figure, this spectre, suggests to me – I will present the argument for this below – is the radical ungraspability of finitude, our inability to lay hold of death and make of it a work and to make that work the basis for an affirmation of life. The event of our death is always too late for us. As Blanchot has recently expressed it in a confessional text, 'l'instant de ma mort désormais toujours en instance'.[29]

In phenomenological terms, death is not the object or meaningful fulfilment of an intentional act; it is not the *noema* of a *noesis*. Death is ungraspable and exceeds both intentionality and the correlative structures of phenomenology, whether the latter is understood in its Hegelian, Husserlian or Heideggerian senses. Thus, and this is the basis for my extended engagement with Blanchot in Lecture 1, there can be no phenomenology of death because it is a state of affairs about which I can find neither an adequate intention nor intuitive fulfilment. Death is radically resistant to the order of representation. Representations of death are misrepresentations, or rather representations of an absence. The paradox at the heart of the representation of death is best conveyed by the figure of *prosopopeia*, the trope by which an absent or imaginary person is presented as speaking or acting, a form which indicates the failure of presence, a face which withdraws behind the form which presents it. The representation of death is always a mask – a *memento mori* – behind which nothing stands, rather like the way in which the face of Tadzio appears to Von Aschenbach as he dies on the beach at the end of Mann's *Death in Venice*.

Thus, if there can be no phenomenology or representation of death because it is a state of affairs about which I can find neither an adequate intention nor intuitive fulfilment, then *the ultimate meaning of human finitude is that we cannot find meaningful fulfilment for the finite*. In this specific sense, death is meaningless and the work of mourning is infinite. Of course, this is also to say that mourning is not a work, for our relation to the death of the other does not permit any adequation with the dead other such that I might eventually detach myself from the other and work through their memory, becoming 'free and uninhibited', as Freud puts it.[30] This book is part of a *process* of mourning where the

26

unquestionable need for a work is continually outstripped by an inordinate desire that is workless.

To return briefly, in closing, to the problem of nihilism, the difficulty here is that if one accepts, as I hope to show, that one cannot find meaningful fulfilment for the finite, if death (and consequently life) is meaningless, then how does one avoid moving from this claim into the cynical conformism and sheer resignation of passive nihilism?

A response to nihilism and its crisis of meaning will not consist in the restoration of a new totality of meaning derived from the datum of finitude: a new thesis on Being, the creation of new values, the achievement of philosophy as revolutionary praxis, or whatever. Such would be the 'more and more faded positivities' of the true nihilists with their active desire for overcoming. Rather than restoring meaning, a response to nihilism will lie, I believe, in *meaninglessness as an achievement*, as a task or quest, what I describe in Lecture 2 as the achievement of the ordinary or the everyday without the rose-tinted spectacles of any narrative of redemption. This is why Beckett's work is so crucial for the argument of this book – he is, as Heidegger would say, the hero I have chosen.[31] On the interpretation I develop in Lecture 3, Beckett is not a nihilist, that is, he is not flatly stating that life is meaningless or celebrating the meaninglessness of existence, rather he indicates how meaninglessness can be seen as an achievement. Here the task, the labour of interpretation – of interpretation respecting the determinate negation of meaning enacted by Beckett's work – is *the concrete reconstruction of the meaning of meaninglessness*. The world is all too easily stuffed with meaning and we risk suffocating under the combined weight of competing narratives of redemption – whether religious, socio-economic, scientific, technological, political, aesthetic or philosophical – and hence miss the problem of nihilism in our manic desire to overcome it. What Beckett's work offers, I think, is a radical de-creation of these salvific narratives, an approach to meaninglessness as the achievement of the ordinary, *a redemption from redemption*.

The recognition of meaninglessness as an achievement leads to a deeper recognition of the profound limitedness of the human condition, of our frailty and separateness from one another. In relation to Beckett, I claim that his use of language – the syntax of weakness – is a comic evocation of the painful stiffening of the body, the experience of crispation, abjection and senescence. As we will see, 'Nothing is funnier than unhappiness, I grant you that', and I will claim –

27

contra Adorno – that the experience of laughter in Beckett is a node of uncolonizable non-identity in the life-world.[32]

In Lectures 1 and 2, this recognition of limitedness, finiteness and weakness leads to the sketching of a fairly minimal *ethics of finitude*, based on a critical reconstruction of the work of Emmanuel Levinas and Stanley Cavell. Such an ethics – minimal, fragile, refusable – does not open onto the glory of the Infinite or the trace of God, but only onto the night of what Levinas calls the *il y a* (the central topic of Lecture 1), the infinite time of our dying, our breath panting on in the darkness, a murmur in the mud, the experience of what I call *atheist transcendence*. And yet, into this night comes a voice, a weakly messianic injunction that resounds through many of Beckett's writings: *imagine*! This injunction is the core of my interest in the theory of the romantic fragment, and in the various more contemporary inheritors of Jena Romanticism. In Lecture 2, I outline what I call an *unworked romanticism* which has an essential but essentially limited role for the imagination, an imagination that goes on imagining in the knowledge that imagination has come to an end; in Beckett's typically antithetical formulation, *Imagination Dead Imagine*. It is with this minimal resistance of the imagination to the pressure of reality, born out of a deep sense of the ungraspability of finitude, that I would like to fashion a response to nihilism in terms of an affirmation of the ordinary, an extraordinary ordinary, what Wallace Stevens calls a return to the plain sense of things.

Of course, this conclusion is disappointing. Moreover, it *must* be disappointing for this is where I began and to offer anything more would be to exacerbate the very nihilism I am seeking to confront. This is very little . . . almost nothing. Yet, the entirety of the effort here must be directed towards keeping open this 'almost'.

Lecture 1

Il y a

Just as the man who is hanging himself, after kicking away the stool on which he stood, the final shore, rather than feeling the leap which he is making into the void feels only the rope which holds him, held to the end, held more than ever, bound as he had never been before to the existence he would like to leave.

(Thomas the Obscure, revised version)

(a)
Reading Blanchot

Reading Blanchot is, in a sense, the easiest of tasks. His French is limpid and clear, it is daylight itself; almost the French of the *Discours de la méthode*. And yet, as nearly everyone who writes on Blanchot points out, his work seems to defy any possible approach, it seems to evade being drawn into the circle of interpretation. The utter clarity of Blanchot's prose would appear to be somehow premised upon a refusal of the moment of comprehension and the consequent labour of interpretation and judgement. Absolutely clear at the level of reading, yet fundamentally opaque at the level of comprehension; a vague fore-understanding that somehow resists being drawn up into an active comprehension.

Reading Blanchot, and this will be my only hypothesis in what follows, one is drawn from daylight into an experience of the night. An *experience* of the night which is not the sleep which blots out and masters the night, preparing the body for the next day's activity – the sleep of *Dasein*, of heroes and warriors, that allows the night to disappear and transforms it into a reserve of possibility. The latter is what Blanchot calls the *first* night, the night in which one can go unto death, a death one dies each time sleep comes – sleep as mastery, as virility unto death.

Reading Blanchot one is led rather into an experience of the *other* or *essential* night, the night which does not permit the evasion of sleep, the night in which one cannot find a position, where the body refuses to lie still – this is the spectral night of dreams, of phantoms, of ghosts. In the other night, one can neither go to sleep nor unto death, for there is something stronger than death, namely the simple facticity of being riveted to existence without an exit, what Blanchot calls *le mourir* in opposition to *la mort*: the impossibility of death (ED 81). In the other night, one is not permitted the fantasy of suicide, that controlled and virile leap into the void that believes the moment of death is a possibility that can be mastered; a perverse version of the belief that one can die content, in one's bed, with one's boots on. In place of the mastered leap into the void, all the suicide feels is the rope tightening around his neck, binding him ever tighter to the existence he wanted to leave. This condition of being riveted to existence is also the experience of insomnia, a reluctant vigilance in the night, the night that slowly exhausts and sickens the body, thereby preventing sleep the following night and thus engaging insomnia's vicious circle. This is the bodily recollection of the night that one carries around during the day like a thousand invisible aching scars – eyes quietly burning beneath closed lids. Blanchot's original insight, obsessively reiterated in his work, is that the desire that governs writing has for its (impossible) origin this experience of the night, which is the experience of a dying stronger than death, what Levinas will call, and I will keep coming back to this, the *il y a*. Writing is not a desire for the beautiful artwork but for the origin of the artwork, its nocturnal source; which is why Blanchot defines the writer as 'the insomniac of the day' (ED 185).

Reading Blanchot in terms of a prose of daylight that is governed by nocturnal desire, an impossible and insatiable desire for that which is by definition denied to the movement of comprehension, it should be noted that reading Blanchot is not reading *philosophy*. If – with, after and against Hegel, or at least a certain Kojèvian Hegel of the *Phenomenology of Spirit*, the cartoon or comic Hegel of 'Les trois Hs', the Hegel who causes Bataille such mirth: the system as a comedy itself premised upon the *Aufhebung* of tragedy (and let it be noted that there are other, more interesting and more tragic readings of Hegel) – philosophy is fundamentally bound up with the movement of the *Begriff*, which is the movement of comprehension itself, a bipolar movement of negation whereby

32

the Subject comes to Spirit and Spirit to the Subject, a dialectic that is always governed by the horizon of recognition, reconciliation, daylight and the production of the work, *then Blanchot's work is not philosophy*. To paraphrase a passage from the *Phenomenology of Spirit* to be discussed below, if philosophy means that power of the Subject, that absolute and magical power of the negative that ensures its life by enduring death and maintaining itself unto death – that self-consciousness that constitutes itself through a right to death (which is also a right to sleep), and a right to experience itself, the production of *Erfahrung* in the dialectical movement from the in-itself to the for-itself – *then the desire that governs Blanchot's work has its source elsewhere*.

Reading Blanchot's work is, paradoxically, not the reading of a Work; that is, it does not have its horizon in the Subject's constitution of a Work that will allow it a presentation (*Darstellung*) of the Absolute (which, incidentally, is always the desire for the presentation of *community*: Absolute Knowing as the presentation of Spirit in the form of community). Blanchot's writing is the scattering of the work (and of community) in a movement of worklessness. To express this in historical figures anticipating the analyses of Lecture 2, Blanchot's work perhaps retrieves a certain moment of worklessness that can be glimpsed in the fragmentary writing of the Jena romantics against the dialectical *Aufhebung* of the fragment: Schlegel *contra* Hegel. As a Blanchot-inspired reading of Jena Romanticism points out, there is an alteration or oscillation within romanticism, where the systematic intentions of the Work, the desire for the *Gesamtkunstwerk* – for Schlegel, the great novel of the modern world – are interrupted and disseminated in the Work itself, producing instead incomplete chains of fragments.[1] This is what Blanchot identifies as 'the non-romantic essence of romanticism' (EI 524/IC 357). Both Schlegel and Blanchot engage in the production of 'a work of the absence of the work' (EI 517/IC 353), namely *literature*, or, more precisely, *writing outside philosophy*. Writing interrupts the dialectical labour of the negative, introducing into the Subject a certain impotence and passivity that escapes the movement of comprehension, of philosophy's obsession with meaning: the desire to master death and find a fulfilment for human finitude. Writing outside philosophy means ceasing to be fascinated with the circular figure of the Book, the en-*cyclo*-paedia of philosophical science, itself dominated by the figures of unity and totality, which would attempt to master death and complete meaning by letting nothing fall outside of its closure. In writing, one is no longer attracted by the Book, but rather by *the energy of exteriority* that cannot be reduced to either the exteriority

33

of Law – even the written Torah – or to the *Aufhebung* of the exteriority of Law in Christianity or dialectics: neither the Book of God nor the Book of Man. Writing is the experience of language unworking itself in an irreducible ambiguity that points towards an exteriority that would scatter meaning – a dizzying absence, the space of dying itself. The question that I will persistently raise is whether such an exteriority can be tolerated by the human organism, or rather whether there must be a moment of bad faith in the experience of writing in order to protect us from its truth.

Reading Blanchot, one notes a quite determinate and progressive mirroring of what I will call, from force of habit, 'form' and 'content'.[2] Within Blanchot's critical writing, one could mark a 'progression' from the relatively stable subject position of the early essays and *L'espace littéraire* through the polylogue of *L'attente, l'oubli* and parts of *L'entretien infini*, to the complete formal fragmentation of *L'écriture du désastre*. A different progression would have to be noted for Blanchot's fiction, noting the movement from *roman* to *récit* with the two versions of *Thomas l'obscur* to the refinement and eventual disappearance of the *récit*; what is called, in *La folie du jour*, the *pas de récit* (the one step more/ no more of the tale), when Blanchot stops writing 'fiction' altogether (or so it seems). It is interesting to note how Blanchot's fiction and criticism reach a point where both undergo fragmentation and pass into one another, something that can be seen particularly acutely in *L'écriture du désastre*. One way to read Blanchot's work would be in terms of a movement towards a writing that would result in a certain *Aufhebung* of the distinction between fiction and criticism and the conceptions of form and content implicit in both genres. This allows us to avoid some of the rather tedious debates that can arise with questions like 'is Blanchot's fiction superior to his criticism?' Whilst it is certainly true that at times Blanchot's criticism is best read as a commentary on his fiction, and that Blanchot is perhaps the best, and possibly, with Kafka, the *only* example of a writer whose practice comes close to the views expressed in his criticism, it is once again perhaps helpful to place Blanchot's work in the wake of Jena Romanticism, which would have as its central project *the production of literature as its own theory*, and whose genre of expression is the *fragment*. Form and content somehow conspire in Blanchot's work to produce, beyond the criticism/fiction divide, a fragmentary writing, an *Aufhebung* of the *Aufhebung* of the fragment. As we will see in Lecture 2, writing produces itself *ironically* and *wittily* as a refusal of comprehension, an enactment of a field of fragmentation that produces an alterity irreducible to presentation or cognition, an alterity that can variously be named with the words absence, exteriority, the night, the neuter, the outside, dying, and, as we will see, the *il y a*.

Which brings me to my suggestion for a route through the labyrinth of Blanchot's work (and when writing on Blanchot, I confess that I feel very much in the dark, fumbling here and there for a thread). My lecture will be in six parts: I will begin by trying to establish a framework for Blanchot's work by looking at what he means by 'literature' in the early 1943 essay, 'De l'angoisse au langage'. Extending the parameters of this framework, I will then give two close readings of 'Le regard d'Orphée' from *L'espace littéraire* (1955) and 'L'absence du livre' which closes the monumental *L'entretien infini* (1969). This will be followed by an extended commentary on 'La littérature et le droit à la mort', the crucially important essay that concludes Blanchot's second collection of essays, *La part du feu*, in 1949. The discussion of the latter essay will allow me, first, to show how Levinas's notion of the *il y a* can be understood as the origin of the artwork for Blanchot, and secondly to introduce the thesis of the impossibility of death, of the interminability of *le mourir* which is stronger than *la mort*. This will be followed by a consideration of Blanchot's reading of Kafka in *L'espace littéraire*, which focuses on the theme of 'the double death' and brings out the relation of writing to the interminability of dying and criticizes a certain romanticization of suicide as the ecstasy of annihilation. The long, final section of the lecture draws together the insights we have gleaned from the reading of Blanchot into a more thematic discussion of death, which then provides the basis for a critical discussion of Levinas's work. I attempt to show what I think can be defended in Levinas's work – roughly and readily, his quasi-phenomenology of the relation between myself and the other – and what cannot be defended in his work – crudely stated, the words 'God' and 'ethics'. I attempt to redescribe the human relation in terms of what might be called an atheistic 'ethics' of finitude. For me, what opens in the relation to the other is not, as Levinas would have it, the trace of the divine, but rather the trauma of the *il y a*, the night without stars, the scene of immemorial disaster, what I am tempted to call the experience of atheist transcendence.

(b)
How is literature possible?

In 'De l'angoisse au langage', Blanchot is trying to tease out the ambiguities of the writer's situation in order to address the question that heads his 1942 pamphlet on Jean Paulhan's *Les fleurs de tarbes*: 'Comment la littérature est-elle possible?' This strangely transcendental question – What are the conditions of possibility for literature? – can, at least in this essay, be equated with the question, 'How is language possible?', where language is understood as the more or less rule-governed production of meaningful sentences, the possibility of communication. At its simplest, and in a way whose tone will never change but only deepen in the entire destiny of Blanchot's work, the response to the question of the possibility of literature is paradoxically that literature is only possible insofar as it is *impossible*. That is, the possibility of literature is found in the impossibility of what Blanchot here calls 'aesthetic consciousness' (FP 26/ GO 19). Although left undefined by Blanchot, we might think of aesthetic consciousness as the total realization of meaning in an artwork, the comprehension of what Blanchot calls the work in a book, the sensuous presentation of the Absolute in Hegelian terms. For Blanchot, the possibility of literature is found in the radical impossibility of creating a complete work. That is to say, it is *the impossibility of literature that preserves literature as possibility*. Higher than actuality, echoing Heidegger's definition of phenomenology in *Sein und Zeit*, literature is the preservation of possibility *as* possibility. Thus, in one sense, it is the radical incompletion of the artwork that preserves the possibility of literature as possibility, and it is this incompletion that prevents the writer or painter standing back from their work and saying 'at last it is finished, at last there is nothing' (FP 26/GO 20).

However, if the possibility of literature is conditioned by the impossibility of completing the work, then this is still only a superficial, and indeed rather circular, response to the question, 'How is literature possible?' (i.e. literature is the possibility of literature). The title of the essay is 'De l'angoisse au langage'; what about *angoisse* or dread? Does not the title of the essay suggest a movement from dread to language, implying that dread renders both language and literature possible? To express this provisionally, one could say that literature is *the non-literal and ever-incomplete 'translation' of dread into language, a 'translation' that does not provide a representation or intuitive fulfilment of dread, but rather that literature is dread at work in language*. Blanchot writes (incidentally – and insistently – against a tendency in surrealism, if not against surrealism as such), 'The opposite of automatic writing is a *dread-filled desire* (*la volonté angoissé* – my emphasis) to transform the gifts of chance into deliberate initiatives' (FP 24/GO 18). A dread-filled desire, and we have yet to define these terms, is somehow the source of literature and literature is dread's failed expression in language.

36

Blanchot begins his meditation on literature, as he will do in *L'espace littéraire*, with the theme of solitude (although, as we will see presently, solitude in Blanchot's later work is the essential solitude of the work and not, as in this early essay, the solitude of the artist). Is there not a performative contradiction at the heart of literature insofar as its use of language is premised upon the generality of meaning and communication, but where what is expressed in language is the writer's solitude? Blanchot takes as axiomatic for the experience of literature – and one might well want to criticize this silent substitution of a highly determinate conception of literature arising at a particular historical moment (i.e. aesthetic modernism) for literature as such – Rimbaud's statement 'je suis seul'; that is, the condition of the writer is solitude and the function of literature is the articulation of this solitude. But how can a person be alone, if he confides to us that he is alone? 'Is the writer only half sincere' (FP 9/GO 3)? No, Blanchot insists, the writer is caught in a double bind, where he 'is not free to be alone without expressing the fact that he is alone' (FP 10/GO 4). That is to say, solitude can only be expressed by means of that which precisely denies solitude: language. But solitude is only solitude with respect to its other, it only has meaning as a privation whose absence is the rule. The writer is thus caught in a vicious circle, 'a person who writes is committed to writing by the silence and the privation of language that have stricken him' (FP 11/GO 5). Note here that the condition of possibility for literature is a certain silence, the silence of solitude. Silence is then equated by Blanchot with the theme of the nothing (*le rien*), the silent essence of solitude is a nothingness. Nothing, then, is the material of the writer and *the writer has nothing to express*: a statement that must be read in the same way as Heidegger reads Leibniz's Principle of Sufficient Reason, with the emphasis on *nothing* and *express*. The writer has an obligation to say or to bring to language, to literature, the nothing or silent solitude that is the source of literature. Such is the tragic-comic situation of the writer (one is reminded of Beckett), 'having nothing to write, of having no means of writing it, and of being forced by an extreme necessity to keep writing it' (FP 11/GO 5).

The solitude of the writer that literature seeks to bring to language is then equated by Blanchot – drawing discreetly on a whole network of allusions to the theme of dread in Kierkegaard and Heidegger – with dread or anguish: 'it sometimes seems, in a strange way, as though dread characterised the writer's function' (FP 12/GO 6). For Blanchot, and here we find a refinement of Heidegger's analysis in *Sein und Zeit*, the *Grund-Stimmung* of *Angst* that discloses

37

the human being to itself for the first time, that wrenches *Dasein* from the gravitational pull of *das Man*, that allows freedom to surge up as the vertiginous nothingness of possibility, is something essentially linked to the experience of writing: 'dread, which opens and closes the sky, needs the activity of a man sitting at his table and forming letters on a piece of paper' (FP 12/GO 6). In the previous paragraph, Blanchot tells us that it does not occur to anyone that the same dread would characterize a man who repairs shoes. Writers are not cobblers; and writers, unlike cobblers or all non-writing humans, have a privileged access to the *Grund-Stimmung* of dread. Although it is not my purpose in this lecture, one might want to press Blanchot's work quite hard at this point and see, first, whether and to what extent he is giving an ontological privilege to the writer – the writer is the only being capable of authentic *Dasein* – and second, whether he is justified in making this move. What does it mean to make quite general ontological claims for a highly specific and determined – culturally, socially, historically – form of activity, like literary writing?

Nevertheless, for the writer – and *only* for the writer, the experience is different again not only for the cobbler but even for the reader, where reading is a kind of second order writing (FP 25/GO 19) – literature is the attempt to attain the emptiness that, in the medium of art, will be the response to the dread that fills the writer's life. Writing engages a movement towards the nothingness opened by the experience of dread. Literature is an attempt at saying nothing. Such an attempt calls on the writer – in terms that reappear in *The Gaze of Orpheus* – to *sacrifice* himself. Blanchot writes, in words redolent of Bataille:

> The writer is called upon by his dread to perform a genuine sacrifice of himself. He must spend (*dépense*), he must consume, the forces that make him a writer. The spending must also be genuine. Either to be content with not writing any more, or to write a work in which all the values that the mind held in potential reappear in the form of effects, is to prevent the sacrifice from being made or to replace it by an exchange.
>
> (FP 14/GO 7–8)

Without remuneration or return, writing must be a pure sacrifice or pure gift that does not collapse back into the restricted economy of exchange. Writing must be an excessive gift in a general economy, like the potlatch that so intrigued Mauss and Bataille. The above quote has one devastating consequence whose force will never change in Blanchot's later work, namely *what has to be sacrificed by the writer in writing is the work itself, a work that is exceeded by desire.* Like Empedocles (to stay with the cobbler motif – that pair of sandals left on the rim of Mount Etna), the writer must sacrifice himself and his wish for a work out of a fidelity to the source from which the work comes. Blanchot writes, in an anticipation of the notion of *désoeuvrement*, 'The work he makes signifies that there is no work made' (FP 14/GO 8). The writer's loyalty to the dread that characterizes his life demands a work that must sacrifice itself and become workless. The goal of writing is not the work, the production of meaning and beauty, rather the writer writes out of a desire for the origin of the work, which means that the work must be sacrificed in fidelity to the pursuit of its origin. It is this origin that calls the writer in the *Grund-Stimmung* of dread.

For Blanchot, there is no adequation between the source of literature and its response, the writer cannot express in writing the dread that haunts him. 'Man cannot describe his torment' (FP 22/GO 15): dread is incommunicable, unrealizable and unrepresentable. If this were not the case, then literature would be some form of therapy for coming to terms with or overcoming dread; recall that Blanchot writes, alluding to the unhappy consciousness in Hegel's *Phenomenology*, 'L'art est d'abord la conscience du malheur, non pas sa compensation' (EL 85/SL 75). Blanchot wants to aggravate and not appease the ambiguous situation of the writer and show the necessity that governs this ambiguity: dread is nothing that can be expressed and yet the only thing that causes me to desire expression, writing is useless and yet nothing is more serious. The writer full of dread is bound to a necessity that cannot be governed by the simple 'yes' or 'no' of reality.

One of Blanchot's most insistent themes in these pages is the steadfast refusal of any practice of writing based upon chance as an appropriate response to dread (both Mallarmé's *Un coup de dès* and the automatic writing of the Surrealists are major reference points here). For Blanchot, the very difficulty of writing entails working with necessity, that is, the necessity of employing the traditional rules of writing – form, genre, etc. – in order to show the inadequacy of those rules. Traditional forms must be observed in order to show the limitations of such forms. One can try, in the manner of automatic writing, to escape rules by subjecting oneself to pure chance, and it would seem to the writer that by proceeding in this way, 'he is closer to his nocturnal passion'. 'But', Blanchot continues, 'the point is that for him, *the day is still there next to the night* [SC's emphasis], and he needs to betray himself through fidelity to the norms of clarity, for the sake of what is without form and without law' (FP 24/GO 17–

18). As well as being an interesting self-description of Blanchot's practice as a writer, one sees introduced here the metaphors of day and night that are constantly present in Blanchot's work: it is not a matter of giving oneself the illusion of merging with the night in some sort of ecstatic loss of consciousness. Such an option is easily enough achieved with the use of the right hallucinogenic drugs, a congenial climate and adequate leisure time. For Blanchot, however, such an aesthetic practice is an *evasion* of the *essential* night, which is the experience of being riveted to existence without exit. As we will see presently, the fundamental experience of the night is insomniac vigilance, a passive watching that extends the day into the night, drawing the laws of lucidity into the nocturnal space where they are transformed and made to serve that which exceeds all law.

Thus, Blanchot is not exhorting the writer to blind obedience to the traditional rules that govern literary production, for rules can easily become habits and lose their force, 'most of the time to give oneself to language is to abandon oneself' (FP 24/GO 18). And herein lies the problem with automatic writing for Blanchot: 'True automatic writing is the habitual form of writing, writing that has used the mind's deliberate efforts and its erasures to create automatisms' (FP 24/GO 18). That is to say, automatic writing risks slipping into the very *Gerede* it seeks to subvert. In opposition to this, Blanchot is proposing a form of writing governed by a dread-filled desire and obedient to the necessity of following the traditional laws of literary production, experiencing their limitations and then going on to posit a new law in which the writer can believe.

At this early stage of Blanchot's critical development, his account of writing indeed resembles an existentialist account of Kantian autonomy (which is one possible – if somewhat partial – reading of what Heidegger is proposing in *Sein und Zeit*). He writes:

> The instinct that leads us, in dread, to flee from the rules . . . comes, then, from the need to pursue these rules as true rules, as an exacting kind of coherence, and no longer as the conventions and means of a traditional commodity. I try to give myself a new law . . . because its novelty is the guarantee that it is really a law, for me, a law that imposes itself with a rigour I am aware of and that impresses more heavily upon me the feeling that it has no more meaning than the toss of the dice.
>
> (FP 24–25/GO 18)

Thus, chance is not an adequate aesthetic response to dread because it reduces writing to the toss of a dice and freedom to the experience of arbitrariness. I must find for myself a law that imposes itself upon me with a necessity and which I feel to be the law I give to myself, a law to which I freely submit. Thus the task of writing becomes one of 'setting words free' and freeing words 'from a rule one no longer submits to, in order to subject them to a law one really feels' (FP 25/GO 18). In this early essay, writing seems to move within the horizon of individual autonomy, of giving myself a law I freely submit to, even though it is clear that autonomy can never achieve complete self-identity through the alterity of the artwork; aesthetic consciousness must always remain structurally incomplete.

Turning to Blanchot's more mature criticism, any residual claims to individual autonomy would seem to evaporate. For example, in an Appendix to *L'espace littéraire*, Blanchot makes the distinction between essential solitude and solitude in the world (EL 341–44/SL 251–53). Essential solitude is not the worldly, artistic solitude of Rimbaud's 'je suis seul' or that of Rilke's isolation during the composition of the *Duino Elegies*. Such solitude is the existential solipsism that, in Heideggerian terms, *Dasein* undergoes in the *Grund-Stimmung* of *Angst*, which is always, essentially, self-communion or self-relation. Rather, the essential solitude is that of the Work, a solitude upon which the writer is dependent but to which he necessarily has a self-deceptive relationship, mistaking the Work for the book that he writes, or, like Valéry, misunderstanding the interminability of the Work for the infinity of the Spirit (EL 10/SL 21–22). For the Blanchot of *L'espace littéraire*, the solitude of the Work is expressed by the 'word' *être* (EL 10–11/SL 22–23). This transformation in the meaning of solitude should perhaps be read in terms of the influence of the later Heidegger on Blanchot, and one feels the continual presence of 'The Origin of the Work of Art' in *L'espace littéraire* – where Heidegger turns from the alleged anthropologism of the *Dasein*-analytic to the thinking of the truth of Being as that event of self-occultation disclosed and sheltered in and as language, and which emerges when worldly solitude slips away. However, if it is plausible to follow Blanchot's development in terms of shadowing Heidegger's *Kehre*, then this in no way discredits the insights of 'De l'angoisse au langage', just as Heidegger's work after the *Kehre* is not a refutation but a deepening of the claims of fundamental ontology. The analyses of dread-filled desire, the necessary incompletion of the work, writing as dread at work(lessness) in language, the gift and sacrifice, are already on the way to *L'espace littéraire*, to which I should now like to turn.

41

(c)
Orpheus, or the law of desire

Every book has a centre, even if it is only an imagined one. The writer writes the book out of a desire for this centre and in the hope that one will achieve identification with this centre and with oneself through the creation of an artwork. In Hegelian terms, the beauty of art is born of the Spirit and then born again from the Spirit in being recognized in objective form, standing over against self-consciousness: beautiful art exemplifies the dialectical formula of self-recognition in absolute otherness. However, and this is an insistent theme in Blanchot, the writer is in a profound sense ignorant of the centre towards which his work tends and the feeling of having attained it is always illusory. The writer can only exist in bad faith, mistaking the published book for the work of which the book is but the failed instantiation. In *L'espace littéraire*, the paradigm example employed to illustrate the writer's fate is the gaze of Orpheus, which also, as Blanchot points out in the untitled *avertissement au lecteur*, provides the (imagined) centre for that book (EL 227–34/GO 99–104). Of course, this raises Paul de Man's question about the circularity of Blanchot's claims about bad faith, and I shall come back to this.

There is a law that governs the artwork, a prohibition imposed upon Orpheus by Pluto and Persephone, that, if obeyed, will permit Orpheus to complete his work, that is to say, to bring Eurydice into the daylight. Eurydice is Orpheus' Work, and his work – the production of beauty – will be achieved when she escapes from Hades and comes to stand in the daylight. Orpheus must submit to the law of the underworld in order to produce the artwork. Thus, the presentation or unconcealment of the beautiful form in the daylight – what one can call, with Heidegger, 'world' – can only be achieved by submitting to the prohibition against looking Eurydice in the face, by recognizing that she can only be approached by turning away. That is to say, there is a law of concealment, the dark ascent out of Hades, which is necessary to the production of the work – we might think of this concealment as 'earth' for Heidegger, the nocturnal material substratum of the artwork. Thus the law that governs the production of the artwork demands an obedience to the creative strife of world and earth, of unconcealment and concealment: *alētheia*.

However, Orpheus' *gaze* – the moment when he turns around to look at Eurydice in the night, as the night – transgresses the law through the movement of desire. Desire, for Blanchot, is always in excess of the law. Orpheus' desire is not to see Eurydice in the daylight, in the beauty of a completed aesthetic form that has submitted to the passage by way of the law of concealment, but rather to see her in the night, as the heart of the night prior to daylight, 'her body closed, her face sealed' (almost like a fetish – EL 228/GO 100). Orpheus does not want to make the invisible visible, but rather (and impossibly) to see the invisible as invisible. Orpheus' 'mistake', as it were, lies in the nature of his desire, which desires to see Eurydice when he is only destined to *sing* about her – *parler ce n'est pas voir.* He loses her through his desire and is forced to forgo both his art – his song – and his dream of a happy life.

Yet, the paradox of Orpheus' situation is that if he did not turn his gaze on Eurydice he would be betraying his desire and thus would cease to be an artist. Thus, the desire which destroys his art is also its source. Such is the ambiguous double bind of *inspiration* for Blanchot. Inspiration is precisely this irresistible and impatient desire that transgresses the law that governs the artwork. Inspiration, far from completing the artwork, and bringing it to formal perfection, destroys the possibility of the artwork by transgressing its law in an act of impatience. Orpheus' gaze sends Eurydice back to Hades and destroys the possibility of the artwork. Blanchot asks rhetorically:

> Does this mean that inspiration changes the beauty of the night into the unreality of the void, makes Eurydice into a shade and Orpheus into someone infinitely dead? Does it mean that inspiration is therefore that problematic moment when the essence of the night becomes something inessential and the welcoming intimacy of the first night becomes the deceptive trap of the other night? That is exactly the way it is.
>
> (EL 231/GO 102)

Inspiration is both the source of the artwork and its ruination, it leads us through the comforting experience of the first night, the night to which Novalis addressed his hymns, to the other night, the unwelcoming night in which one can neither sleep nor die. To the night of Novalis, one might oppose the nocturnal *Angst* of Bonaventura's *Nachtwachen*, the nadir of poetic nihilism.[3] Orpheus' gaze is the realization of failure as the destiny of art, an essential inessentiality that, Blanchot suggests – in a curious remark commented on by Levinas when he is desperately trying to prise apart Blanchot and Heidegger – 'could reveal itself as the source of all authenticity' (EL 231/GO 102).[4]

One can here draw together the double bind of inspiration with what Blanchot writes about *fascination* earlier in *L'espace littéraire*. 'The undecided moment of fascination' (EL 15/GO 67) describes that experience when we are caught by something that we can neither grasp fully nor relinquish. Fascination is preoccupied, claims Blanchot, with the *image*. It is the image which becomes perceptible through the mediation of the writer in a manner which can neither be seized nor refused – in this case the vanishing face of Eurydice. Orpheus' gaze is fascinated by something which its desire cannot resist and over which it has no power: 'Fascination is the gaze . . . in which blindness is still vision, vision that is no longer the possibility of seeing, but the impossibility of not seeing' (EL 26/ GO 75). The fascinated gaze does not perceive any real object or form, it is like seeing with eyes open in the insomniac night, when familiar objects take on strange and terrible contours in the darkness, where they seem to attract the gaze to the extent that they continue to evade it – the experience of the uncanny. This is the night when the inanimate becomes animate, where toys come to life and terrify the sleepless child. Indeed, Blanchot goes on to link fascination to the experience of childhood and to the figure of the mother, who, Blanchot claims, is the first figure of fascination (EL 26–27/GO 76). We might ask, with Hélène Cixous, what is the gender of the child fascinated by the mother: is it a boy or a girl? Is the experience of the artist or the writer gendered or gender specific in Blanchot's work? Is the regard of the poet a male gaze on female alterity, and is this not the most traditional and pernicious of aesthetic conventions?[5]

Orpheus' gaze is fascinated by that which exceeds the law that governs the artwork, and thus his desire brings about its destruction. Blanchot insists – and this reintroduces themes we saw above – that Orpheus *sacrifices* the artwork and makes of it a radical and excessive *gift*, for which there will be no remuneration or exchange (EL 232–34/GP 103–4). But to whom or to what is this sacrifice made and this gift given? It is now clear that the Work is sacrificed and made a gift out of *a desire for the source or origin* (Blanchot's words – EL 232/GO 103) *of the Work*. Thus, and the Heideggerian resonances of these formulations should be noted, *the artwork is sacrificed because of the desire for the origin of the artwork, and the origin of the artwork is not a work, it is the betrayal, failure and scattering of the Work before its origin in worklessness.* The source of the artwork, its workless origin, is the experience of the other night – 'the profoundly dark point towards which art, desire, death and the night all seem to lead' (EL 227/GO 99) – an experience which introduces not death, but the interminable facticity of dying. After the failure of his work in Hades, Orpheus is finally torn to pieces by a band of Thracian women. Workless, his remains are scattered and his body thrown into the River Hebrus where it still mutters 'Eurydice, Eurydice'.

(d)
Blanchot's genealogy of morals: exteriority as desire, exteriority as law

This conception of writing as the sacrifice of the Work to its workless origin is continued in different terms in 'The Absence of the Book', the difficult concluding text from *L'entretien infini*. As Blanchot repeatedly emphasizes, the act of writing does not find its fulfilment in the Book, whether the Book of God (the Bible), or the Book of Man (Hegel and Mallarmé are the examples given – EI 621/IC 423). Rather, writing is related to and directed towards the absence of the Book, that is, the production of worklessness in the Work. Thus, writing passes through the Book, but the Book is not the destiny of writing. Furthermore, Blanchot also insinuates that writing *must* pass through the Book, insofar as occidental culture is a civilization of the Book. That is to say, in terms similar to the opening theses of Derrida's *Of Grammatology*, occidental civilization is founded upon the Book as the condition of possibility for meaning, knowledge, totality, presence, memory and systematicity. It matters little which transcendental signified – God, the Subject, History, the Proletariat, the Nation, the American Family – is claimed as the origin of meaning; what is essential here is that the Book is a strategy for evading the radical absence at the heart of language and culture. Blanchot writes, 'The book: a ruse by which writing goes towards *the absence of the book*' (EI 623/IC 424). The book is a ruse, an act of cunning, whereby what Blanchot calls the *energy* (EI 624/IC 425) of writing, what we described above as desire or inspiration, is displaced into the Book: logocentrism is bibliocentrism.

However, what summons us when we write, Blanchot claims, using the safety curtain of parenthesis, is 'The attraction of (pure) exteriority' (EI 625/IC 426). The law of the Book, what we saw above as the prohibition that governs the possibility of the artwork, is the displacement of pure exteriority into an order of meaning. A distinction is here established between the law of the Book, what Blanchot also calls the exteriority of the Law, and the pure exteriority of writing, whereby the former is the *slackening* of the latter's energy. The energy and desire of writing always work against the law, and the law of desire is lawlessness itself.

Behind these seemingly baroque distinctions, Blanchot is intimating a genealogical critique of morality in terms of a discreet account of the origin of Judaism; because the moment when exteriority slackens, it appears as the exteriority of the Law, or written Torah, which takes the form of the Book – the Bible – and provides the condition of possibility for monotheism and a universalistic morality. Thus, the institution of a covenant based upon the written Law and the establishment of a people of the Book, is, for Blanchot, the substitution of a limited exteriority for the unlimited exteriority of writing. The law as the written Torah replaces and displaces the lawlessness of the writing of desire. Blanchot writes:

> In other words, the breaking of the first tablets is not a break with a first state of unitary harmony; on the contrary, what the break inaugurates is the substitution of a limited exteriority (where the possibility of a limit announces itself) for an exteriority without limitation – the substitution of a lack for an absence, a break for a gap, an infraction for the pure–impure fraction of the fragmentary.
>
> (EI 633/IC 432)

Once this substitution has been made and a moral and religious order has been grounded in the Book and the Law, then the pure exteriority of writing – 'the primordiality of difference' – is thrust aside as 'impious' (EI 635/IC 433), and the postulation of a writing of desire outside the Law is made to appear as 'an irresponsible gesture, an immoral game' (EI 636/IC 434).

With more than a little hermeneutic violence, one can delineate a threefold structure in Blanchot's implied genealogy of morals: in the beginning, there was writing – the pure exteriority, worklessness and absence towards which inspiration and desire tend. Second, this pure exteriority slackens and is displaced into the exteriority of the Law, which is the moment of Judaism. However, I would claim, and the many references to Hegel in 'The Absence of the Book' could be used to buttress my argument here, that a third step is implied when Blanchot writes, 'the law in its turn will dissolve' (EI 633/IC 432). Christianity, or at least Hegel's understanding of it, is the *Aufhebung* of Judaism, that is, the dissolution of the exteriority of Law as exterior and its translation into the interiority of *love*, the *Grund-Stimmung* of Christianity. This dissolution and translation are achieved through the person of Christ, in whom the abstraction of the Law becomes incarnated into a living divine subjectivity with whom human self-consciousness can enter into a reciprocal, loving intersubjectivity: the form of Spirit itself. Of course, within Hegel's (a)theo-teleo-logical schema even the exteriority of Christ is *aufgehoben* insofar as our relation with him remains in the sphere of *Vorstellung*, picture thinking. After

46

religion comes philosophy, self-consciousness of the Absolute or Spirit become Subject in and as community. Beneath the *Aufhebung* of religion by philosophy – as Feuerbach and the young Marx clearly perceived – the stench from the decay of God's corpse is already nauseating.

Despite the violence of this genealogy, it can be seen that Blanchot's work is an *attempt* at a retrieval of the origin of desire – energy itself – as a (pure) exteriority of writing prior to its slackening into Law. Yet, Blanchot continues, perhaps this slackening is necessary, perhaps the expenditure of energy in pure exteriority would be intolerable to the human organism (EI 632/IC 431), like the pure energy of the Dionysian without the redemptive *Schein* of the Apollonian. Our feet are still very firmly stuck in the epoch of the Book and the transition to what Blanchot means by writing would demand a transformation of historical–social–cultural–economic conditions that, to say the very least, would not seem to be likely at the present time. To recall the enigmatic prefatory 'Note' to *L'entretien infini*, the advent of writing, in Blanchot's sense, would presuppose a radical transformation of the epoch, 'an end of history', and the establishment of communism: 'a communism being always still beyond communism' (EI vii–viii/IC xi–xii). Such remarks could lead to what one might call an *apocalyptic* reading of Blanchot, that is, an interpretation that would emphasize the interdependence of writing and revolution – writing as the enabling of revolutionary action and revolution as the transformation of the epoch of the Book into the epoch of Writing (with a capital 'W').

However, such an interpretation is extremely limited and risks reducing what I believe to be the fundamental lesson of Blanchot's work, namely, *the irreducibility of ambiguity or equivocity*. In the concluding lines of 'The Absence of the Book', Blanchot writes, 'One cannot go back (*remonter*) from exteriority as law to exteriority as writing' (EI 636/IC 434). That is to say, one must accept the fall into Law and the epoch of the Book: 'The law is the summit, there is no other. Writing remains outside the arbitration between high and low.' Reading Blanchot apocalyptically would risk positing the achieved revolution as a Work, and construing post-revolutionary forms of community in terms of the very unity and totality that Blanchot's writing seeks to undermine. In the terms introduced above, it would be to read Blanchot in terms of the first night and not the other, essential night. It would escape the interminable facticity of dying through some virile, revolutionary death fantasy – the fantasy of automatic writing, of creation by sheer chance without regard for rules and aesthetic criteria. Such a reading would posit a successful end to desire – and it should have been established by now that 'success' and 'end' are words that contradict what Blanchot means by desire – and participate in the therapeutic fantasy of the cure.

The reading of Blanchot that I would like to develop places emphasis on the *ambiguity* of our (historical–political–cultural–economic) situation, that is, of being in the epoch of the Book but without a belief in the Book. We must accept our fall within the epoch of the Book and the Law and begin to negotiate our position *critically*; that is to say, through writing, speaking, thinking and acting. Modernity, for Blanchot, is perhaps this fundamental experience of equivocity, of the kind that Lacoue-Labarthe and Nancy find in their reading of Jena Romanticism (AL 419–25/LA 121–27) – what was called above the *alteration* between the desire for the Work and the worklessness that leaves the Work in fragments. Perhaps Blanchot's writing participates in and deepens the aporias of this romanticism, returning us to the margins of a modernity we are unable to leave and in which we are unable to believe: 'The Athenäum is our birthplace' (AL 17/LA 8).

(e)
Il y a – the origin of the artwork

In *L'entretien infini*, Blanchot often employs a double plus and minus sign ($\pm\ \pm$) to indicate that someone is speaking, in place of the single dash (-) that is customary in French. What does this simultaneity of the positive and the negative signify? An oblique response to this question can be found in the concluding pages of 'Literature and the Right to Death', where Blanchot makes the following remark about the power or force of literature:

> Then where is literature's power? It plays at working in the world and the world regards its work as a worthless or dangerous game. It opens a path for itself towards the obscurity of existence and does not succeed in pronouncing the 'Never more' which would suspend its curse. Then why would a man like Kafka decide that if he has to fall short of his destiny, being a writer was the only way to fall short of it truthfully? Perhaps this is an unintelligible enigma, but if it is, *the source of the mystery is literature's right to affix a negative or positive sign indiscriminately to each of its results. A strange right – one linked to the question of ambiguity in general* [SC's emphasis]. Why is there ambiguity in the world? Ambiguity is its own

answer. We can't answer it except by rediscovering it in the ambiguity of our answer, and an ambiguous answer is a question about ambiguity.

(PF 342/GO 58–59)[6]

Literature, Blanchot goes on to write, is language turning into ambiguity; or again, literature is the form in which the original double meaning at the heart of meaning has chosen to show itself (PF 345/GO 62). My hypothesis here is that the above sign – the simultaneity of the positive and the negative – provides a *formula* for the linguistic ambiguity expressed in and as literature. The power of literature is located in the irreducibility of ambiguity and the maintenance of this ambiguity is literature's *right*. Literature always has the right to mean something other than what one thought it meant; this is, for Blanchot, both literature's treachery and its cunning version of the truth (*'sa vérité retorse'*).

In order to elucidate this ambiguity I would like to sketch in some detail the two differing conceptions or, to use Blanchot's word, 'slopes' (*pentes* or *versants*) of literature that constitute the poles of this ambiguity – two slopes of literature that also entail two conceptions of death and two voices often heard in the background of 'Literature and the Right to Death', those of Hegel and Levinas. It should be noted at the outset that these two slopes, two conceptions of death and two names cannot be divided and continually risk passing into one another in the experience of literature.[7]

(i)
First slope: Hegel avec Sade

For Blanchot, the ambiguity of literature is indissolubly linked to the maintenance of the *question* of literature as a question. Although Blanchot is prepared to concede that one can write without asking why one writes, he begins 'Literature and the Right to Death' with the hypothesis, 'Let us suppose that literature begins at the moment when literature becomes a question' (PF 305/GO 21). The essay is thus going to be concerned with literature questioning itself or contemplating itself. However, the question is: what is literature's question? How and when does literature contemplate itself? To begin to find a response to these questions and ascend the first slope of literature, we have to understand what, for Blanchot, is the ultimate temptation of the writer and introduce the themes of *revolution* and *terror*.

The influence of Hegel's *Phenomenology of Spirit* can be felt at many points in 'Literature and the Right to Death' and indeed the first half of the essay was initially published in the November 1947 number of *Critique* – which also included a double review of Hyppolite's and Kojève's commentaries on Hegel – under the very Hegelian title, 'The Animal Kingdom of the Spirit' (*'Le règne animal de l'esprit'*). P. Adams Sitney calls Blanchot's essay a 'near parody' or 'ironic aestheticization' of the *Phenomenology of Spirit* (GO 175), and whilst this is not implausible, I feel that a stronger word than 'parody' would be required to convey the extent of Blanchot's proximity to Hegel. Blanchot *mimics* the dialectical procedure of the *Phenomenology*, insofar as one cannot read 'Literature and the Right to Death' as defending a particular position, as much as letting truth unfold in the totality of possible positions. Blanchot works in the spirit, if not the letter, of Hegel (and incidentally reads Hegel as literature, which means – as was so common in France at this time – privileging the *Phenomenology* over the *Logic* or the *Encyclopaedia*) by engaging in a phenomenology of the various temptations available to the writer and articulating them in terms of the categories of the *Phenomenology*. Blanchot writes, as if this were self-evident:

> As we know, a writer's main temptations are called stoicism, scepticism and the unhappy consciousness.
>
> (PF 321/GO 37)

If the stoic views writing as the exercise of absolute freedom, and the sceptic sees literature as the total negation of all certitude, then the unhappy consciousness – the truth of stoicism and scepticism – best describes the situation of the writer, 'ce malheur est son plus profond talent' (PF 320/GO 37). The writer's consciousness is unhappily divided against itself by an array of irreconcilable temptations which are as justifiable as they are contradictory.

'But', Blanchot adds, 'there is another temptation.' This ultimate temptation, that outstrips all the others, is articulated through a series of allusions to the 'Absolute Freedom and Terror' chapter of the *Phenomenology*, which, of course, is Hegel's discussion of the French Revolution. In this temptation, literature is the passage from nothing to everything, that is to say, the writer is no longer satisfied with the aesthetic pleasure of manipulating mere words, but wishes to realize writing in the world by negating something real, by annulling *everything* hitherto considered real: the state, the law, institutions, religion. Thus, writing comes to see itself in the mirror of *revolution*, where the latter is understood as both the absolute negation of previously existing reality, and the exercise of absolute freedom. Thus, revolution is the realization of *absolute freedom* in the world, and the writer succumbs to the temptation to become a revolutionary. Therefore, the choice facing the writer, according to this temptation, is either absolute freedom or death, because anything less than freedom would be a concession to the established order. This choice of freedom or death soon becomes an identification of freedom *with* death, with a certain *right* to death, whereby death becomes the perfection of one's free existence. Hegel is thinking of the fates of revolutionaries like Robespierre or Saint-Just (but one might also think here of David's painting of the death of Danton, or of photographs of Che Guevara's Christ-like corpse). But a second identification is also at work here: if death is the expression or realization of one's freedom, then this is only an abstract, insubstantial and one-sided freedom, where death no longer has any real importance. This devaluation of death leads Hegel to identify absolute freedom with the Terror, where individuals are slaughtered mean- inglessly, in Hegel's famous words, 'It is thus the coldest and meanest of all deaths, with no more significance than cutting off a head of cabbage or swallowing a mouthful of water.'[8]

The writer who succumbs to this ultimate temptation becomes a revolutionary and a terrorist, 'The terrorists are those who, desiring absolute freedom, know that in this way they desire their own death' (PF 323/GO 39). If one had the expertise and the inclination, one might read these remarks autobiographically, because Blanchot had, in 1936, as the frenzied culmination of his political activism, advocated terrorism as a means of public salvation.[9] However, in 'Literature and the Right to Death', as elsewhere in Blanchot's work, the writer *par excellence* is the Marquis de Sade, or 'Citoyen Sade', as he later called himself: held captive in the Bastille and calling out (through a urine funnel) to the revolutionary crowds that prisoners were being massacred inside the prison. Sade's writing is the exercise of absolute freedom as total negation: the denial of God, of other people, of nature. A negation that is driven to blood, cruelty and terror as the most faithful expression of absolute freedom.

> He writes, all he does is write, and it doesn't matter that freedom puts him back into the Bastille after having brought him out, he is the one who understands freedom the best, because he understands that it is a moment when the most aberrant passions that turn into political reality, have a right to be seen, are the law.

> (PF 324/GO 40)

Sadism is a perversion of the Hegelian dialectic of intersubjectivity, where recognition is forced through sexual domination, and where identification with the other is obtained through their humiliation. Literature here becomes a bacchanal of absolute sovereignty, and writing becomes a solitary masturbation that negates reality and posits a fantasized reality in its place. The perversion of the dialectic of intersubjectivity takes place in solitude, *as* solitude.[10] Indeed, Sade's writing begins after his imprisonment, when his only sexual gratifications are solitary and where writing – as was also the case for Rousseau, another confessed masturbator – is a supplement for something lacking in reality. One is also reminded here of Genet's *Notre dame des Fleurs* and Sartre's description of the latter as 'the epic of masturbation'.[11] Both Sade and Genet are obsessed with a rape fantasy, which is – surprise, surprise – deeply misogynist, and centred on a scene of anal penetration, whether the desire is to penetrate (in Sade) or to be penetrated (in Genet), a scene itself banalized through endless repetition and the prolix cataloguing of sexual exploits – think also of the enumeration of sexual conquests in Mozart's *Don Giovanni*. The final crucial element in this mini-psychopathology of the literary terrorist is that although the writer loudly and repeatedly negates God, events culminate in the elevation of the writer to an identification with the Messiah, or, even better, the Crucified, an identification made by Nietzsche in *Ecce Homo* with the kind of self-lacerating irony all too lacking in his imitators.

We are here ascending the first slope of literature, and as a response to the initial questions raised above – What is the question of literature? What is the question that literature poses itself? How and at what moment does literature question itself? – it is by now clear that the question that literature contemplates is presented in revolution and terror:

> Literature contemplates itself in revolution, it finds its justification in revolution, and if it has been called the *Terror*, this is because its ideal is indeed that historical moment when 'life endures death and maintains itself in death' in order to gain from death the possibility and the truth of speech. This is the 'question' that seeks to pose itself in literature, the 'question' that is its being.
>
> (PF 324/GO 41)

I want to pick up on the sentence in quotation marks, the 'life [that] endures death and maintains itself in death', which is repeated at least four times in Blanchot's essay, and is taken from the Preface to Hegel's *Phenomenology*.[12] Hegel is discussing the power and work of the Understanding (*die Kraft und Arbeit des Verstandes*), the absolute power, which is also identified with the Subject. The

52

Subject, for Hegel, is the power of the negative, in Sartrean terms a nothingness set free in the world, which is able to dissolve that which stands over against it as an object in-itself and translate it into something for-itself, to mediate the immediate. Dialectical thought – the active dynamic of *Erfahrung* and the movement of the *Begriff* – consists in the emergence of new, true objects for consciousness through the labour of negation. What Hegel calls the Life of the Spirit (*das Leben des Geistes*) is this magical power (*Zauberkraft*) to live through the negative, to produce experience out of a labour of negation. This work of negation whereby the in-itself becomes for-itself and the immediate mediated is then likened, by Hegel, to *death*:

> Death, if that is what we want to call this non-actuality, is of all things the fearful, and to hold fast to what is dead demands the greatest power.[13]

Thus, the Subject produces itself through a relation with death; the Life of the Spirit endures death and maintains itself in death.

Thus, on Blanchot's reading of Hegel, dialectics is a form of murder that kills things *qua* things-in-themselves and translates them into things-for-consciousness. Dialectics is a conceptual Sadism, which forces recognition on things through domination. Furthermore, the murder weapon that dialectical thought employs is *language*, the very *Dasein* of Spirit for Hegel. Thus, the life of language is the death of things as things:

> When we speak we gain control over things with satisfying ease. I say, 'This woman', and she is immediately available to me, I push her away, I bring her close, she is everything I want her to be.
>
> (PF 325/GO 41)

Blanchot is here alluding to a passage from Mallarmé's *Crise de vers*, but where the latter writes 'Je dis: une fleur',[14] Blanchot strangely and perhaps (to be extremely generous) only to force the connection between dialectics and Sadism, substitutes 'woman' for 'flower'. However, Blanchot would here seem to be advancing the proposition that language is murder, that is, the act of naming things, of substituting a name for the sensation, gives things to us, but in a form that deprives those things of their being. Human speech is thus the annihilation of things *qua* things, and their articulation through language is truly their death-rattle: Adam is the first serial killer. 'Therefore', Blanchot continues:

It is accurate to say that when I speak death speaks in me. My speech is a warning that at this very moment death is loose in the world, that it has brusquely arisen between me, as I speak, and the being I address.

(PF 43/GO 326)

There is a paradox here: namely that the condition of possibility for the magical power of the understanding to grasp things as such entails that those things must be dead on arrival in the understanding. In speaking, I separate myself from things and I separate myself from myself: 'I say my name, and it is as though I were chanting my own dirge' (PF 326–27/GO 43). What speaks, then, when I speak? In a sense, and this returns us to our earlier analysis of 'From Dread to Language', *nothing speaks*. Negation is the very work of language and thus when I speak a nothing comes to speak in me. Thus, for Blanchot, the work of literature could be seen as having nothing to express, of having no means of expressing it and being forced by an extreme necessity to keep expressing it. Literature's right to death – its absolute freedom, its terrifying revolutionary power – is a Hegelian–Sadistic right to the total negation of reality taking place in and as language, 'a strange right' (PF 325/GO 42).

(ii)
Second slope – a fate worse than death

Such is the first slope of literature and the first right to death. However, literature does not stop here, for it simultaneously works on a second slope, where it attempts to recall the moments leading up to the murder of the first moment, and where literature becomes 'a search for this moment which precedes literature' (PF 329/GO 46) – the trembling, pre-linguistic darkness of things, the universe before the creation of the human being. If, in the experience of the first slope of literature, ultimately in Sade, literature's right to death results in the death of God and the identification of the writer with God, then the second slope of literature seeks God *qua* God. To express this differently, literature seeks that moment of existence or Being prior to the advent of the Subject and its work of negation. If consciousness is nothing but this work of negation, then the second slope of literature wants to attain that point of unconsciousness, where it can somehow merge with the reality of things. Literature here consists, in the words of Francis Ponge, in *Le parti pris des choses*, that is, in seeking to recover the silence and materiality of things as things before the act of naming where they are murdered by language and translated into

54

literature.[15] Using the Mallarméan example, literature no longer wants to say 'a flower', but desires this flower as a thing prior to its fatal act of naming. In relation to Blanchot's use of the Orpheus myth, this second slope is not satisfied with bringing Eurydice into the daylight, negating the night, but rather by wanting to gaze at her in the night, as the heart of the essential night. Literature here becomes concerned with the presence of things before consciousness and the writer exist; it seeks to retrieve the reality and anonymity of existence prior to the dialectico-Sadistic death drive of the writer.

The occasion that prompts Blanchot's account of the second slope of literature is the publication of Emmanuel Levinas's *De l'existence à l'existent*, in 1947. The second half of 'Literature and the Right to Death' was originally published, under the same title, two months after the first half, in the January 1948 number of *Critique*. As can be clearly seen from two of Blanchot's infrequent footnotes, he appropriates two ideas from Levinas's book: first the *il y a* (PF 334/GO 51), which I shall discuss presently, and, second, the related anti-Heideggerian thought that dread is not dread in the face of death — *Sein-zum-Tode* — but rather that dread is had in the face of existence itself, of being riveted to existence, *the impossibility of death* (PF 338/GO 55).

What is the *il y a*? In the 1978 Preface to the Second Edition of *De l'existence à l'existent,* Levinas calls the *il y a* 'le morceau de résistance' of that work (DEE 10). In his Introduction, Levinas notes that his reflections find their source in Heidegger's renewal of philosophy as a fundamental ontology centred on the relation that the human being maintains with Being, in Levinas's (questionable) terms the relation of the existent to existence. However, if Levinas's initial philosophical position is Heideggerian, something that can be more clearly seen in his 1930 Doctoral thesis and his essays prior to 1933 (this is a very decisive 'prior'), then it is also, and with an ever increasing insistence, 'governed by a profound need to leave the climate of that philosophy' (DEE 19/EE 19). As Paul Davies points out, 'The *il y a* is a contribution to ontology that ruins ontology'.[16] The concept (if it is one) of the *il y a* is Levinas's response to Heidegger, and what he is trying to describe with this concept is the event of Being in general. He asks, 'What is the event of Being, Being in general, detached from the "beings" which dominate it?' (DEE 17/EE 18). In other words, what does the generality, impersonality or, most importantly, *neutrality* of Being mean?

For Levinas, such neutrality — and here we begin to touch upon the essential difference between Levinas and Blanchot — must be surmounted through the advent of the subject in the event of what Levinas calls *hypostasis*, an event that will culminate in the establishment of the ethical relation as the basis of sociality. As the title of *De l'existence à l'existent* indicates, Levinas's path of thinking follows a counter-Heideggerian trajectory from existence to the existent, or in Heidegger's terms, from *Sein* to *Dasein*, a trajectory that ultimately comes to question the fundamentality of ontology as first philosophy. Blanchot's thought – at least on the picture given above, that is to say, prior to the emergence of the 'Levinasian' problematic of *autrui* that comes to dominate *L'entretien infini* and which haunts all of Blanchot's *récits* – remains dominated by the thought of neutrality (*le neutre*) and wants to block the passage beyond neutrality into the hypostasis of the subject. In this connection, we should note the highly ambiguous compliment that Levinas pays Blanchot in *Totality and Infinity*, namely, 'The Heideggerian Being of the existent whose impersonal neutrality the critical work of Blanchot has so much contributed to bring out' (TeI 274/TI 298). The ambiguity of this remark would seem to be equalled by Blanchot in *L'entretien infini* when he places question marks around Levinas's notions of 'ethics' and 'God' at the same time as trying to maintain the radicality of the absolute relation to the Other. Blanchot (or, more precisely, the interlocutors in his *entretien*) writes (or speak), ' – Would you fear the shaking that can come to thought by way of morality? – I fear the shaking when it is provoked by some Unshakable' (EI 83/IC 58). And again, 'Is the general name "ethics" in keeping with the impossible relation that is revealed in the revelation of *autrui*?' (EI 78/ IC 55).

Are we here on the point of recognizing the limit of any rapprochement between Levinas and Blanchot, a rapprochement that they generously and repeatedly offer one another in a series of texts extending over five decades? Does their work, as Derrida suggests in 'Violence et métaphysique', only have an affinity in its critical or negative moment – the critique of the Same, of Unity, the suspicion of the generosity and luminosity of Heidegger's thought – which ceases when Levinas asserts the *ethical* positivity of the relation to the Other?[17] Or is the relation between Blanchot and Levinas perhaps to be understood as the paradigm of a philosophical friendship, a pattern for any future *entretien*? I would like to leave these questions open for the moment and return to them in the conclusion to this lecture.

With the *il y a*, Levinas asks us to undertake a thought-experiment, 'Let us imagine all beings, things and persons, reverting to nothingness' (DEE 93/EE 57). Such a situation would be the complete annihilation of all existents, all

Seienden. But what would remain after this annihilation? Nothing? Levinas claims that this very nothingness of all existents would itself be experienced as a kind of presence: an impersonal, neutral and indeterminate feeling that '*quelque chose se passe*', what he calls in *Le temps et l'autre*, 'An atmospheric density, a plenitude of the void, or the murmur of silence' (TA 26/TO 46). This indeterminate sense of something happening in the absence of all beings can be expressed, Levinas claims, with the neutral or impersonal third person pronoun, that designates an action when the author of that action is unknown or unimportant, for example, when one says '*il pleut*' or '*il fait nuit*'. This impersonality or neutrality is then designated by Levinas as the *il y a* and equated with the notion of Being in general (DEE 94/EE 57). In Heideggerian terms, the *il y a* is Levinas's word for Being, even if he insists that it must not be assimilated to Heidegger's *es gibt*, whose full elaboration it precedes. For Levinas, Heidegger's interpretation of the *es gibt*, as with Rimbaud's use of the *il y a* in *Les illuminations* − itself discussed by Heidegger[18] − emphasizes the generosity and joyfulness of the *il y a* as an event of donation (*Gegebenheit*), of the gift of *Ereignis*, or the opening of a world to the poet, and hence misses the fundamental *Stimmung* of the *il y a* for Levinas: *horror*.[19]

To illustrate phenomenologically the experience of the *il y a*, Levinas writes, 'We could say that the night is the very experience of the *il y a*' (DEE 94/EE 58). As I have already discussed earlier in this lecture, the essential or other night for Blanchot is that experience towards which the desire of the artist tends. In the night, all familiar objects disappear, something is there but nothing is visible; the experience of darkness is the presence of absence, the peculiar density of the void, where the things of the day disappear into an uncanny 'swarming of points' (DEE 96/EE 59). This is the night of insomnia, the passive watching in the night where intentionality undergoes reversal, where we no longer regard things, but where they seem to regard us:

> La veille est anonyme. Il n'y a pas *ma* vigilance à la nuit, c'est la nuit elle-même qui veille. Ça veille.
>
> (DEE 111/EE 66)

This is particularly difficult to translate because *la veille* denotes wakefulness, watchfulness, a vigil, staying up in the night or watching over the night, the state of being on the brink or verge, as well as meaning 'eve' or 'preceding day'. It is difficult to find one expression in English that combines both wakefulness and watchfulness. However, in the experience of *la veille*, the subject is no longer able to achieve cognitive mastery over objects, to exercise its strange right to death. In a formulation that Blanchot seems to take up, the *il y a* is the experience of consciousness without a subject (DEE 98/EE 60), or my consciousness without me (PF 330/GO 47). In the *il y a*, I am neither myself nor an other, and this is precisely the abject experience of horror, 'the rustling of the *il y a* is horror... horror is somehow a movement which will strip consciousness of its very "subjectivity"' (DEE 98/EE 60). In order to reinforce his analysis, Levinas calls upon the whole genre of horror literature, citing classical examples from Shakespeare's tragedies – *Hamlet*, *Macbeth* – and Racine's *Phaedra*, and modern examples from Poe and Maupassant.

Parenthetically, what is fascinating here with regard to Levinas's relation to Blanchot, is that the moment of the *il y a*, the neutrality that has to be faced and surmounted, is *the moment of literature in Levinas's work*. Insofar as Blanchot employs the *il y a* to describe the experience of literature, there would seem to be perfect accord between them. Indeed, the pattern of assimilation and cross-addressing is yet more complex as, in the only footnote to Levinas's discussion, he cites Blanchot's *Thomas l'obscur* as an example of the *il y a* (DEE 103/EE 63). Thomas's world could indeed be described as a world of reversed intentionality, where things – the sea, the night, words and language itself – regard us, where the Subject dissolves into its objects, becoming 'the radiant passivity of mineral substances, the lucidity of the depths of torpor' (PF 330/GO 47).

A further provisional way of articulating the difference between Levinas and Blanchot would be to say that, for the former, literature, as the experience of neutrality par excellence, is something to be overcome – and overcome, moreover, through a certain retrieval of philosophy, ultimately of ethics as first philosophy – whereas for the latter there is a quasi-phenomenological fundamentality to the experience of literature or writing, whose overcoming would only constitute a strategy of evasion, motivated by fear. Blanchot asks us at the beginning of his discussion of Levinas in *L'entretien infini* – and this is not intended as a criticism, but as a restatement of the *Grund-Stimmung* that begins philosophy – 'What is a philosopher?', responding with Bataille that 'It is someone who experiences fear' (EI 70/IC 49). Thus, the debate between Levinas and Blanchot would seem, at a profound level, to repeat the ancient Platonic quarrel between philosophy and literature. However, the substantive question here is: Can philosophy overcome literature? Can it reduce (does it seek to reduce) the moment of writing, rhetoric and ambiguity that is necessary to its constitution? Is this the lesson of Platonic dialogue? Is Socrates *serious* in privileging living speech over dead writing, a privilege piously invoked in the trembling language of *Totality and Infinity*? This is another way of asking: Can Levinas surmount the neutrality of the *il y a*? Or is not Levinas's depiction of the ethical relation dependent at each step upon an experience of writing understood as the enigmatic ambiguity of the Saying and the Said? Is it not rather the case that Levinas's work requires the moment of the *il y a* – the ghost of writing – as its condition of possibility and perhaps impossibility? (But we are already getting ahead of ourselves.)

What is the nature of the horror undergone in the *il y a*? What does Levinas mean by calling it tragic? As is often the case, Levinas is using Heidegger as a lever to open his own thought; for the latter, *Angst* is a basic mood had in face of nothingness, it is the anxiety for my Being experienced in being-towards-death. Therefore, the most horrible thought, for Heidegger, would be that of conceiving of the possibility of my own death, of that moment when I pass over into nothingness. Against this, Levinas claims that 'horror is in no way an anxiety about death', and that what is most horrible is not the possibility of my own death, but, much worse, *the impossibility of my death*. Levinas produces two classical examples to back up this claim: first, the apparition of Banquo's ghost to Macbeth after his murder, as the haunting return of the spectre or phantom after death:

> The times have been that when the Brains were out, the man would dye, and there an end; but now they rise again . . . and push us from our stools. This is more strange than such a murder is.
>
> (DEE 101/EE 62)

Second, Phaedra's desperate cry that there is no place in which she can hide to escape her fate, not even in death:

> Le ciel, tout l'univers est plein de mes aïeux./Où me cacher? Fuyons dans la nuit infernale!/Mais que dis-je? Mon père y tient l'urne fatale.
>
> (DEE 102/EE 62)[20]

A third example might be added to this list, in Manuel Gutiérrez Nájera's poem, translated by Samuel Beckett as 'To Be':

> Life is pain. And life persists, obscure,/but life for all that, even in the tomb . . . Suicide is unavailing. The form/is changed, the indestructible

being endures . . . There is no death. In vain you clamour for death,/souls destitute of hope.[21]

Thus, horror is not the consequence of anxiety about death, rather it flows from the impossibility of death in an existence that has no exits and no escape, 'Demain, hélas!, il faudra vivre encore' (DEE 102/EE 63). The world of horror is that of existence beyond death, of awakening underground in a coffin with nobody to hear your sobbing or your fingers scratching on the wood. Horror is possession by that which will not die and which cannot be killed – something beautifully exploited by Maupassant in 'The Horla' and 'The Hand'. Such is the spectral logic of ghosts and phantoms, the world of the undead, where, as Levinas points out in a stunning passage from 'Reality and its Shadow', 'It is as though death were never dead enough'.[22] Even the final act of brutal penetration, where the stake pierces the Vampyre's heart, fails to assuage us and we await the next instalment in the tale.

For Levinas, as for Edgar Allan Poe – I am thinking in particular of 'The Facts in the Case of M. Valdemar' – there is a fate worse than death.[23] Therefore dread, or anxiety, is not fear of nothingness; rather dread is dread of existence itself, the facticity of being riveted to existence without an exit. What is truly horrible is not death but the irremissibility of existence, immortality within life, as Jonathan Swift perfectly understood in his description of the Struldbruggs or Immortals in *Gulliver's Travels*. In this regard, the possibility of death – or death as possibility – would be a civilizing power or a metaphysical comfort, the possibility of achieving dignity, of rising up in the face of existence, of dying content in one's bath like a good Roman after a bad day. But what if tomorrow does not bring death, but only the infinity of today, the irremissibility of an existence one is unable to leave? What if the rope with which the suicide leaps into the void only binds him tighter to the existence he is unable to leave? What if there is something stronger than death, namely dying itself?

(iii)
Ambiguity – Blanchot's secret

We are now in a position to understand what Blanchot means when he writes that 'From a certain point of view, literature is divided (*partagée*) between two slopes' (PF 332/GO 48).[24] On the one hand, literature is that Sadistic–dialectical labour of negation that defines the Subject itself, whereby things are killed in order to enter the daylight of language and cognition. The first slope is that of meaningful *prose*, which attempts to express things in a transparent language that designates them according to a human order of meaning (PF 334–35/GO 51). (Incidentally, might this not go some way to explaining what is most shocking about Sade's writing, namely its prosaic *reasonableness*?) On the other hand, literature is that concern for things prior to their negation by language, an attempt to evoke the reality of things – the opacity of the night, the dim radiance of materiality. For Blanchot, doubtless thinking of Rilke and Ponge (I would think of Wallace Stevens and Seamus Heaney), this is the task of poetry.

Blanchot's very Hegelian purpose in delineating these two slopes of literature is that they both represent irresistible temptations for the writer and yet each of them is a tragic endeavour. The first, Sadeian temptation of literature as the revolutionary imperative of absolute negation results in either the cruelty and vacuity of terrorism – Blanchot produces the stunning, if apocryphal, image of Robespierre and his ministers reading a few passages from Sade's *Justine* when they had grown weary of murders and condemnations and needed a break (EI 338/IC 227) – or, more likely, masturbatory writing in a prison cell or suburban bedroom. The second temptation of literature as the desire to reveal that which exists prior to all revelation – which revelation destroys – is destined to fail because each poem is a revelation and hence conceals that which it meant to reveal. The writer, even the most delicate of poets, always has the Midas touch, which simultaneously renders things precious and kills them. This is why literature is *divided* or *shared* between these two slopes; it is the space of a certain *partage*, an experience of both sharing and division.

(It would be extremely interesting to connect this understanding of literature as *partage* with Jean-Luc Nancy's discussion of community as *partage*, expressed in the polysemic, near-dialectical formula 'toi (e(s)t) (tout autre que) moi', which expresses both the sharing or commonality of community, in the relation between you and me (*toi et moi*), where you are me (*toi est moi*), but where this sharing is itself sustained by the recognition of division, where you are wholly other than me (*toi est tout autre que moi*). Perhaps this link between Blanchot and Nancy goes some way to explaining the latter's use of the notion of *communisme littéraire*, a notion that can be traced to Bataille's attempts to think an anti-fascist and anti-aestheticist conception of community.)[25]

The *partage* of literature is its treachery. Literature cannot simply be divided up and one's location is always uncertain. If you write, believing yourself to know where you are and what slope you are going to follow, then literature will insidiously cause you to pass from one slope to the other:

if you convince yourself that you are indeed there where you wanted to be, you are exposed to the greatest confusion because literature has already insidiously caused you to pass from one slope to the other and changed you into what you were not before.

(PF 335/GO 52)

The situation of the writer is thus always caught between the two slopes. For example, one could be a writer who believed, like Flaubert, in the absolute transparency of prose, but whose entire work, Blanchot claims, evokes the horror of existence deprived of a world (PF 335/GO 52). Alternatively, one could desire, like Ponge or Heaney, to write poetry faithful to the intangible grain of things and only produce gobbets of utter transparency that reduce the elusive to the banal.

For Blanchot, the situation of literature, the experience of this *partage* between its two slopes, is *ambiguity*, which is the secret to 'Literature and the Right to Death'. Which is why, when Blanchot writes of literature's treachery, he also adds that this very ambiguity is 'sa vérité retorse' – its devious, wily, crafty, cunning, twisted truth. To put this in the form of a hypothesis, we can say that for Blanchot *ambiguity is the truth of literature, and perhaps also the truth of truth, which is to say that truth is something duplicitous and bivalent* – like *physis*, it loves to hide.

With this thought of literature as ambiguity, one can begin to see, I would claim, the deeper function that the *il y a* plays in Blanchot's work, because, as Levinas points out, the *il y a* is the very experience of ambiguity:

There is no determined being, anything can count for any thing else. In the equivocation, the threat of the pure and simple presence of the *il y a* takes form.

(DEE 96/EE 59)

Thus, the *il y a* is not, as it might seem at first glance, simply placed on the side of the second slope of literature. If the first slope of literature wants to reduce all reality to consciousness – pure daylight – through a labour of negation, then the second slope of literature wants to achieve a total unconsciousness – pure night – and fuse with the reality and materiality of things. The fact that literature can achieve neither total consciousness nor total unconsciousness, leads, Blanchot claims, to a fundamental *discovery*:

By negating the day, literature reconstructs the day as fatality; by affirming

62

the night, it finds the night as the impossibility of the night. This is its discovery.

(PF 331/GO 48)

One can approach this discovery through Levinas's account of insomnia. The second slope of literature desires the night, the first or pure night of Novalis's hymns, but discovers only the *impossibility* of the night. Instead of some rapturous merging or ecstatic fusion with the night of unconsciousness, one is unable to sleep, and hence the essential night is discovered as the fatality or necessity of that which cannot be evaded, a consciousness without subjectivity, but a consciousness, nonetheless, that draws out diurnal activity to the point where it turns over into the utter neutrality of fatigue and sleepless exhaustion.[26] On the other hand, the first slope of literature desires a total grasp of the day, as a world of absolute freedom, but discovers the day not as freedom but as fatality. This is the insomniac's experience of the day: the day stupefied by lack of sleep, the day as something to which one is riveted, what Blanchot calls the madness of the day. *Literature is thus the discovery of the world of the insomniac, as the double impossibility and double necessity of the day and the night.* This is why, in *L'écriture du désastre*, Blanchot defines the writer as 'l'insomniaque du jour' (ED 185). The experience of the writer, this insomniac of the day, is divided/shared between two slopes of literature that are simultaneously necessary and impossible. Ambiguity – the truth of literature – consists in the experience of being suspended between day and night, of watching with eyes open in the night, of eyes stupefied by the spectre of insomnia in the day. The fundamental experience towards which literature tends is the ambiguity of the *il y a*.

Thus my claim here is that the *il y a* is a kind of primal or primitive scene in Blanchot's work, something to which it keeps returning as its secret, its unstable point of origin, *as the origin of the artwork*. This claim can be supported anecdotally with reference to *Ethique et infini*, where Levinas says that although Blanchot prefers to speak of 'the neuter' or 'the outside', the *il y a* is '*probablement là le vrai sujet de ses romans et de ses récits*' (EeI 40). However, it can be more interestingly illuminated by looking at a much-discussed and highly significant passage – a kind of parable – from *L'écriture du désastre*, entitled '*Une scène primitive?*' (ED 117).[27]

(A primitive scene?) *You who live later, close to a heart that no longer beats, suppose, suppose this: the child – is he perhaps seven or eight – standing, drawing the curtain and looking through the window. What he sees, the garden, the winter* trees, the wall of a house: whilst he is looking, in the way a child does, at his playing space, he gets bored and slowly looks up towards the ordinary sky, with clouds, the grey light, the drab and distance-less day.

What happens next, the sky, the same sky, suddenly open, absolutely black, revealing (as through a broken window) such an absence that everything has been lost since always and for ever, to the point where the vertiginous knowledge is affirmed and dissipated that nothing is what there is and above all nothing beyond. The unexpectedness of this scene (its interminable trait) is the feeling of happiness that immediately overwhelms the child, the ravaging joy to which he can only testify through tears, an endless streaming of tears. They think that the child is sad, they try to console him. He says nothing. He will henceforth live in the secret. He will weep no more.

(ED 117)

So, in this passage, a seven- or eight-year-old child – is it a boy or a girl? Cixous argues that it is the former and places the masculinity of the child and its consequent relation to the law of the phallus at the centre of her reading – looking out of the window on its familiar playing space and letting its eyes wander upwards, is suddenly presented with the openness and absolute blackness of the sky, with the vertiginous knowledge of utter absence, namely that 'rien est ce qu'il y a, et d'abord rien au-delà'. In his oblique commentary on 'Une scène primitive', which appears some sixty pages later in *L'écriture du désastre*, and which reads as if the text had been written by somebody else, Blanchot writes:

For my part, I hear the irrevocability of the *il y a* that being and nothingness roll like a great wave, unfurling it and folding it back under, inscribing and effacing it, to the rhythm of the anonymous rustling.

(ED 178)

This link between the *il y a* and the primal scene of childhood is hinted at in the 1978 Preface to *De l'existence à l'existent*, where Levinas remarks that the *il y a* 'goes back to one of those strange obsessions that one keeps from childhood and which reappear in insomnia when the silence resounds and the voids remain full' (DEE 11). In the insomniac horror that defines the experience of writing for Blanchot, the claim is that we have a vague memory of this primal scene of childhood, a dim reminiscence of being alone at night in one's cot, lying frightened in the murmuring darkness, undergoing the agony of separation, what Levinas calls 'le remue-ménage de l'être' ('the bustle or hubbub of being').[28] The primal scene of the *il y a* is the experience of disaster, of the night without stars, the night that is not the starry heaven that frames the Moral Law, but the absence, blackness and pure energy of the night that is beyond law. In Blanchot's parable, what is unexpected is the child's feeling of happiness, the ravaging joy that follows the disclosure or the *il y a*, this vertiginous knowledge of finitude. We might connect this *sentiment de bonheur* with another more recently disclosed primitive scene, namely that described in Blanchot's tantalizingly brief 1994 text *L'instant de ma mort*, where the protagonist in this seemingly autobiographical, confessional narrative describes 'un sentiment de légèreté extraordinaire, une sorte de béatitude' felt at the point of being executed by soldiers believed to be German (who turn out to be Russian). The protagonist then describes this feeling as 'the happiness of being neither immortal nor eternal', the vertiginous knowledge of finitude which opens onto 'the feeling of compassion for suffering humanity'.[29] Returning to the passage from *L'écriture du désastre*, Blanchot concludes that the child testifies to the knowledge of finitude in an endless stream of tears, at which point they (*on* – presumably his parents) try to console him, believing him to be sad. The child says nothing, 'he will henceforth live in the secret. He will weep no more.'

My claim has been that the *il y a* – this vertiginous knowledge of finitude – is the secret of Blanchot's work. To write is to learn to live in this secret. Literature is the life of the secret, a secret which must be and cannot be told. The secret, in order to remain a secret, cannot be revealed; that is, literature cannot be reduced to the public realm, to the daylight of publicity and politicization, which is not at all to say that literature is reducible to the private realm. Rather, literature is essentially heterogeneous to the public realm, essentially secretive, which is paradoxically to claim that it is the *depoliticizing condition for politicization*, the precondition for a space of the political based on the vertiginous knowledge of finitude, a space that remains open and, dare one add, democratic.[30]

(f)
The (im)possibility of death – or, how would Blanchot read Blanchot if he were not Blanchot?

If ambiguity is to become the truth of literature, then we have to begin with *death*. Blanchot writes:

If we want to bring back literature to the movement which allows all its ambiguities to be grasped, that movement is here: literature, like ordinary speech, begins with the end, which is the only thing that allows us to understand. In order to speak, we must see death, we must see it behind us.

(PF 338/GO 55)

We have already seen how each of the two slopes of literature entails a certain right to death. On the first slope, the life of the Subject is produced through a work of negation which is equated with death; it is 'The life that endures death and maintains itself in death'. Death is therefore the most fundamental *possibility* of the Subject, which enables consciousness to assume its freedom. This is why Blanchot writes that 'death is the greatest hope of human beings, their only hope of being human' (PF 338/GO 55). Death is a civilizing power and the condition of possibility for freedom, projection and authentic existence. With the second slope of literature, and the notion of the *il y a*, we introduced the idea of a fate worse than death, namely the interminability of existence where I lose the ability to die and where the dead seem to rise up from their graves. Dread, on this second slope, cannot be characterized as Being-towards-death, but is rather dread in the face of the irremissibility of Being itself. In the *il y a*, death is impossible, which is the most horrible of thoughts. Ambiguity, therefore, is ultimately an ambiguity about death, where the writer is suspended between two rights to death, *death as possibility and death as impossibility*. The writer, like the narrator in Maupassant's 'The Horla', senses that 'he is the prey of an impersonal power that does not let him either live or die' (PF 341/GO 58), a situation that Blanchot baptizes with the phrase 'the double death' (EL 126/SL 103).

I would now like to analyse this notion of the double death as it appears in *L'espace littéraire* and tease out certain of its important consequences. As is so often the case in Blanchot, the writer who best exemplifies the ambiguous situation of the writer is Kafka (who is surely the implied subject of much of 'Literature and the Right to Death'). Blanchot cites a passage from Kafka's *Diaries*, where he reports a conversation with Max Brod: Kafka writes that on his deathbed he will be very content, and, moreover, that all the good passages in his writing, where someone is undergoing an agonizing or unjust death (Kafka seems to be thinking of 'In the Penal Colony' and *The Trial*), might well be very moving for the reader, 'But', he continues, 'for me, since I think I can be content on my deathbed, such descriptions are secretly a game. I even enjoy dying in the character who is dying' (EL 106/SL 90). This passage, precisely because of its 'irritating insincerity' (EL 106/SL 91), is revealing for Blanchot. It reveals an economy of death at work in the writer: on the one hand, Kafka's heroes inhabit a space − *une espace littéraire* − where death is not possible and is not my project. One thinks here of the dog-like death of Josef K; of the vast writing machine that executes the inhabitants of the penal colony by inscribing their punishment into their flesh; of Gregor Samsa, who does not die, but who is reborn as a giant insect; of K's vain struggle for death, that great unattainable castle; of 'Die Sorge des Hausvaters', where the spectral figure of Odradek is unable to die. Yet, on the other hand, although Kafka's characters inhabit what Blanchot calls '*(le) temps indéfini du "mourir"*' (EL 108/GO 92), Kafka himself claims that his art is a means to attain mastery over death, to die content, to have death as a possibility. With a pathos that comes close to the Hegelian position discussed above − indeed, in these pages Blanchot once again cites Hegel's phrase on the life that endures death and maintains itself in death (EL 122/SL 101) − Kafka judges that the goal of his art is a certain mastery of death, and that, in writing, he is death's equal, 'I do not separate myself from men in order to live in peace, but in order to be able to die in peace' (EL 110/SL 93). The wages of art are a peaceful death. The writer here enters a circular relation with death, what we might think of as a thanatological circle, that is premised upon the belief that death is a possibility. The writer, in this case Kafka, writes in order to be able to die, and the power to write comes from an anticipated relation with death. Writing is what permits one to master death − to die content − and yet death is what provokes one to write: '*Write to be able to die − Die to be able to write*' (EL 111/SL 94).

For all systems of thought that take the question of finitude seriously, that is to say, for all non-religious systems of thought, which do not have an escape route from death (and *ressentiment* against life) through the postulates of God and immortality (let me just state polemically that I agree with Sade when he writes that 'The idea of God is the one fault that I cannot forgive man' − EI 340/IC 229), the fundamental question is that of finding a *meaning* to human finitude. If death is not just going to have the contingent character of a brute fact, then one's mortality is something that one has to project freely as the product of a resolute decision. As Blanchot reminds us:

Three systems of thought − Hegel's, Nietzsche's, Heidegger's − which

67

attempt to account for this decision and which therefore seem, however much they may oppose each other, to shed the greatest light on the destiny of modern man, are all attempts at making death possible.

(EL 115/SL 96)

The acceptance of the ubiquity of the finite is not simply expressed in the fact that the human being is mortal; rather the human being must *become* mortal. Death, therefore, is something to be achieved; it is, for Heidegger, a possibility of *Dasein*, the most fundamental possibility (of impossibility) which allows us to get the totality of our existence in our grasp. However, the question here must be: *Is* death possible? *Can* I die? Can I say, 'I can', with respect to death?

Blanchot approaches this question by considering the problem of suicide. Surely the test case as to whether death is a possibility and is therefore something of which I am able, is suicide. If I can say 'I can' with respect to death, then I *can* kill myself. The act of suicide would be the perfection or highest realization of death as a possibility, a possibility which, Blanchot writes, is like a supply of oxygen close at hand without which we would smother. Can I kill myself? Have I the power to die? Can I go to my death resolutely, maintaining death, in Heideggerian terms, as *the possibility of impossibility*? Or is death more truly the experience of not being able to die, of not being able to be able, in Levinasian terms *the impossibility of possibility*?

Cruelly and crudely, there is an almost logical contradiction at the heart of suicide, namely that if death is my ownmost possibility, then it is precisely the moment when the 'I' and its possibilities disappear. In suicide, *the 'I' wants to give itself the power to control the disappearance of its power*. If the resolute decision of the suicide is to say, 'I withdraw from the world, I will act no longer', then he or she wants to make death an act, a final and absolute assertion of the power of the 'I'. Can death be an object of the will? Blanchot writes:

> The weakness of suicide lies in the fact that whoever commits it is still too strong. He is demonstrating a strength suitable only for a citizen of the world. Whoever kills himself could, then, go on living: whoever kills himself is linked to hope, the hope of finishing it all.

(EL 125/SL 103)

The desire of the suicide is too strong and too hopeful because it conceives of death as the action of an 'I' in the realm where the 'I' and its action no longer pertain. The contradiction of the suicide is analogous to that of the insomniac, who cannot will him or herself to sleep because sleep is not an exercise of the will – sleep will not come to the person who wills it.

Paradoxically, the suicide, in desiring to rid him or herself of the world, acts with an affirmativeness that would equal the most resolute, heroic and Creon-like of worldly citizens. Blanchot continues:

> He who kills himself is the great affirmer of the *present*. I want to kill myself in an 'absolute' instant, the only one which will not pass and will not be surpassed. Death, if it arrived at the time we choose, would be an apotheosis of the instant; the instant in it would be that very flash of brilliance which mystics speak of, and surely because of this, suicide retains the power of an exceptional affirmation.
>
> (EL 126/SL 103)

Suicide is the fantasy of total affirmation, an ecstatic assertion of the absolute freedom of the Subject in its union with nature or the divine, a mystical sense of death as the *scintilla dei*, the spark of God. Obviously, one finds this line of thought in Dostoevsky's depiction of Kirilov in *The Devils*, where the latter says, 'He who dares to kill himself is a god. Now everyone can make it so that there shall be no God and there shall be nothing. But no one has done so yet.'[31] In his Diary, Dostoevsky calls Kirilov's position 'logical suicide' that necessarily follows the loss of belief in the 'loftiest' 'sublime' idea: the immortality of the soul.[32] However, one can find analogies in Hölderlin's fascination with the death of Empedocles or more widely in the Jena romantics, where Friedrich Schlegel writes of 'the enthusiasm of annihilation', where 'the meaning of divine creation is revealed for the first time. Only in the midst of death does the lightning bolt of eternal life explode' (ID 106). The moment of annihilation is the becoming-enthused, possession by and identification with the god – rapture, fervour, intensity. The moment of the controlled extinction of the Subject is also paradoxically the moment when the Subject swells to fill the entire cosmos, becoming, like Walt Whitman, a cosmos, and the uncreated creator of the cosmos. The death of the self confirms its deathlessness. As Baudelaire defines pantheism in his 'Fusées', 'Panthéisme. Moi, c'est tous; tous c'est moi.'[33] Such is also the death ecstasy of eternal return in Nietzsche, expressed in a stunning fragment from the *Nachlass*:

> Five, six seconds and no more: then you suddenly feel the presence of eternal harmony. Man, in his mortal frame cannot bear it; he must either

physically transform himself or die . . . In these five seconds I would live the whole of human existence, I would give my whole life for it, the price would not be too high. In order to endure this any longer one would have to transform oneself physically. I believe man would cease to beget. *Why have children when the goal is reached?* [34]

The romantic and post-romantic affirmation of annihilation is an attempt at the appropriation of *time*, to gather time into the living present of eternity at the moment of death. By contrast, the person who *actually* lives in despair, that quiet resignation that makes up so much of the untheorized content of everyday life, dwells in the interminable temporality of dying, in *le temps mort*, where time is experienced as passing, as slipping away – the wrinkling of the skin, the murmuring of senescence, crispation. Such a person has no time and, in a wonderful image, 'no present upon which to brace himself in order to die' (EL 126/SL 103).

As we will see in detail in Lecture 3, this temporality of dying is evoked in Beckett's *Malone Dies*. The 'I' that speaks in Beckett's books has no time and yet has all the time in the world, 'I could die today, if I wished, merely by making a little effort. But it is as well to let myself die, quietly, without rushing things' (T 166). The point here can be made with reference to the theme of *laughter*. On the one hand, there is the laughter of eternal return, laughter *as* eternal return, the golden Nietzschean laughter of affirmation, which laughs in the face of death; a laughter that I always suspect of emanating from the mountain tops, a neurotic laughter: solitary, hysterical, verging on sobbing. On the other hand, there is Beckett's laughter, which is more sardonic and sarcastic, and which arises out of a palpable sense of impotence, of impossibility. But, for me, it is Beckett's laughter that is more joyful (not to mention being a lot funnier), 'If I had the use of my body I would throw it out of the window. But perhaps it is the knowledge of my impotence that emboldens me to that thought' (T 201).

To want to commit suicide is to want to die *now*, in the living/dying present of the *Jetztpunkt*. As such, within suicide, *there is an attempt to abolish both the mystery of the future and the mystery of death*. Suicide – or euthanasia for that matter – wishes to eliminate death as the prospect of a contingent future that I will not be able to control, to avoid the utter misery of dying alone or in pain. 'But', as Blanchot points out, 'this tactic is vain' (EL 127/SL 104). The ultimate (but perhaps necessary) bad faith of suicide is the belief that death can be achieved – and eliminated, that in Chaucer's words 'deeth shal be deed', or Donne's 'death, thou shalt die'[35] – through a controlled leap into the void. However, once this heroic leap is taken, all the suicide feels is the tightening of the rope that binds him more closely than ever to the existence he would like to leave, the horror of the irremissibility of Being which we discussed above. Death is not an object of the will, the *noema* of a *noesis*, and one cannot, truly speaking, *want* to die. To die means losing the will to die and losing the will itself as the motor that drives the deception of suicide. This means no longer conceiving of death as possibility and attempting to accept the harder lesson of the impossibility of death, which will open the time of an infinite future and the space of the other night. Through its very weakness, the thought of *le mourir* proves itself stronger than *la mort*. But is it possible to face up to the impossibility of death, this most horrible of thoughts?

To respond to this question, we must introduce Blanchot's notion of 'the double death'. Blanchot writes:

> There is one death which circulates in the language of possibility, of liberty, which has for its furthest horizon the freedom to die and the power to take mortal risks – and there is its double, which is ungraspable, it is what I cannot grasp, what is not linked to me by any relation of any sort, that never comes and toward which I do not direct myself.
>
> (EL 126/SL 104)

The experience of death is double, and the most extreme exposure to the first slope of death as possibility in suicide, opens onto the second slope of the impossibility of death. In believing that death is something that can be grasped – in placing the noose around my neck or the gun in my mouth – I expose myself to the radical ungraspability of death; in believing myself able to die, I lose my ability to be able.

And yet, is one to conclude from this that the second conception of death as impossibility is the *truth* of death for the writer? If so, what has happened to the irreducibility of ambiguity as the truth of literature that was insisted upon above? To illuminate these problems, Blanchot proposes an analogy between the suicide and the artist that will return us once more to the problem of the writer's bad faith or self-deception. The suicide's self-deception is to mistake the second conception of death for the first and hence to believe that death is a possibility. This bad faith is analogous to that of the writer, who always mistakes the book that is completed and published for the work that is written. The writer undergoes an unacknowledged form of *désoeuvrement*, where 'The writer belongs to the work, but what belongs to him is the book' (EL 12/SL 23). The writer is a priori ignorant of the nature of his work, as is revealed by Kafka in his *Diaries*, and will have recourse to the journal or diary form as a way of arresting the worklessness of literature in literature. In the journal, the writer desires to remember himself as the person he is when he is not writing, 'when he is alive and real, and not dying and without truth' (EL 20/SL 29). Therefore, both the artist and the suicide are deceived by forms of possibility, both want to have a power in the realms where power slips away and becomes impossible: in writing and dying.

Thus, there would seem to be a two-fold claim being made by Blanchot's work: first, writing has its unattainable source in an experience of worklessness and a movement of infinite dying; this has variously been described as the desire of Orpheus' gaze, the energy of pure exteriority prior to law, the experience of the other night and the impossibility of death. And yet, second, the extremity of this experience cannot be faced, it would be intolerable to the human organism, and the writer is therefore necessarily blind to the guiding insights of his or her work, requiring, in Nietzschean terms to be developed below, the metaphysical comfort of the Apollonian to save them from the tragic truth of the Dionysian. The writer necessarily experiences bad faith with regard to what takes place in writing, and is therefore maintained in an ambiguous relation, divided between two slopes, and drawn by two opposing temptations. Perhaps the task of the *reader*, however, is to see this ambiguity *as* ambiguity and to point towards its source.

In his justly celebrated essay on Blanchot, and in what would appear to be intended as a criticism, Paul de Man argues that Blanchot's critical writings are ultimately directed towards an impossible act of self-reading, where his work seeks an ontological impersonality that is self-defeating, because it cannot eliminate the self, because the self cannot be defeated. Hence, Blanchot is caught in an unavoidable circularity, which is more clearly signalled in the original title of de Man's essay, 'La circularité de l'interprétation dans l'œuvre critique de Maurice Blanchot'.[36] However, on my reading of Blanchot, which has sought to emphasize the irreducibility of ambiguity, bad faith and the impossibility of self-reading in the writer's experience, Blanchot would seem to have predicted these criticisms and, indeed, made them the cornerstone of his approach to literature. Which raises the fascinating speculative question: how would Blanchot read Blanchot if he were not Blanchot?

(g)
Holding Levinas's hand to Blanchot's fire[37]

(i)
A dying future

Death is not the *noema* of a *noesis*. It is not the object or meaningful fulfilment of an intentional act. Death, or, rather, dying, is by definition ungraspable; it is that which exceeds intentionality and the noetico-noematic correlative structures of phenomenology. There can thus be no phenomenology of dying, because it is a state of affairs about which one could neither have an adequate intention nor find intuitive fulfilment. The ultimate meaning of human finitude is that we cannot find meaningful fulfilment for the finite. In this sense, dying is meaningless and, consequently, the work of mourning is infinite.

Since direct contact with death would demand the death of the person who entered into contact, the only relation that the living can maintain with death is through a representation, an image, a picture of death, whether visual or verbal. And yet, we immediately confront a paradox: namely, that the representation of death is not the representation of a presence, an object of perception or intuition – we cannot draw a likeness of death, a portrait, a still life, or whatever. Thus, representations of death are *misrepresentations*, or rather they are representations of an absence.[38] The paradox at the heart of the representation of death is perhaps best conveyed by the figure of prosopopeia, that is, the rhetorical trope by which an absent or imaginary person is presented as speaking or acting. Etymologically, prosopopeia means to make a face (*prosopon* + *poien*); in this sense we might think of a death mask or *memento mori*, a form which indicates the failure of presence, a face which withdraws behind the form which presents it.[39] In a manner analogous to what Nietzsche writes about the function of *Schein* in *The Birth of Tragedy*, such a prosopopeic image allows us both to glimpse the interminability of dying in the Apollonian mask of the tragic hero, and redeems us from the nauseating contact with the truth of tragedy, the abyss of the Dionysian, the wisdom of Silenus: 'What is best of all is . . . not to be born, not to *be*, to be *nothing*. But the second best for you is – to die soon.'[40] I believe that many of the haunting images – or death masks – in Blanchot's *récits* (I am thinking of the various death scenes in *Thomas l'obscur*, *L'arrêt de mort* and *Le dernier homme*, but also of the figures of Eurydice or the Sirens) have a prosopopeic function, they are a face for that which has no face, and they show the necessary inadequacy of our relation to death. To anticipate myself a little, my question to Levinas will be: *must the face of the other always be a death mask?*

However, as I show above with reference to Blanchot's reading of Kafka's *Diaries*, the writer's (and philosopher's) relation with death is necessarily self-deceptive; it is a relation with what is believed to be a possibility, containing the possibility of meaningful fulfilment, but which is revealed to be an impossibility. The infinite time of dying evades the writer's grasp and he or she mistakes *le mourir* for *la mort*, dying for death. Death is disclosed upon the horizon of possibility and thus remains within the bounds of phenomenology, or what Levinas would call 'the economy of the Same'. To conceive of death as possibility is to conceive of it as *my* possibility; that is, the relation with death is always a relation with *my* death. As Heidegger famously points out in *Sein und Zeit*, my relation to the death of others cannot substitute for my relation with my own death, death is in each case *mine*.[41] In this sense, death is a self-relation or even self-reflection that permits the totality of *Dasein* to be grasped. Death is like a mirror in which I allegedly achieve narcissistic self-communion; it is the event in relation to which I am constituted as a Subject. Being-towards-death permits the achievement of authentic selfhood, which, I have elsewhere argued,[42] repeats the traditional structure of autarchy or autonomy, allowing the self to assume its fate and the community to assume its destiny. One might say that the community briefly but decisively envisaged in paragraph 74 of *Being and Time* is a community of death, where commonality is found in a sharing of finitude, where individual fates are taken up into a common destiny, where death is the Work of the community.

The radicality of the thought of dying in Blanchot is that death becomes impossible and ungraspable. It is meta-phenomenological. In Levinas's terms, dying belongs to the order of the enigma rather than the phenomenon (which, of course, passes over the complex question as to whether there can be a phenomenology of the enigmatic or the inapparent). Dying transgresses the boundary of the self's jurisdiction. This is why suicide is impossible for Blanchot: I cannot *want* to die, death is not an object of the will. Thus, the thought of the impossibility of death introduces the possibility of an encounter with some aspect of experience or some state of affairs that is not reducible to the self and which does not relate or return to self; that is to say, something other. The ungraspable facticity of dying establishes an opening onto a meta-phenomenological alterity, irreducible to the power of the Subject, the will or *Dasein* (as I see it, this is the central argument of *Time and the Other*). Dying is the impossibility of possibility and thus undermines the residual heroism, virility and potency of Being-towards-death. In the infinite time of dying, all possibility becomes impossible, and I am left passive and impotent. Dying is the sensible passivity of senescence, the wrinkling of the skin – crispation: the helplessly ageing face looking back at you in the mirror.

In this way, perhaps (and this is a significant 'perhaps') the guiding intention of Levinas's work is achieved; namely that if death is not a self-relation, if it does not result in self-communion and the achievement of a meaning to finitude, then this means that a certain plurality has insinuated itself at the heart of the self. The facticity of dying structures the self as Being-for-the-other, as substitution, which also means that death is not revealed in a relation to my death but rather in the alterity of death or the death of the other. As Levinas writes in a late text, it is 'As if the invisible death which the face of the other faces were *my* affair, as if this death regarded me'.[43]

This relation between dying and plurality allows us to raise the question of what vision of community could be derived from this anti-Heideggerian account of dying, from this fundamental axiom of heteronomy. If, as Levinas suggests, the social ideal has been conceived from Plato to Heidegger in terms of fusion, a collectivity that says 'we' and feels the solidarity of the other at its side, what Nancy calls 'immanentism', then a Levinasian vision of community would be 'a collectivity that is not a communion' (TA 89/TO 94), *une communauté désoeuvrée,* a community unworked through the irreducibility of plurality that opens in the relation to death. This is a point made by Alphonso Lingis:

> Community forms when one exposes oneself to the naked one, the destitute one, the outcast, the dying one. One enters into community not by affirming oneself and one's forces but by exposing oneself to expenditure at a loss, to sacrifice.[44]

To conceive of death as possibility is to project onto a future as the fundamental dimension of freedom and, with Heidegger, to establish the future as the basic phenomenon of time. Yet, such a future is always *my* future and *my* possibility, a future ultimately grasped from within the solitary fate of the Subject or the shared destiny of the community. I would claim that such a future is *never future enough for the time of dying,* which is a temporality of infinite delay, patience, senescence or *différence.* Dying thus opens a relation with the future which is always ungraspable, impossible and enigmatic; that is to say, it opens the possibility of a future without me, an infinite future, *a future which is not my future.*[45]

75

What is a future that is not my future? It is another future or the future of an other, that is, the future that is always ahead of me and my projective freedom, that is always to come and from where the basic phenomenon of time arises, what Levinas calls dia-chrony. But what or who is the other? Does the word 'other' translate the impersonal *autre* or the personal *autrui*? For Blanchot, writing establishes a relation with alterity that would appear to be strictly impersonal: a relation with the exteriority of *le neutre*. It would seem that the latter must be rigorously distinguished from the personal alterity sought by Levinas, the alterity of *autrui*, which is ultimately the alterity of the child, that is, of the son, and the alterity of illeity, of a (personal) God.[46] It would seem that although the experience of alterity in Blanchot and Levinas opens with the impossibility of death, that is, with their critique of Heidegger's Being-towards-death, one might conclude that there is only a formal or structural similarity between the alterity of the relation of the neuter and the alterity of *autrui* and that it is here that one can draw the line between Levinas and Blanchot. However, in opposition to this, I would like to muddy the distinction between Blanchot and Levinas by tracking an alternative destiny for the *il y a* in Levinas's work and indicating the direction that could be taken by a Blanchot-inspired re-reading of Levinas.

(ii)
Atheist transcendence

I have shown above that the experience of literature has its source in 'the primal scene' of what Blanchot variously calls 'the other night', 'the energy of exteriority prior to law' or 'the impossibility of death', and that this experience can be understood with reference to Levinas's notion of the *il y a*. However, although Levinas's thinking begins with the *il y a*, which is his deformation of the Heideggerian understanding of Being (an appropriation and ruination of the *Seinsfrage*), his entire subsequent work would seem, on a first reading, to be premised upon the necessity to surmount the *il y a* in order to move on to the hypostasis of the Subject and ultimately the ethical relation to the other, a relation whose alterity is underwritten by the trace of illeity. In order to establish that ethics is first philosophy (i.e. that philosophy is *first*), Levinas must overcome the neutrality of the *il y a*, the ambiguous instance of literature.

Now, to read Levinas in this way would be to adopt 'a linear narrative',[47] that would begin with one ('bad') experience of neutrality in the *il y a* and end up with another ('good') experience of neutrality in illeity, after having passed through the mediating moments of the Subject and *Autrui* (roughly, Sections II and III of *Totality and Infinity*). To read Levinas in this way would be to follow a line from the *il y a* to the Subject, to *Autrui*, to illeity. However, the question that must be asked is: can or, indeed, *should* one read Levinas in a linear fashion, as if the claim to ethics as first philosophy were a linear ascent to a new metaphysical summit, as if *Totality and Infinity* were an anti-Hegelian rewriting of the *Phenomenology of Spirit* (which might yet be true at the level of Levinas's intentions)? Is the neutrality of the *il y a* ever decisively surmounted in Levinas's work? And if this is so, why does the *il y a* keep on returning like the proverbial repressed, relentlessly disturbing the linearity of the exposition? As I show above, this is also to ask: Is literature ever overcome in the establishment of first philosophy? Is the moment of writing, the instance of the literary, of rhetoric and ambiguity, in any way reducible or controllable in Levinas's work? Or might one track an alternative destiny of the *il y a*, where it is not decisively surmounted but where it returns to interrupt that work at certain critical moments? Might this not plot a different itinerary for reading Levinas, where the name of Blanchot would function as a clue or key for the entire problematic of literature, writing, neutrality and ambiguity in the articulation of ethics as first philosophy? Let me give a couple of instances of this tracking of the *il y a* before provisionally sketching what I see as the hugely important consequences of such a reading.[48]

The problem with the *il y a* is that it stubbornly refuses to disappear and that Levinas keeps on reintroducing it at crucial moments in the analysis. It functions like a standing reserve of non-sense from which Levinas will repeatedly draw the possibility of ethical significance, like an incessant buzzing in the ears that returns once the day falls silent and one tries to sleep. To pick a few examples, almost at random: (i) in the 'Phenomenology of Eros', the night of the *il y a* appears alongside the night of the erotic, where 'the face fades and the relation to the other becomes a neutral, ambiguous, animal play' (TeI 241/TI 263). In *eros*, we move beyond the face and risk entering the twilight zone of the *il y a*, where the relation to the other becomes profane and language becomes lascivious and wanton, like the speeches of the witches in *Macbeth*. But, as is well known, the moment of eros, of sexual difference, cannot be reduced or by-passed in Levinas's work, where it functions as what Levinas calls in *Time and the Other* an 'alterity content' (TA 14/TO 36) that ensures the possibility of fecundity, plurality within Being and consequently the break with Parmenides.

(ii) More curious is the way in which Levinas will emphasize the possible ambivalence between the impersonal alterity of the *il y a* and the personal alterity of the ethical relation, claiming in 'God and Philosophy' that the transcendence of the neighbour is transcendent almost to the point of possible confusion with the *il y a*.[49] (iii) Or, again, in the concluding lines of 'Transcendence and Intelligibility', where, at the end of a very conservative and measured restatement of his main lines of argumentation, Levinas notes that the account of subjectivity affected by the unpresentable alterity of the infinite could be said to announce itself in insomnia, that is to say, in the troubled vigilance of the psyche in the *il y a*.[50] It would appear that Levinas wants to emphasize the sheer radicality of the alterity revealed in the ethical relation by stressing the possible confusion that the subject might have in distinguishing between the alterity of the *il y a* and that of illeity, a confusion emphasized by the homophony and linked etymology of the two terms.

In *Existence and Existents*, Levinas recounts the Russian folk tale of Little John the Simpleton who throws his father's lunch to his shadow in order to try and slip away from it, only to discover that his shadow still clings to him, like an inalienable companion (DEE 38/EE 28). Is not the place of the *il y a* in Levinas's work like Little John's shadow, stretching mockingly beneath the feet of the philosopher who proclaims ethics as first philosophy? Is not the *il y a* like a shadow or ghost that haunts Levinas's work, a revenant that returns it again and again to the moment of nonsense, neutrality and ambiguity, like Banquo's ghost returns Macbeth to the scene of his crime, or like the ghostly return of scepticism after its refutation by reason? Thus, if the *il y a* is the first step on Levinas's itinerary of thought, a neutrality that must be surmounted in the advent of the Subject and *Autrui*, then might one not wonder why he keeps stumbling on the first step of a ladder that he sometimes claims to have thrown away? Or, more curiously – and more interestingly – *must* Levinas's thought keep stumbling on this first step in order to preserve the possibility of ethical sense? Might one not wonder whether the ambiguity of the relation between the *il y a* and illeity is essential to the articulation of the ethical in a manner that is analogous to the model of scepticism and its refutation, where the ghost of scepticism returns to haunt reason after each refutation? Isn't this what Levinas means in 'God and Philosophy' (but other examples could be cited) when he insists that the alternating rhythm of the Saying and the Said must be substituted for the unity of discourse in the articulation of the relation to the other (DQVI 127/CPP 173)?

Which brings me to a hypothesis in the form of a question: might not the *fascination* (in Blanchot's sense) that Levinas's writing continues to exert, the way that it captivates us without us ever feeling that we have captured it, be found in the way it keeps open the question of ambiguity, the ambiguity that defines the experience of language and literature itself for Blanchot, the ambiguity of the Saying and the Said, of scepticism and reason, of the *il y a* and illeity, that is also to say – perhaps – of evil and goodness?

(Let us note in passing that there is a certain thematization, perhaps even a staging, of ambiguity in Levinas's later texts. For example, when he speaks in *Otherwise than Being* of the beyond of being 'returning and not returning to ontology... becoming and not becoming the meaning of being' (AE 23/OB 19). Or again, in the discussion of testimony in Chapter Five of the same text, 'Transcendence, the beyond essence which is also being-in-the-world, needs ambiguity, a blinking of meaning which is not only a chance certainty, but a frontier both ineffaceable and finer than the outline (*le tracé*) of an ideal line' (AE 194/OB 152). Transcendence *needs* ambiguity in order for transcendence to 'be' transcendence. But is not this thematization of ambiguity by Levinas an attempt to *control* ambiguity? My query concerns the possibility of such control: might not ambiguity be out of control in Levinas's text?)

What is the place of evil in Levinas's work? If I am right in my suggestion that the *il y a* is never simply left behind or surmounted and that Levinas's work always retains a memory of the *il y a* which could possibly provoke confusion on the part of the subject between the alterity of the *il y a* and the alterity of illeity, then one consequence of such confusion is the felt ambiguity between the transcendence of evil and that of goodness. On a Levinasian account, what is there to choose experientially between the transcendence of evil and the transcendence of goodness?[51] This is not such a strange question as it sounds, particularly if one recalls the way in which ethical subjectivity is described in *Otherwise than Being...* in terms of trauma, possession, madness and even psychosis, predicates that are not so distant from the horror of the *il y a*. How and in virtue of what – what criterion, as Wittgenstein would say, or what evidence as Husserl would say – is one to decide between possession by the good and possession by evil in the way Levinas describes it?

(Of course, the paradox is that there can be no criterion or evidence for Levinas for this would presume the thematizability or phenomenologizability of transcendence. But this still begs the question as to how Levinas convinces his readers: is it through demonstration or persuasion, argumentation or edification, philosophy or rhetoric? Of course, Levinas is critical of rhetoric in conventionally Platonic terms, which commits him, like Plato, to an anti-rhetorical rhetoric, a writing against writing.)

Let me pursue this question of evil by taking a literary example of possession mentioned in passing by Levinas in his discussion of the *il y a*, when he speaks of 'the smiling horror of Maupassant's tales' (DEE 97/EE 60). In Maupassant, as in Poe, it is as though death were never dead enough and there is always the terrifying possibility of the dead coming back to life to haunt us. In particular, I am thinking of the impossibility of murdering the eponymous Horla in Maupassant's famous tale. The Horla is a being that will not die and which cannot be killed, and, as such, it exceeds the limit of the human. The Horla is a form of overman, 'After man, the Horla'.[52] What takes place in the tale – suspending the temptation to psychoanalyse – is a case of possession by the other, an invisible other with whom I am in relation but who continually absolves itself (incidentally, the Horla is always described using the neutral, third person pronoun – the *il*) from the relation, producing a trauma within the self and an irreducible responsibility. What interests me here is that in Maupassant the possession is clearly intended as a description of possession by evil, but does not this structure of possession by an alterity that can neither be comprehended nor refused not closely resemble the structure of ethical subjectivity found in substitution? That is to say, does not the trauma occasioned in the subject possessed by evil more adequately describe the ethical subject than possession by the good? Is it not in the excessive experience of evil and horror – the insurmountable memory of the *il y a* – that the ethical subject first assumes its shape? Does this not begin to explain why the royal road to ethical metaphysics must begin by making Levinas a master of the literature of horror? But if this is the case, why is radical otherness goodness? Why is alterity ethical? Why is it not rather evil or an-ethical or neutral?[53]

Let us suppose – as I indeed believe – that Levinas offers a convincing account of the primacy of radical alterity, whether it is the alterity of *autrui* in *Totality and Infinity* or the alterity within the subject described in *Otherwise than Being*.... Now, how can one conclude from the 'evidence' (given that there can be no evidence) for radical alterity that such alterity is goodness? In virtue of what further 'evidence' can one predicate goodness of alterity? Is this not, as I suspect, *to smuggle a metaphysical presupposition into a quasi-phenomenological description*? Such a claim is, interestingly, analogous to possible criticisms of the *causa sui* demonstration for the existence of God.[54] Let us suppose that I am convinced that in order to avoid the vertigo of infinite regress (although one might wonder why such regress must be avoided; why is infinite regress bad?) there must be an uncaused cause, but in virtue of what is one then permitted to go on and claim that this uncaused cause is God (who is, moreover, infinitely good)? Where is the argument for the move from an uncaused cause to God *as* the uncaused cause? What necessitates the substantialization of an uncaused cause into a being that one can then predicate with various other metaphysical or divine attributes? Returning the analogy to Levinas, I can see why there has to be a radical alterity in the relation to the other and at the heart of the subject in order to avoid the philosophies of totality, but, to play devil's advocate, I do not see why such alterity then receives the predicate 'goodness'. Why does radical otherness have to be determined as good or evil in an absolute metaphysical sense? Could one – and this is the question motivating this critique – accept Levinas's quasi-phenomenological descriptions of radical alterity whilst suspending or bracketing out their ethico-metaphysical consequences? If one followed this through, then what sort of picture of Levinas would emerge?

The picture that emerges, and which I offer in closing as one possible reading of Levinas, as one way of arguing with him, is broadly consistent with that given by Blanchot in his three conversations on *Totality and Infinity* in *The Infinite Conversation* (EI 70–105/IC 49–74).[55] In the latter work, Blanchot gives his first extended critical attention to a theme central to his *récits*, the question of *autrui* and the nature of the relation to *autrui*.[56] What fascinates Blanchot in his discussion of Levinas is the notion of an absolute relation – *le rapport sans rapport* – that monstrous contradiction (that refuses to recognize the principle of non-contradiction) at the theoretical core of *Totality and Infinity*, where the terms of the relation simultaneously absolve themselves from the relation. For Blanchot, the absolute relation offers a *non-dialectical account of intersubjectivity* (EI 100–1/IC 70–71), that is, a picture of the relation between humans which is not – *contra* Kojève's Hegel – founded in the struggle for recognition where the self is dependent upon the other for its constitution as a Subject. For Levinas, the interhuman relation is an event of radical asymmetry which resists the symmetry and reciprocity of Hegelian and post-Hegelian models of intersubjectivity (in Sartre and Lacan, for example) through what Levinas calls, in a favourite formulation, 'the curvature of intersubjective space' (TeI 267/TI 291).

For Blanchot, Levinas restores the strangeness and terror of the interhuman relation as the central concern of philosophy and shows how transcendence can be understood in terms of a social relation. But, and here we move onto Blanchot's discreet critique of Levinas, the absolute relation can *only* be understood socially and Blanchot carefully holds back from two Levinasian affirmations: first, that the relation to alterity can be understood *ethically* in some novel metaphysical sense and, second, that the relation has '*theological*' implications (i.e. the trace of illeity). So, in embracing Levinas's account of the relation to *autrui* (in a way which is not itself without problems), Blanchot places brackets around the terms 'ethics' and 'God' and hence holds back from the metaphysical affirmation of the Good beyond Being. Blanchot holds to the ambiguity or tension in the relation to *autrui* that cannot be reduced either through the affirmation of the positivity of the Good or the negativity of Evil. The relation to the Other is neither positive nor negative in any absolute metaphysical sense; it is rather neutral, an experience of neutrality that – importantly – is *not* impersonal and which opens in and as that ambiguous form of language that Blanchot calls literature. (If I had the space and competence, it is here that one could begin a reading of Blanchot's *récits* in terms of the absolute relation to the *autrui*.)

Where does this leave us? For me, Levinas's essential teaching is the primacy of the human relation as that which can neither be refused nor comprehended and his account of a subjectivity *disposed* towards responsibility, or better, responsivity (*Responsivität* rather than *Verantwortung*, following Bernhard Waldenfels's distinction).[57] Prior to any metaphysical affirmation of the transcendence of the Good or of the God that arises in this relation, and to which I have to confess myself quite deaf (I have tried hard to listen for many years), what continues to grip me in Levinas is the attention to the other, to the other's claim on me and how that claim changes and challenges my self-conception.[58] Now, how is this claim made? Returning to my starting point with the question of death, I would like to emphasize something broached early in Levinas's work, in *Time and the Other*, but not satisfactorily pursued to my mind, where the first experience of an alterity that cannot be reduced to the self occurs in the relation to death, to the ungraspable facticity of dying (TA 51–69/ TO 67–79). Staying with this thought, I would want to claim, with Blanchot, that what opens up in the relation to the alterity of death, of my dying and the other's dying, is not the transcendence of the Good beyond Being or the trace of God, but is the neutral alterity of the *il y a*, the primal scene of emptiness, absence and disaster, what I am tempted to call, rather awkwardly, atheist transcendence.

We are mortals, you and I. There is only my dying and your dying and nothing beyond. You will die and there is nothing beyond. I shall slowly disappear until my heart stops its soft padding against the lining of my chest. Until then, the drive to speak continues, incessantly. Until then, we carry on. After that there is nothing.

Lecture 2

Unworking romanticism

(a)
Our naïveté

'Romanticism is our naïveté' write Lacoue-Labarthe and Nancy in *The Literary Absolute* (AL 27/LA 17). What is romanticism's naïveté? But, first, what is romanticism?

By romanticism, I mean Jena or early German Romanticism, particularly the work of Friedrich Schlegel, more particularly the publication of the journal *Athenäum* between 1798 and 1800, and more particularly still the ensembles of fragments published in that journal. Thus, I will be working with quite a narrow understanding of romanticism, which might be provisionally defined as the attempt, and, as we will see, *only* the attempt, to unify philosophy and poetry, or to heal the wound which has been festering since Plato's *Republic* between the claims of philosophy and literature.

Such a desire for unification itself arose as a response to the perceived crisis of the modern world at the end of the eighteenth century: the eviscerated bequest of the Enlightenment that Hegel would later perceive as the amphibious world of *Moralität* and that Nietzsche would later call nihilism. In shorthand, the problem facing those we now call the romantics (although, of course, they didn't employ this term pejoratively as a self-description) was how to take up and continue 'the greatest tendencies of the age' (AF 216),[1] namely the inheritance of Kant in philosophy, of Goethe in poetry and the French Revolution in politics. The problem to which romanticism attempts to provide a solution is that of how to reconcile the values of the Enlightenment – secularization, humanism, the

85

libertarian and egalitarian values of republicanism, the primacy of reason and the ubiquity of science – with the disenchantment of the world that those values seem to bring about. The post-religious or post-traditional values of the Enlightenment somehow fail to connect with the fabric of moral and social relations, with the stuff of everyday life, and lead instead to the progressive degradation of those relations. Such is, as I said above, the dialectic of nihilism.

The problem faced by romanticism is what might count as a meaningful life, or as a meaning for life, after one has rejected the founding certainties of religion. To return to the theme with which I began these lectures, philosophy – and this is its unhappy consciousness – asks questions and should ask questions which have the same form as religious questions, but without the possibility of finding a religious response to those questions. This is philosophy's essential disappointment. Philosophy is atheism arising out of the experience of nihilism, but it is an uneasy atheism.

The naïveté of romanticism is the conviction that the crisis of the modern world can best be addressed in the form of art. More specifically, the crisis can be addressed through poetry, broadly conceived, where the *novel* would be the ideal romantic poetic form ('*Progressives Gedicht ist der Roman*'[2]), what Schlegel elsewhere refers to, in a revealing metaphor, as 'an eternally developing book, the gospel of humanity and culture' (ID 95). The unification of philosophy and literature would be the writing of a novel. A number of points already clamour for our attention here:

1   As Walter Benjamin points out, when Friedrich Schlegel 'speaks of art, he thinks above all of poetry';[3] although poetry must be understood in its broadened Greek sense as *poiesis*, as creation or production. But there is a continual slippage in the romantics between poetry in the broad sense, as creation, and poetry in the narrow sense as specific literary genres (epic, lyric, drama).

2   If the novel is the ideal romantic poetic form, then what is a novel or what counts as a novel? As we will see, this is an open question, because the great romantic novel was never written by the romantics themselves, although attempts were made, notably Friedrich Schlegel's *Lucinde* and Novalis's *Heinrich von Ofterdingen*.[4]

3   Most importantly, although the precursors for the romantic artwork might well be derived from antiquity, which for Schlegel meant the wit and irony of Socratic dialogue rather than the Sophoclean tragedy so important to Hegel,

Hölderlin and Schelling (Schlegel notes that 'Novels are the Socratic dialogues of our time' (CF 26); Nietzsche says almost the same thing, with a slightly more barbed intent in *The Birth of Tragedy*[5]), romanticism does not attempt to retrieve the art of antiquity. What Schlegel saw as the fusion of art and raw beauty amongst the Greeks was no longer possible or *even* desirable in modernity, insofar as such art would constitute nothing more than a pale imitation of the ancients. Thus, Jena Romanticism is not engaged in an attempted *mimesis* of the ancients, where, according to Hegel, the art of antiquity is characterized by an alleged immediacy or sensuous unification of form and content, but rather in what would be impossible for Hegel (and extremely improbable for Heidegger): namely, the production of a specifically *modern* artwork, that would be world-disclosive, self-conscious and self-critical. Schlegel calls such an artwork variously 'the philosophy of poetry', 'transcendental poetry' or 'the poetry of poetry', and the 'modern' precursors of this romantic artwork (and we might begin to wonder about what periodization of modernity is at work here) would be the great triptych of Dante, Shakespeare and Cervantes. The romantic artwork would stand in relation to its world in a manner that is analogous to the relation of Dante to the world of mediaeval Florence or the relation of Shakespeare to Elizabethan London. The naïveté of romanticism is the belief that the crisis of the modern world can be addressed in the form of art. It is the belief in the possibility of producing a modern artwork that would be the peer, but not the imitation, of the art of antiquity.

Now, as has been very well documented, the philosophical conditions for romantic naïveté lie in the reception of Kant, specifically in the new articulation of the relation between aesthetics and philosophy that opens up in the Third Critique. As Lacoue-Labarthe and Nancy write, 'Kant opens up the possibility of romanticism' (AL 42/LA 29). The preparation for the romantic and idealist inheritance of Kant can be seen, in nascent and almost symbolic form, in the 'Oldest Systemprogramme of German Idealism', an anonymously or collectively authored fragment from 1796, although reflecting the ideas to be systematically presented four years later in Schelling's *System of Transcendental Idealism*.[6]

Of course, it is more customary and perhaps philosophically more justified to follow Hegel and Benjamin and trace Jena Romanticism to Fichte's early conception of reflection in the *Wissenschaftslehre*.[7] Reflection is the activity of the intelligence, or *free* action, defined as the *form* of thinking itself without regard to specific contents. A notion whose potential limitlessness was seen by Schlegel

— in distinction from Fichte — as positive. I come back to the notion of infinite reflection later in this lecture and try and link it to Blanchot's notion of *désoeuvrement*. However, for the purposes of this lecture I will follow Lacoue-Labarthe and Nancy and trace romanticism to Kant rather than Fichte.

(i)
Kantian fragmentation

Now, as is well known, the philosophical actuality of the 1790s in Germany was the perceived fragmentation of the Kantian critical system. The source of this fragmentation was the division between ethics and epistemology, the border separating the First and Second Critiques, namely that Kant had drawn tight the bounds of knowledge in order to make room for faith, the primacy of practical reason. This distinction produced a crisis (in the etymological sense) or splitting at the heart of the Kantian subject, leaving it in what Hegel might have called an amphibious existence, swimming in the sea of causality whilst simultaneously breathing the oxygen of freedom. Let me try to explain this more carefully.

For Kant, the principle of apperception — where I can only grasp the manifold of representations insofar as they are mine, where the 'I think' must accompany all my representations — is 'the highest principle in the whole sphere of human knowledge'.[8] However, the 'I think' cannot itself be represented, the ground of the subject cannot be known for this would demand, for Kant, an impossible act of intellectual intuition or *inspectio sui*. Thus, although Kant maintains the primacy of the epistemological subject, this subject is de-substantialized or weakened, becoming something logically rather than ontologically entailed as a place holder in the argument of the transcendental deduction. Thus, Kant is methodologically, but not metaphysically, Cartesian. The Kantian subject is a *cogito* without an *ergo sum*.

However, this weakening of the subject in the epistemological domain is paralleled by a strengthening of the subject in the ethical domain, the subject of freedom claimed by the Moral Law. The weakening of the epistemological subject is carried out *for the sake of* the ethical subject. But this raises a serious and potentially devastating problem at the heart of the Kantian project: that is, if Kant is committed to the primacy of practical reason, to our life as free moral subjects, then *there is no evidence for freedom*. We act *as if* we were free, we propose and universalize maxims, but there is no evidential or epistemic certainty for freedom. I cannot intuit freedom. Freedom is blind. All Kant offers is 'the fact of reason', understood as the consciousness of the way in which the objectivity of the moral law determines the subjective will, but which is based on no empirical intuition.[9] As Bowie remarks, Kant is like Moses — the Moses of the German nation, according to Hölderlin; structurally Jewish rather than Christian according to both Hegel and Derrida — trying to make people believe in a God they cannot see.[10] Adapting one of Schleiermacher's *Athenäum* Fragments, which uncannily predicts Hegel's critique of Kant, we might say that Kant discovered a point outside of the earth but lost the earth itself. That is, the preoccupation with *Sollen* leads to the obscuring of the situation of 'der sittliche Mensch' (AF 355).

The romantic and idealist inheritance of Kant — which perhaps conspires with what I have elsewhere called a logic of *incarnation* whose force is irreducibly Christian[11] — will therefore be obsessed with the question as to whether there could be an intuition or a presentation of the subject to itself, an auto-presentation or objective instantiation of the subject's freedom. This question is powerfully and continually linked to an ontology of *praxis* and *Wirklichkeit* and casts a shadow that stretches beyond Hegel to Feuerbach, the Young Hegelians, Marx and well into this century. It is this desire for a practical instantiation of freedom that lies behind Marx's celebrated eleventh thesis on Feuerbach. It is within this disappointment — the disappointment to realize philosophy as praxis — that thinking continues to move and have its being. But, *felix culpa*.

Incipit Kant's Third Critique — for it is through the category of the aesthetic or the beautiful that the possibility of the subject's auto-presentation will be pursued. It is the aesthetic that will be the locus for the attempt at a systematic unification or, better, *harmonization* of the elements of the critical project.[12] In the words of the 'Systemprogramme', '*Truth and Goodness are brothers only in Beauty*'.[13] That is, the epistemological project of the First Critique and the ethical project of the Second Critique will only be reconciled in the Third Critique. As Schelling expresses it four years after the 'Systemprogramme' in 1800, 'The general organon of philosophy — and the keystone of its whole arch — is the philosophy of art'.[14] Aesthetics is the bridge that spans epistemology and ethics. In Platonic terms, beauty is the bridge that unites the domains of the sensuous and the intelligible. As Coleridge puts it, the Beautiful or Fair is what unites the Good and the True in the Philosophical Trinity:

> Where'er I find the Good, the True, the Fair,
> I ask no names — God's spirit dwelleth there!

The unconfounded, undivided Three,
Each for itself, and all in each, to see
In man and Nature, is Philosophy.[15]

Passing over the curious slippage that divides Kant from his romantic and idealist inheritors, namely the move from the Kantian concern with the aesthetic as such, particularly the beauty of nature – the much-derided tulips and daffodils that decorate the pages of the Third Critique – to the post-Kantian identification of the aesthetic with art, that leads ultimately to Hegel's exclusion of nature as an object of aesthetic regard at the beginning of the *Aesthetics*, it can be said that *the artwork will provide a sensuous image of freedom.*[16] The artwork is evidence for freedom. The work of art is purposively produced through free human activity *and* it is intuitively available in the form of an object, *it is the object in which the subject finds its own freedom reflected back to it and realized.* As such, the work of art partakes in and unites the realms of necessity and freedom, epistemology and ethics or the sensuous and the intelligible that Kant had sundered. This produces what Bernhard Lypp calls an *aesthetic absolutism*, where the aesthetic is the medium in which the oppositions of the Kantian system – which, by implication, are the antinomies of the Enlightenment – are absolved and overcome.[17] The category of the aesthetic is the place where the problem of nihilism – the dilemma as to what might count as a meaningful life without the founding certainties of religion – is broached. Of course, the question can be raised, thinking in particular of Kierkegaard, as to whether the aesthetic can perform this lofty function and whether it is only through art that we respond to nihilism.

(ii)
Deepest naïveté – political romanticism

Of course, none of what I have said so far should exactly be news. But, it is with this aesthetic absolutism in mind that one can begin to make sense of certain propositions from the 'Systemprogramme': 'I am convinced that the supreme act of reason, in which all other acts are included, is an aesthetic act', 'The philosophy of spirit is an aesthetic philosophy'.[18] The category of the aesthetic solders and sublates all oppositions and antinomies, it permits what we might call, with Hegel, the *spiritual* identification of the subject insofar as self-recognition is achieved in the absolute otherness of the artwork, where art is, in Hegel's words, *'born of the Spirit and born again'*.[19] This means that philosophy must complete itself in and through an artwork – 'The philosopher must possess as much aesthetic power as the poet'[20] – philosophy and poetry must become one. In the 'Systemprogramme', this unification of philosophy and poetry is pursued through the theme of the 'mythology of reason', which is an important theme in post-Kantian philosophy, most obviously in Schelling. The mythology of reason entails a two-way movement of reconciliation or harmonization, where the philosopher must learn to swim in the sea of aesthetic sensuousness and the non-philosopher – identified with the newly emergent mass of the people (*das Volk*) – must learn to breathe the oxygen of reason. The duck-billed platypus becomes an image of reconciled humanity. The mythology of reason would be the aesthetic unification of philosophy and poetry, of the intelligible and the sensible and epistemology and ethics, whose horizon would be the unity of a people. When the people become rational through the activity of the new mythology and the philosophers become sensuous, then 'eternal unity will reign amongst us'.[21]

With this in mind, we can approach what is doubtless the deepest naïveté of romanticism, that is, the linking of its aesthetic absolutism to the *work* of politics, to politics conceived on analogy to aesthetics and the inception of what Paul de Man has called an 'aesthetic ideology'.[22] The reasoning that binds aesthetics to politics is impeccable enough: if the artwork is a sensuous image of freedom, then it provides us with an image of what the world might be like if freedom were realized – it is through art that we intimate the dimensions of a politically transfigured everyday life (think, for example, of Coleridge's early sonnets on Pantisocracy[23]). The revolutionary political character of the aesthetic can be seen in the 'Systemprogramme' through its invocation of what Lacoue-Labarthe and Nancy call a 'speculative Rousseauism' (AL 48/LA 34), where the form of the modern state must be overcome in order to establish a moral sociality, 'We must therefore also overcome the state! For every state must treat free man like a mechanical cog; and it should not do this; therefore it should *disappear*.'[24] Although this Rousseauism has little to do with Rousseau's political philosophy – which was premised upon the impossibility and even the undesirability of both a return to nature or an overcoming of the state – what is being described here is the organicist fantasy of an overcoming of the state and an end to politics, the proto-totalitarian dream of a society without power, antagonism and capital, the utopia of a post-bourgeois order that is shared by Fourier in France, the Pantisocrats in England and their Situationist heirs in 1968.

Of course, the paradox here is that at the moment when, in Blanchot's words, 'literature declares that it is taking power' (EI 520/IC 354), at the moment when, in the wake of the French Revolution, the poet declares himself legislator for humanity, a moment when literature becomes identified with terror in a way that is repeated on the political right in the 1930s and on the left in 1968, he or she is utterly marginal to society, like 'Citoyen' Sade calling through a urine funnel to the crowds assembled outside the Bastille. The protestations of the philosopher–artist are merely the cries of the drowning man, sinking beneath the waters of generalized bourgeois indifference – otherwise known as the nineteenth century. Romanticism's audacity is only matched by the extent of its failure. In Emersonian terms, to which I return later in this lecture, it is the failure to transform genius into practical power, to unify philosophy and poetry through revolutionary praxis, a failure to carry through Marx's eleventh thesis on Feuerbach, a failure symbolized by the text of the 'Systemprogramme' itself, this fragment of theoretical radicalism that lay gathering dust in a pile of Hegel's papers for 120 years until a chance discovery by Franz Rosenzweig.

The almost inconceivable naïveté of Jena Romanticism is perhaps best captured by Lukács in a brilliant and very early essay from 1907, 'On the Romantic Philosophy of Life':

> Jena at the end of the eighteenth century. An episode in the lives of a few human beings, of no more than episodic significance for the world at large. Everywhere the earth resounds with battles, whole worlds are collapsing, but here, in a small German town, a few young people come together for the purpose of creating a new, harmonious, all-embracing culture out of the chaos. They rush at it with that inconceivable, reckless naïveté that is given only to people whose degree of consciousness is morbidly high, and to these only for a single cause in their lives and then only for a few moments. It was a dance on a glowing volcano, it was a radiantly improbable dream; after many years the memory of it still lives on in the observer's soul as something bewilderingly paradoxical. For despite all the wealth of what they dreamed and scattered, 'still there was something unearthly about the whole thing'. A spiritual tower of Babel was to be erected, with nothing but air for its infrastructure; it had to collapse, but when it did, its builders broke down too.[25]

From a rather different political orientation to that of Lukács, a powerful conservative critique of romanticism is proposed by Carl Schmitt in *Political*

Romanticism.[26] For Schmitt, romanticism is rooted in a fatal double bind: on the one hand, it repudiates the aesthetic principles of the past, thereby becoming autonomous art, but on the other hand, it absolutizes art and aestheticizes every sphere of culture. Thus, art is absolutized and yet it is rendered problematic because there is no obligation, as there is in neo-classicism, to achieve a grand or strict form. This collapse of objective aesthetic criteria leads ineluctably to a subjectivization and privatization of aesthetic experience. Schmitt's thesis is that romanticism is a subjectified occasionalism. In the classical metaphysical occasionalism of Malebranche, God is posited as the occasion for the interaction of mental and physical events. In romanticism, however, God or any comparable objective metaphysical authority is abandoned and the human subject occupies centre stage, which means that anything and everything that appears to the romantic subject can become an occasion. For Schmitt, romanticism is a metaphysical narcissism, where there can be no reference to an authority or source of legitimation outside the play of the subjective imagination.

This aestheticization of existence, this occasionalist attitude, where the substantial conflicts of the real world are aesthetically transposed into data capable of generating a pleasing aesthetic response or into becoming material for the great romantic novel (and anything and everything can become a subject for the great novel of the world), explains why *political* romanticism is characterized by extreme vacillation and indecision. A romantic might support the French Revolution in 1789, then endorse the restoration in 1806, only to then endorse the revolutions after 1830 or in 1848. Political romanticism is infinitely plastic. As such, in Schmitt's terms, romanticism is incapable of *thinking the political*, that is, of making a decision in a situation of conflict, 'Where political activity begins, political romanticism ends'.[27] Of course, and this is Schmitt's real target in *Political Romanticism* and elsewhere, romanticism is dependent upon liberalism and protestantism, where the emancipated private individual of the bourgeois social order is the only metaphysical authority. Thus, romanticism can only arise in an individualistically disintegrated society where each person has become their own priest, where 'the ultimate roots of romanticism . . . lie in the private priesthood'. In liberal protestant society each individual is 'our own master builder in the cathedral of our personality'.[28]

It's a good thing that Carl Schmitt didn't read Walt Whitman. In the Introduction to the first edition of *Leaves of Grass*, after claiming that 'The Americans of all nations at any time upon the earth have probably the fullest poetical nature. The United States themselves are essentially the greatest poem',

Whitman goes on to confirm Schmitt's thesis that 'There will soon be no more priests. Their work is done . . . A new order shall arise and they shall be the priests of man, and every man shall be his own priest.'[29] I shall return to this connection between romanticism, liberal democracy and America in my discussion of Stanley Cavell.

(iii)
Hegel, Schlegel

So, romanticism is naïve. Bewilderingly naïve. The question is: can one therefore dismiss this naïveté, laying it aside as a childish aberration, in Lukács's words as a 'radiantly improbable dream'? Yes. One can. Romanticism fails. And for two very good reasons, one based on internal criteria, the other on external criteria.

First, on internal criteria, romanticism fails because neither Friedrich Schlegel, Novalis, nor the other romantics, made good on their promise for an artwork, a new mythology, a literary absolute that would reconcile the crisis of post-Kantian modernity and overcome nihilism. The romantic literary absolute would be the great novel of the modern world, a total book that would be the peer of Dante, Shakespeare and Cervantes and the superior of Goethe (of course, the status of Goethe in relation to Jena Romanticism is much more complicated than I am allowing here). But, unsurprisingly perhaps, this ambition was never realized and the great novel was never written. As Schmitt remarks, with perhaps greater perspicacity than he intended, romanticism is 'an art without works'.[30] This aesthetic failure can perhaps be paralleled with the already indicated political failure of romanticism, where Friedrich Schlegel, the republican, atheist (or at least mystic), individualist, aesthete; the man whose brother, August Wilhelm, said of him that he has a theory ovarium in his brain, where, like a hen, he lays a theory each morning (AF 269); this man ends up, in Blanchot's words, 'a fat philistine' (EI 51/IC 352), a convert to Catholicism and civil servant to Metternich. Romanticism ends badly, in England as well as Germany, with Coleridge sailing south to Malta into self-imposed exile and Wordsworth appointed Distributor of Stamps for Westmorland. Is this because, as Blanchot suggests, 'Romanticism is essentially what begins and what cannot but finish badly: an end that is called suicide, madness, loss, forgetting' (EI 517/IC 352–53)? The question then is: does one judge romanticism by its beginning or its end, by its radicalism or its conservatism? Or should romanticism be judged, with Schmitt, by the political vacuity that permits such vacillation?

Secondly, romanticism could also be said to fail when judged by external criteria. In this regard, the sternest and most persuasive critic of romanticism is, of course, Hegel. One, admittedly partial, way of reading Hegel would be to claim that the whole edifice of the system exists to ensure the impossibility of romanticism: the celebrated, if much misunderstood, thesis that art is a thing of the past, that the absolute can no longer be presented aesthetically in sensuous form as in the tragic age of the Greeks, that philosophy is the truth of art and that consequently art is only a moment in the history of truth. Might not a hostility to romanticism explain why Hegel strangely – and perhaps even spitefully – categorizes all post-classical, i.e. Christian, art as *romantic*, a category which culminates in poetry – the most spiritual aesthetic medium – only to pass over into philosophy and the prose of thought?

However, the clearest picture of Hegel *contra* Schlegel [31] can be found in a few devastating pages from the Introduction to the *Aesthetics* and a couple of oblique and irritable broadsides in the Preface to the *Phenomenology*.[32] Of course, Schlegel is not referred to by name in the *Phenomenology*, and there is nothing surprising in this, as all of Hegel's targets in the *Phenomenology* are obliquely addressed or cross-dressed in someone else's garments – Descartes is dressed as a sceptic, Kant as a stoic, etc. However, it is clear that what Hegel objects to in Jena Romanticism is its exclusive emphasis on feeling and genius, which reduces the labour of the concept to the discourse of edification, and where the romantic hitches the highway of despair in the robes of the high priest. As Hegel writes, not without a little *ressentiment*:

> It is not a pleasant experience to see ignorance, and a crudity without form or taste, which cannot focus its thought on a single abstract proposition, still less on a connected chain of them, claiming at one moment to be freedom of thought and toleration, and at the next to be even genius.[33]

And again, in a tone we have already heard in Schmitt:

> The high sense for the Eternal, the Holy, the Infinite strides along in the robes of a high priest, on a road that is from the first no road, but has immediate being as its centre, the genius of profound, original ideas and lofty flashes of inspiration. But just as profundity of this kind still does not

95

reveal the source of essential being, so too these sky rockets of inspiration are not yet the empyrean. True thoughts and scientific insight are only to be won through the labour of the Concept.[34]

Hegel opposes romantic inspiration to conceptual perspiration. In the *Aesthetics*, the essence of Hegel's critique of Schlegel was that he is a good critic but a bad philosopher. The philosophical insights of the romantics, such as they are, testify to an intellectual magpieism and paucity of speculative seriousness. By tracing the source of romantic irony to Fichte's conception of the ego, Hegel makes the predictably 'Hegelian' claim that romanticism remains abstract and formal, and represents an abstract freedom divorced from any specific content. That is to say, romanticism remains quite alien to the ethico-social sphere of *Sittlichkeit*. Like its Kantian and Fichtean antecedents, romanticism is ultimately neither *wirklich* nor *sittlich*. It is, in Lukács's words, 'a dance on a glowing volcano'.

For Hegel, there are two paths that the romantic poet can follow from this conclusion. First, he or she can refuse the seriousness of *Sittlichkeit*, of conventional laws and morals, by employing irony to maintain an infinitely evasive relation to the world that views morality as a product of contingency and caprice, and which regards humanity as poor, deceived, stupid creatures unable to attain the lofty standpoint of the romantic ironist. (Sadly, there is some truth in this claim, when one reflects on the nagging and narrow élitism of many of the fragments.) Second, and perhaps more insightfully, the blissful self-enjoyment of the romantic ironist can collapse into the feeling of longing (the celebrated *Sehnsucht*) for a lost substance to life, which accounts for the mood of *melancholy* which, I feel (and I will return to this below), pervades the fragments and provides what we might call their ambience.[35] In this sense, the ironical romantic poet becomes the morbidly beautiful soul, whose effect, unlike what Hegel calls the *truly* beautiful soul – i.e. Hölderlin – borders on the comic. In short, the Jena romantics are 'worthless yearning natures'.[36]

(iv)
Romantic modernity

Romanticism is naïve. We have seen that this naïveté can be refuted on internal and external criteria, and that this could provide a plausible basis for claiming that romanticism is a thing of the past. One should not be naïve about naïveté. If romanticism remains naïvely naïve, then an awareness of the internal aesthetic failure of romanticism, its reactionary political destiny and the external power of Hegelian or Schmittian critiques might lead one, with Cavell, to define romantics as those who 'dream revolution, and break their hearts' (CR 464).

However, the thought that I want to try and slowly unravel in the following parts of this lecture, and which will lead me to the work of Stanley Cavell, via a reading of Friedrich Schlegel's fragments, concerns the possibility of presenting and defending another version of romanticism, what I will call an *unworked romanticism*. The fact that romanticism does not work, rather than being a proof of weakness, will be interpreted instead as a sign of its strength. Its very weakness is its strength (a theme that will be taken up again in my discussion of Beckett in Lecture 3). Such a romanticism will still be naïve, but it will be rooted in a self-consciousness of naïveté. That is, an acute awareness of failure and the limitedness of thought.[37] The genre for the expression of this self-conscious naïveté is the fragment. It is, I believe, this self-consciousness of failure and limitation that leads Schlegel to define the effectivity of romantic fragments as 'Nothing but a Lessingean salt against spiritual sloth . . . marginal glosses to the text of the age' (AF 259). This will hopefully lead to my real motivation in this lecture, namely the contribution that an unworked romanticism can make to the thinking of finitude – of the finiteness of the finite – where romanticism would be less concerned with a complete transformation or aesthetic revolution of life and culture and more with an acceptance of finitude and an acknowledgement of the other that will lead to a less radiant but perhaps more probable account of the relation between thought and everyday life, what I call in Lecture 3 the achievement of meaninglessness.

Romanticism is naïve. But my claim, echoing that of Lacoue-Labarthe and Nancy, is that it is *our* naïveté; that is, *we* (and I will leave the limits of this *we* deliberately vague) still belong to the epoch opened up by romanticism. Romanticism is not a thing of the past, it is rather the trace of a past that continues to haunt our living present, in Paul de Man's words:

> We carry it within ourselves as the experience of an *act* in which, up to a certain point, we ourselves have participated.[38]

My broad claim, that I will hopefully begin to make good below, is that we are inheritors of what we might call a *romantic modernity*: that romanticism provides the profile for a modernity in which we are both unable to believe, but which we are unable to leave.[39]

(b)
Digression I: Imagination as resistance (Wallace Stevens)

What would it mean to give up on romantic naïveté? Let us recall the situation in Jena, so eloquently described above by Lukács: the naïveté of early German romanticism – that tiny explosion of the intellect that lasted for barely three years, that pure consciousness of the moment where what was essential was that everything was said and done very quickly – is centred in the belief, as Lacoue-Labarthe and Nancy write, that politics passes through the aesthetic or the literary (AL 27/LA 17). That is, the belief that artworks are or can be effective; that theoretical or artistic interventions in the domain of culture are politically necessary; that poetry can transfigure everyday life; that, to cite Wallace Stevens, 'After one has abandoned a belief in God, poetry is that essence that takes its place as life's redemption'.[40]

The naïveté of Jena Romanticism is that shared by all avant-garde movements – from 1789 to 1968 – of which Jena is perhaps the first modern instantiation. The naïveté is centred in the belief that a small group of highly educated men and women,[41] working together collectively and anonymously in a 'para-academic' context, could theorize and hegemonize new cultural forms and effect a new vision of social relations. Of course, this irreducible naïveté, which is the precondition for any avant-garde, also goes together with what the Situationists called 'recuperation', where the status quo, particularly under capitalist conditions of production, is able to recuperate any potentially subversive avant-garde movement and make it serve its purposes by commodifying it – although commodification is always open to ironization, exemplified in Malcolm McLaren's slogan, 'cash from chaos'.

To give up on the naïveté of romanticism would be to give up on a form of resistance to what Wallace Stevens calls 'the pressure of reality'(NA 36). It would lead to the complete privatization of literature and all artistic production; it would be the end of philosophy understood as the *imaginative* effort to link the public and the private (obviously, I am thinking of Rorty here); it would lead to the total bureaucratization or professionalization of politics and the banalization of everyday life. To say the very least, such is the risk of the contemporary situation, where we are living through what Stevens called 'a leaden time' (NA 63), what Heidegger called after Hölderlin 'a time of dearth' and Wittgenstein, in the Preface to the *Investigations,* called the 'dearth and darkness of this time'.[42] Romantic naïveté is the resistance of the philosophical, poetic and political imagination to our somewhat chastening contemporary circumstances. Knowing itself to be naïve, romanticism is still, I believe, the most plausible response to nihilism. Romantic naïveté is the consciousness of the tranquillized bustle and anaemic pallor of everyday life, and the attempt to resist the disenchantment of the everyday with the violence of the imagination – *imagination au pouvoir*!

(*Excursus*: This violence of the imagination is perhaps most immediately evidenced by contemporary popular music. Examples would be too numerous to mention, but I am thinking in particular of the late situationism of the Sex Pistols.[43] It is, to say the least, an uncanny and slightly depressing experience to witness one's own past being recuperated as cultural and social history, but Jon Savage has brilliantly elucidated the sheer romanticism of early punk: its pure consciousness of the moment expressed through fragments of explosive and abusive noise, above which utopian heresies were screamed or sneered. Punk, like romanticism, began well, for a few moments acting like an oxygen tank for those being suffocated by what passes for life in English suburbia. But, like romanticism, it also ended badly, in a nihilistic stupor of distrust and drug abuse, its *spectacular* energy recuperated by the very music industry whose codes and conventions it had, if only for a few months, so beautifully subverted. The fact that punk's despairing romanticism was continuous with the attempt of the Situationist International to transfigure everyday life through aesthetic and political creation is not incidental, I believe. The difference between punk and '68 Situationism might be characterized precisely in terms of the former's self-consciousness of naïveté and a recognition of the limits of any radical political and cultural transformation of the everyday. Whereas Raoul Vaneigem is able to write in 1966 that 'We have a world of pleasures to win and nothing to lose but boredom',[44] punk is a working through of the creative possibilities of boredom that resist any easy translation into pleasure. Boredom as the self-consciousness of naïveté is the *Grund-Stimmung* of punk. Vaneigem's work is charmingly marked by a tone reminiscent of Fourier, where everyone is a potential revolutionary artist and 'the work of art of the future will be the construction of a passionate life'.[45] But by the autumn of 1976 the celebrated Situationist reversal of perspective was clearly no longer possible, the British economy had fallen through the floor, and the only resort was a nihilism whose bastard progeny was Thatcherism.)[46]

In a wonderfully precise formulation, Stevens defines poetry as 'the imagination of life' (NA 65), a definition that we might align with one of Stanley Cavell's definitions of philosophy, which he describes as the effort 'to bring my own language and life into imagination' (CR 125). The task of poetry and philosophy, then, might be defined as the continual imaginative transfiguration of reality through language, a language that, crucially, does not take flight from the real but *adheres* to it in the 'supreme fictions' without which, for Stevens, life would be inconceivable. Continuing the quote from Cavell, he insists that what is required in philosophy is

> A convening of my culture's criteria, in order to confront them with my words and life as I pursue them and as I may imagine them; and at the same time to confront my words and life as I pursue them with the life my culture's words may imagine for me: *to confront culture with itself, along the lines in which it meets in me.* This seems to me a task that warrants the name of philosophy. It is also the description of something we might call education . . . *In this light, philosophy becomes the education of grown-ups.*
>
> (CR 125, SC's emphasis)

Handsome words. Yet, we are grown-ups and we know that this is a time of dearth, a time of darkness, a leaden time. Has there ever been any moment less naïve than the present? Or is the present moment always experienced as lacking naïveté, as lacking the exercise of the poetic, philosophical and political imagination? Are we today experiencing a peculiar drought or poverty of the imagination? This is not exactly a falsifiable thesis. Yet even if it were true, even if, as Stevens puts it in 'The Plain Sense of Things',

> . . . it is as if
> We had come to end of the imagination
> Inanimate in an inert savoir,

we should note that he immediately adds the rejoinder:

> Yet the absence of the imagination had
> Itself to be imagined.
>
> (CP 502–3)

Consider the apparent contradiction here: it is as if we had come to an end of the imagination, yet the absence of the imagination had itself to be imagined. Are we therefore at the end of the imagination? Or is the end of the imagination itself an act of imagination? As Stevens writes in *The Necessary Angel*, 'It is one of the peculiarities of the imagination that it is always at the end of an era' (NA

22). The ambiguity here is that suggested by Beckett in his antithetical formula, *Imagination Dead Imagine.*

And yet, wherever one puts the emphasis, let us momentarily grant Stevens his premise that the contemporary resources of the imagination are scarce. As he puts it, we are living 'After the leaves have fallen'. Ours is the 'poverty/Of autumnal space'. One is reminded of the climate of coldness, specifically the late autumn, winter and very early spring of New England that defines the season of Stevens's last poems, 'this blank cold, this sadness without cause', where 'A fantastic effort has failed':

> Weaker and weaker, the sunlight falls
> In the afternoon.
>
> (CP 504)

And again

> The effete vocabulary of summer
> No longer says anything.
>
> (CP 506)

Yet despite (or even because of) this climate of coldness or leaden time, despite the peculiar drought of the imagination, perhaps it is with these scant resources that we can return to what Stevens calls 'a plain sense of things'. Yet, what is a return to a plain sense of things? Is it a return? For Stevens, and this will be amplified when we come to Cavell, the return to a plain sense of things is not a return to the banal, or to the world of common sense; rather it is a turn – a conversion, a turning about – to a sense of things that has already been transfigured by poetic language, that is, by the violence of the imagination.

Stevens's response to the Heideggerian/Hölderlinian question *Wozu Dichter in dürftiger Zeit?* ('What are poets for in a time of dearth?') is that at this time of dearth and darkness, the effort of the imagination will not allow the poet to take wing beyond the world of sense, to identify with the Charioteer in Plato's image from *Phaedrus*; an image that Stevens thinks has lost its vitality, because it is imagination working without reference to reality (NA 7). In this sense, for Stevens, as for Heidegger and Hölderlin, we are too late for the gods. So, at this historical moment, with these scant resources, within this drought of the imagination, the poet cannot turn us away from the world of sense, but must rather (re)turn us to the plain sense of things, to 'plain men in plain towns', to 'The eye's plain version', to 'A view of New Haven, say, through the certain eye' (CP 467, 465, 471). Such plainness is what Stevens calls, in a revealing metaphor, that I elsewhere connect to Schlegel, 'The Vulgate of Experience' (CP 465).

In this leaden time, the task of the poet is the saying of the plainest things, 'plainly to propound' (CP 389) the simplest elements of everyday life: 'pond', 'mud', 'water', 'rat', 'lilies'. Two interesting links to classical American sources suggest themselves here: first, to Emerson where the turn to a plain sense of things seems to be consonant with Emerson's preference for 'the near, the low, the common' as that which the *American* Scholar should poeticize.[47] Second, to Walt Whitman, where the democratic imperative of the American poet is to make himself commensurate with the people, and to speak plainly of plain things.[48]

The task of Stevens's poetry, a task that is clearly continuous with romantic modernity, is the imaginative transfiguration of the real through poetic saying, a language that does not take flight from the real, but which both adheres to the real most closely and resists it in the supreme fictions that it writes. As Stevens puts it:

> We keep coming back and coming back
> To the real: to the hotel instead of the hymns
> That fall upon it out of the wind. We seek
>
> The poem of pure reality, untouched
> By trope or deviation, straight to the word,
> Straight to the transfixing object.
>
> (CP 471)

The poem of pure reality would be the imaginative transfiguration of the real in language, a poem that would be 'part of the *res* itself and not about it', that would take us to the plain object, 'to the hotel instead of the hymns that fall upon it out of the wind'.

In this sense, the task of poetry – and philosophy? And why not? (and why not not?) – at the present historical moment is that paring down of language that transfigures things and draws them into a queer poverty, an eerie plainness, so that we might stand transfixed by them and see them anew, renewed. In a stunning formulation, Stevens describes poetry as a force 'capable of bringing about fluctuations in reality in words free from mysticism' (NA viii). The fidelity of the poet is to what Merleau-Ponty calls the perceptual faith, a faith in the visible alone – in-visibility – in 'the difficulty of the visible', and the enigmas to which it gives rise.[49] As Stevens puts it:

> We seek
> Nothing beyond reality. Within it
> Everything . . .
>
> (CP 471)

Consider Stevens's figure of The Necessary Angel, that appears in 'Angel Surrounded by Paysans' (CP 496–97) and which provided the title for his only collection of essays and lectures. The necessary angel, itself a *figura* for the poet, is that oddly weighty 'angel of reality', who has neither 'ashen wing' nor 'tepid aureole'. The angel speaks:

> I am one of you and being one of you
> Is being and knowing what I am and know
>
> Yet I am the necessary angel of earth,
> Since, in my sight, you see the earth again,
>
> Cleared of its stiff and stubborn, man-locked set,
> And, in my hearing, you hear its tragic drone.

The Angel is a transitional or half-figure, a figure half-seen, or glimpsed for a half-moment, and half-understood, whose 'watery words' risk dissolving into half-meanings. As the Angel says, 'I am one of you', it is not only surrounded by *paysans*, but is one of their species and a member of their society. And yet, the figure is an angel, *ein Halbgott*, an angel of earth, but unearthly because half-seen, an apparition or spectre retreating before the gaze, like Eurydice, like the ghost of Hamlet's father. And necessary, because in the sight of the angel, through the seeing and saying of the poet, the earth is re-viewed, as if for the first time, but this time cleared of human prejudice and presupposition, temporarily freed from Blake's 'mind-forged manacles'. In the hearing of the angel, we do not return to some beatific vision or natural innocence, but we hear the earth's 'tragic drone', we hear the cries that fill the air – human suffering, inhuman suffering.

Moving momentarily from Stevens to Rilke, and remarking a reversal of intentionality (in Stevens the Angel speaks to the *paysans*, whilst in Rilke the poet speaks to the Angel), the figure of the necessary angel can obviously be linked to, and might even be based on, Rilke's imperative from the Ninth Duino

Elegy, 'Preise dem Engel die Welt, nicht die unsägliche' ('Praise this world to the Angel, not the unsayable').[50] That is to say, praise *this* world to the Angel, the visible world, and do not speak of the invisible world or of unsayable things, like love, suffering, the stars or the difficulty of being (*Schwersein*). We should speak, rather, of the sayable; that is, *things*: 'Sag ihm die Dinge. Er wird staunender stehn' ('Tell him things. He'll stand more astonished'). But which things? Rilke provides a possible list:

> Sind wir vielleicht *hier*, um zu sagen: Haus,
> Brücke, Brunnen, Tor, Krug, Ostbaum, Fenster, –
> höchstens: Säule, Turm . . .

> (Are we perhaps *here*, just to say: House,
> Bridge, Fountain, Gate, Jug, Fruit tree, Window, –
> At most: Pillar, Tower. . .)

What will astonish the Angel will be the saying of *things*, the most fleeting of things, seen for a half-moment by ourselves who are the most fleeting of beings:

> vergänglich
> traun sie ein Rettendes uns, den Vergänglichsten, zu.
> (Fleeting,
> they look for rescue through something in us, the most fleeting of all.)

A fleeting saying of a fleeting thing by a fleeting being – such is poetry. And it is spoken *here*, at this time and at this place:

> *Hier* ist die *Säglichen* Zeit, *hier* seine Heimat.
> Sprich und bekenn.
> (*Here* is the time for the *Sayable*, *here* is its home.
> Speak and proclaim.)

To conclude, Stevens's undoubted romantic naïveté resides in his offer of a resistance to reality through the violence of the imagination. This offer is minimal. It is not the offer of a new place, new habitat, or *Ur-Heimat*. Nor is it the promise of a utopia, a new Pantisocracy on the banks of the Susquehanna River, or the promise of a New America, to which I shall return in my discussion of Cavell. It is rather the offer of a new way of inhabiting *this* place, at *this* time, a place that Stevens names, in his last poem and piece of prose, 'the spare region of Connecticut', a place inhabited after the time when mythology was possible.[51] As Stevens puts it:

> A mythology reflects its region. Here
> In Connecticut, we never lived in a time
> When mythology was possible.

Without mythology we are offered the inhabitation of this autumnal or wintry sparseness, this Connecticut, what Stevens calls 'a dwindled sphere':

> The proud and the strong
> Have departed.
>
> Those that are left are the unaccomplished,
> The finally human,
> Natives of a dwindled sphere.
>
> (CP 504)

'A dwindled sphere' . . . this is very little, almost nothing. Yet, it is here that we become 'finally human natives'.

(c)
Romantic ambiguity

The limping of philosophy is its virtue. True irony is not an alibi; it is a task; and the very detachment of the philosopher assigns to him a certain kind of action among men.[52]

Romanticism fails. We have already seen how the project of Jena Romanticism is riddled with ambiguity. On the one hand, romanticism is an aesthetic absolutism, where the aesthetic is the medium in which the antinomies of the Kantian system – and the Enlightenment itself – are absolved and overcome. For Schlegel, the aesthetic or literary absolute would have the poetic form of the great novel of the modern world, the Bible of secularized modernity. However, on the other hand, the audacity of romantic naïveté goes together with the experience of failure and incompletion: the great romantic novel of the modern world is never written, and the romantic project can be said to fail by internal and external criteria.

However – and here we begin to approach the heart of romanticism's ambiguity – what the Jena romantics succeed in completing is a new literary genre based neither on the model of the novel nor the *Gesamtkunstwerk* ('total artwork'), nor on that of the philosophical system or organon that haunts the 'Systemprogramme'. The romantic model for the literary absolute, the genre par excellence for romantic expression, is the *fragment*. Now, the specificity of the fragment, its uniqueness, is that it is a form that is both complete and incomplete, both a whole and a part. It is a form that embodies interruption within itself. That is to say, the fragment fails. Thus, the success of Jena Romanticism is the development and deployment of a genre that embodies failure within itself, whose completion is incompletion, whose structure is essentially ambiguous. As Blanchot writes, romanticism's greatest merit is that it has 'the keenest knowledge of the narrow margin in which it can affirm itself' (EI 522/IC 356). That is, it is self-conscious of the possibility of its own failure. In what follows, I will approach the romantic fragment by following Lacoue-Labarthe and Nancy's discussion in the first chapter of *The Literary Absolute*, a discussion which draws heavily from Blanchot's conception of literature.

However, another kindred trajectory of romantic recovery would trace a lineage through Benjamin's doctoral thesis to Adorno's remarkable piece, 'The Essay as Form' (NL 9–33/NTL 2–23), where the genre of the essay assumes many of the predicates of the romantic fragment: 'The essay allows for the consciousness of non-identity, without expressing it directly', 'Its weakness bears witness to the very nonidentity it had to express', 'The essay is ... the critical form par excellence ... it is critique of ideology' (NL 17, 18, 27/NTL 9, 11, 18). However, at one point in Adorno's essay, the proximity between the form of the essay and the fragment becomes explicit:

> The romantic conception of the fragment as a construction that is not complete but rather progresses onward into the infinite through self-reflection champions this anti-idealist motive in the midst of idealism ... it thinks in fragments, just as reality is fragmentary, and finds its unity in and through the breaks and not by glossing them over.
>
> (NL 24–25/NTL 16)

In this sense, the possibility of non-identity and a certain critique of Hegelianism are persistently linked to a recovery of the Schlegelian fragment. The fragment is the form of negative dialectic. Perhaps a meditation on Schlegel provides a pre-Hegelian critique of Hegel that anachronistically anticipates many post-Hegelian critiques.

(i)
The fragment

What is a fragment? Obviously, the genre of the fragment was not invented in Jena. It is inherited from a tradition whose past extends to Chamfort, La Rochefoucauld, Pascal, and ultimately to the ruins of antiquity, and whose future influences a tradition bequeathed by the romantics to Kierkegaard, Nietzsche, Wittgenstein, Adorno and Blanchot. In many ways, the virtue of the Jena romantics is not to offer a theory of the fragment, or even a stable definition, but rather a *practice* of the fragment, an enactment of a literary genre. Although the Jena romantics provide no theoretical definition of the fragment, we might say provisionally that what the form of the fragment opens up is the possibility of discontinuous writing. An *ensemble* of fragments – for a fragment is never written in isolation – is a discontinuous and uneven *field*. Texts of varying length and worth are typographically, if not thematically, organized across intervals and this lends a certain staccato rhythm or abrupt musicality to their reading. As such, an ensemble of fragments enables a vast number of topics to be treated, and this would seem to be its relative privilege in regard to that other fragmentary form, the essay, that is habitually restricted to the treatment of a single theme, whether one thinks of Montaigne or Emerson. An ensemble of fragments can treat a potentially infinite number of topics that do not have to stand in any agreement or constitute any coherent argument but simply testify to the unceasing alternation and differentiation of thoughts. Fragments are traces of an intense and agile aphoristic *energy*, a power of absolutely unlimited extension and intensity.

However, if the fragment enables a plurality of topics to be treated in a single text, it also allows the possibility of a plurality of voices and authors. The fragment opens up the possibility of *collective* and *anonymous* writing, the possibility of genius as a multiple personality (a proposition that should in no circumstances be reversed). Although evidence suggests that this emphasis on collectivity and anonymity was essentially Friedrich Schlegel's ideal conception of the genre, and although only one set of fragments corresponds to this ideal – the 'Athenäum Fragments', as all the other collections, the 'Lyceum Fragments', 'Ideas' and Novalis' 'Blütenstaub' have a signature – the romantic aspiration is for a mind 'that contains within itself simultaneously a plurality of minds and a whole system of persons' (AF 121), where 'several complementary minds create communal works of art' (AF 125). In the fragments, this

107

collective, anonymous ideal is often expressed with the notion of *symphilosophy* (AF 112), where philosophy would be defined as a *communal* or *mutual* search for omniscience (AF 344), as an 'art of amalgamating individuals' (AF 125). This emphasis on mutuality and communality provides an almost Pantisocratic vision of community rooted in *friendship*, which is a theme that haunts the fragments (AF 342, 359). Friendship is the glue that fixes the social bond of a properly romantic community.

(A word on Pantisocracy, which was Coleridge's and Southey's plan, hatched in 1794, to follow Joseph Priestley and establish an 'all-equal' and 'aspheratist' community of friends on the banks of the Susquehanna River in Pennsylvania. Of course – for better or worse[53] – the plan was never realized, although the vision of a small-scale community rooted in friendship remains determinate for an understanding of romanticism and for its religious antecedents, descendants and analogues. In Coleridge's defence, it should be recalled that what he failed to achieve with Southey in Pennsylvania was at least partially realized in the Quantock Hills in Somerset in the company of the Wordsworths.)

The communitarian vision at the heart of Jena Romanticism does not dissolve the singularity of the individual into the anonymous work of the community. The virtue of the fragment is that it preserves the idiosyncrasy of the individual within the collectivity of the ensemble. Collections of fragments might well be, in Schlegel's words, merely 'a motley heap of ideas', but they are connected together in

> That free and equal fellowship in which, so the wise men assure us, the citizens of the perfect state will live at some future date.
>
> (CF 103)

The fragment, like poetry, is

> Republican speech: a speech which is its own law and end unto itself, and in which all the parts are free citizens and have the right to vote.
>
> (AF 65)

Thus, the very form of an ensemble of fragments constitutes a field irreducible to unity, where the latter is continually referred back to the chaotic singularities that make it possible – republican speech, republican space. The form of the fragments provides an image of an ideal romantic community, where collective expression and communal production would exist in a creative tension with singularity and individuality. In the vocabulary that Jean-Luc Nancy borrows from Blanchot and Bataille, a perfected romantic society would be *une communauté oeuvrée et désoeuvrée*, a community worked and unworked, where the being-in-common of individuals is irreducible to fusion, unity or totality.[54] This thought might be placed alongside Cavell's suggestion in *This New Yet Unapproachable America*, that the very form of Wittgenstein's *Investigations* is an image of a philosophical culture as a multiple weave of voices: sceptical voices, philosophical voices (NYUA 75). Once again, the American context is illuminating at this point, for one might relate the republican speech of the fragments to the image of American democracy one finds, say, in Whitman, where the United States is 'not merely a nation but a teeming nation of nations', and again, 'Great is the greatest nation . . . the nation of clusters of equal nations'.[55] In this idealization, the United States is a collectivity of fragments or leaves of grass, a union of that which resists unity. This is why, for Whitman, the United States 'are essentially the greatest poem'.[56]

As Rodolphe Gasché has pointed out, the literary fragment does not exist in simple opposition to the philosophical system, nor does it acquiesce in the existential pathos of the individual against the system; rather the fragment is the romantic thought of the systematic.[57] As Benjamin writes:

> The fact that an author expresses himself in aphorisms will not count for anyone of late as proof against his systematic intentions. . . . Schlegel . . . never confessed himself simply and plainly the enemy of systematic thinkers.[58]

Within Jena Romanticism, the systematic is always viewed as taking on an individual form, as being expressed in a singularity that is irreducible to unity. As Schlegel writes, in a tone strongly reminiscent of Pascal:[59]

> It is equally fatal to the spirit to have a system and not to have a system. It will simply have to decide to combine the two.
>
> (AF 53)

The fragment is at once both systematic and anti-systematic, and this constitutes its essential *ambiguity*, or what Lacoue-Labarthe and Nancy call 'romantic equivocity'.

I would now like to try and pinpoint this ambiguity in more detail. On the one hand, the fragment aims at completion: it should be an entirely autonomous artistic droplet, a self-sufficient and self-referential micro-system isolated from the surrounding world, like the celebrated romantic hedgehog:

A fragment, like a miniature work of art, has to be entirely isolated from the surrounding world and be complete in itself like a hedgehog.

(AF 206)

On the other hand, paradoxically, although the fragment turns in on itself like a frightened hedgehog, such fragments do not and perhaps *should* not exist. This can be seen by turning to Schlegel's definition of a *project*, which initially seems to echo the hedgehog fragment. He writes:

A project is the subjective embryo of a developing object. A perfect project should be at once completely subjective and completely objective, should be an indivisible and living individual.

(AF 22)

Thus, a perfect project, like a completed fragment, would be at once completely subjective and objective, it would be a product of individual freedom and genius and yet objectively realized in sensuous form. That is, it would be the sensuous evidence of freedom discussed above in relation to Kant. However, what must be noted is that the project is only the *embryo* of a developing or becoming (*werdende*) object; that is to say, the project does not exist, which is why Schlegel goes on to define projects as 'fragments of the future': they are thrown towards the future but are perhaps incapable of being realized in the present. This is compounded by a later fragment, where, after claiming that

A dialogue is a chain or garland of fragments. An exchange of letters is a dialogue on a larger scale, and memoirs constitute a system of fragments,

Schlegel writes:

But as yet no genre exists that is fragmentary both in form and content.

(AF 77)

That is, the kind of fragment that would reconcile form and content or subject and object *does not exist*. Thus, the 'Athenäum Fragments' are *not* themselves fragments, they *should* not be fragments, they are merely indications or fore-words for future fragments, promissory notes for an infinite work yet to be written. And, as we have already seen, there is no guarantee that the work will be written. As Blanchot puts it, romanticism is 'rich in projects' but 'poor in works' (EI 517/IC 352).

If this view seems odd, then one only has to turn for confirmation to the most quoted of the 'Athenäum Fragments', the passage where Schlegel defines romantic poetry. One's suspicions might be aroused by a preceding fragment, where he writes that 'A definition of poetry can only determine what poetry should be, not what it really was and is' (AF 114). That is, definitions of poetry are not descriptive but prescriptive; they are promissory notes for something in the process of becoming. We might think of the latter, with Schlegel, as 'the categorical imperative of genius' (CF 16). Keeping this problem of definition in mind, Schlegel writes:

> Romantic poetry is progressive, universal poetry. Its aim isn't merely to reunite all the separate species of poetry and put poetry in touch with philosophy and rhetoric. It tries to and should mix and fuse poetry and prose, inspiration and criticism, the poetry of art and the poetry of nature; to make poetry lively and sociable, and life and society poetical.

So far, so good. Such claims for aesthetic absolutism are already familiar to us from what I said above. However, Schlegel continues:

> Other kinds of poetry are finished and are now capable of being fully analyzed. The romantic kind of poetry is still in the process of becoming; that, in fact, is its real essence: that it should forever be becoming and never be perfected. It can be exhausted by no theory and only a divinatory criticism would dare to try and characterize its ideal. It alone is infinite, just as it alone is free; and it recognizes as its first commandment that the will of the poet can tolerate no law above itself. The romantic kind of poetry is the only one that is more than a kind, that is, as it were, poetry itself: for in a certain sense all poetry is or should be romantic.
>
> (AF 116)

Thus, the real essence of romantic poetry, that which distinguishes it from all other definitions of literary genres and which gives it the status of not being a kind of poetry but the *only* kind, is that it remains constantly in the process of becoming. Its unfinishedness is evidence of its infiniteness. Thus, *the romantic fragment or project, defined as the synthesis of form and content or subject and object is the self-consciousness of the perpetual lack of this final synthesis.*[60] Such is the ambiguity of romanticism. Romantic writing – the practice of the fragment itself – is the exploration of this lack of final synthesis of subject and object, a continual process of self-creation and self-destruction. In other words, romantic writing is always written in the promise of romanticism, a promise that might

111

not be kept. To use Deleuze and Guattari's terminology, it is the writing of a *becoming-romanticism*.[61]

Romanticism does not exist, there is no such thing as romanticism, or a romantic work. All the fragments offer is a practice of writing – a speculative, critical, interrogative, limitless field or ensemble – that opens onto the promise of romanticism. This is what we might think of with Blanchot as 'the non-romantic essence of romanticism' (IC 357).

(ii)
Wit and irony

Of course, in saying this we have already taken sides in a crucial critical debate about the meaning of romanticism. In his seminal essay, 'Friedrich Schlegel and Romantic Irony', Peter Szondi argues – with a pathos that we have already glimpsed in Lukács – that Friedrich Schlegel's situation is *tragic*, and that romantic writing results only in a solipsistic longing for an absent reconciliation.[62] Against Szondi, the position I will defend is similar to that offered by Paul de Man in 'The Rhetoric of Temporality', where de Man argues that rather than resulting in a tragic longing for absent reconciliation, the lack of synthesis and endlessness of romantic writing is a permanent *parabasis*; that is, a stepping forward, or stepping aside, originally designating the parts of ancient Greek comedy sung by the chorus. In this sense, the infinition of romantic writing would be the very vertiginousness of freedom.[63] But in order to understand these claims aright, we have to add two more pieces to our picture of romanticism, two concepts that are generative of its essential ambiguity: *wit* and *irony*.

First, *wit*: if you will excuse the bad manners of a little etymology, the German *Witz* is related to *Wissen*, providing a Schlegelian jokey double for Hegel's *absolutes Wissen*. The same etymology is available in English, where wit refers back to the Middle English *witan* (to know), a form preserved in Joyce's references in *Ulysses* to the *agenbite of inwit* as a synonym for conscience or con-*scientia*, a kind of inward sense or knowledge (in German, *Ge-wissen*). Indeed, a cross reference for *con-scientia* as both 'conscience', 'consciousness' or 'mind', might be found in the relation in French between *esprit* and *spirituel*, that is, between 'mind' and being witty; 'cette femme est bien spirituelle', as Molière might have said. Like most words related to knowledge, wit is derived from

112

classical verbs with strong perceptual meanings, *videre* in Latin and *idein* in Greek.

However, what is essential to the romantic concept of wit, as Lacoue-Labarthe and Nancy remind us (AL 74/LA 52–53), is the sudden idea (*Einfall*), as that which falls upon one quickly. As Schlegel notes, 'The flame of the most brilliantly witty idea should radiate warmth only after it has given off light' (CF 22). *Witz* must be like *Blitz*, a lightning wit that must be both sudden and brief. Brevity *and* speed are the soul of wit. What takes place in the suddenness and speed of wit is the combination or unification of seemingly heterogeneous thoughts, the almost chance discovery of previously unperceived similarities, finding like in unlike. Schlegel writes that 'Many witty ideas are like the sudden meeting of two friendly thoughts after a long separation' (AF 37). Friendship can be witty. In the 1804 Windischmann Lectures, Schlegel declares that wit is the faculty to 'detect resemblances between objects otherwise independent and separated'.[64] This is why Schlegel describes wit as *chemical*: it is the unification of disparate elements (AF 355), what Benjamin would call the 'mystical' element in romanticism.[65] If wit is chemical, then understanding is *mechanical* or calculative, and genius – which the philosophy of our age has not yet reached – is *organic* (AF 412, 426). It is noteworthy that Schlegel describes the French as a chemical nation, which presumably explains their capacity for wit (forgive my irony). He also describes the French Revolution as a chemical event, where all the paradoxes of 'French national character' are 'thrust together as the most frightful grotesque of the age . . . a monstrous human tragicomedy' (AF 424).

This emphasis on brevity, rapidity and chemistry means that the fragment becomes the ideal vehicle for the expression of wit, 'Wit is absolute social feeling, or fragmentary genius' (CF 9). Indeed, what makes the romantic notion of wit distinctive from its eighteenth-century predecessor is that it is essentially related to the Kantian notion of genius. That is, wit is not merely a mirror to magnify social foibles in the manner of Pope's mock-heroic ('The Rape of the Lock') or Swift's travesty (*Gulliver's Travels*), but an act of *creatio ex nihilo*. Schlegel goes so far as to claim that 'wit in all its manifestations is the principle and the organ of universal philosophy' (AF 220). Incidentally, this entails the intriguing consequence that Leibniz is the wittiest philosopher, insofar as his work is characterized by fragmentation and unfinishedness. Schlegel admits that Kant might also be witty, the problem being that what has happened to Kant's

113

ideas is the same thing that happens to popular songs, 'The Kantians have sung them to death'.

Irony, on the other hand, is the counter-concept to wit. If wit is *synthetic*, the chemical mixing of disparate elements, then irony is *diaeretic*, the separation or division of those elements. This diaeresis establishes an irreconcilable conflict between separated elements. In metaphysical terms, this means that irony expresses the *paradoxical* relation between the absolute and the relative. As Schlegel writes, paradoxically of course, 'Irony is the form of paradox. Paradox is everything simultaneously good and great' (CF 48). The main precursor for the romantic concept of irony is the figure of Socrates; and when Schlegel writes that 'Philosophy is the real homeland of irony', what he means by philosophy is the urbanity of the Socratic dialogue rather than the rigidity of a system or the monological tedium of a lecture. It is this mixture of urbanity and paradoxicality found in dialogue that the romantic fragment attempts to recover, and which clearly so frustrated Hegel. For Schlegel, Socratic irony encapsulates the essential teaching of philosophy, for it is, paradoxically again, 'the only involuntary and yet completely deliberate dissimulation'. He elaborates this in a chain of oxymorons:

> In this sort of irony, everything should be playful and serious, guilelessly open and deeply hidden. It originates in the union of *savoir vivre* and scientific spirit, in the meeting of a perfectly natural and a perfectly artistic philosophy. It contains and arouses a feeling of indissoluble conflict between the unconditional and the conditioned, between the impossibility and the necessity of complete communication.
>
> (CF 108)

Playful and serious, open and hidden, natural and artistic, unconditional and conditioned, impossible and necessary... Irony is the expression of the double bind at the heart of the human condition. It is the recognition of the simultaneous necessity and impossibility of complete communication, 'Whoever desires the infinite doesn't know what he desires. But one can't turn this sentence around' (CF 47 – a wonderful example of ironical bathos). As Bernhard Lypp reminds us in a formulation to which we shall return in our reading of Cavell, irony is the 'höchste, reinste *skepsis*',[66] it is the *sceptical* dissolution of the markers of certitude by which we attempt to understand the world and others within the world. And yet, as the later collection of fragments, *Ideas*, makes clear, this sceptical conflict between the absolute and the relative at

114

the heart of irony also describes the *religiosity* of being human.[67] Schlegel writes, 'Religion is absolutely unfathomable. One can sound it anywhere and still penetrate more deeply into the infinite' (ID 30). It is this consciousness of irony that drives the philosopher into self-parody or even pseudonymity as the most faithful expression of their religiosity – strategies bequeathed by Schlegel to the seemingly opposed religiosities of Kierkegaard and Nietzsche.

However, although one can treat wit and irony as analytically distinct, it is crucial to show their interdependence. Indeed, one might well say that the originality of Schlegel's theory of wit is its essential link to irony, and vice versa: to show the wit within irony and the irony within wit. The synthesizing chemistry of wit is counteracted by the dissolving diaeresis of irony. The movement of wit and irony is a ceaseless alternation between self-creation and self-destruction that produces a 'divided spirit' (CF 28) and a 'science of the eternally uniting and dividing sciences' (AF 220). Now, this oscillating movement, this alternation between *Witz* or *Wissen* and *Ironie* or *skepsis*, is *almost a dialectics*. That is to say, it is a dialectics without Hegelian reconciliation or *Aufhebung*, and without either a tragic longing for *verlorene Sittlichkeit* or a teleology of reconciliation and Absolute Knowing. The oscillation of wit and irony in the romantic fragment is *almost a speculative sentence* in Hegel's sense, but the specularity of reflection is always outstripped by an endless spectrality, an infinite reflection that is not completed in any intuition or in any coincidence of thought and the object of thought, i.e. the Concept. The rhythm of the romantic fragment is an interminable oscillation devoted to the indissoluble conflict of the absolute and the relative. With Adorno, one might think of this movement as a *negative* dialectic that disrupts the possibility of Hegelianism *avant la lettre*, 'that champions this anti-idealist motive in the midst of idealism'. The privilege that Schlegel enjoys *contra* Hegel is that his critique of Hegel is – anachronistically – pre-Hegelian, and might therefore lead us to see Hegelian dialectics as a *wit-less* and *un-ironical* response to romantic ambiguity.

(iii)
The non-romantic essence of romanticism

With these insights, I believe, we approach the unworking that is the heart of Jena Romanticism. The genre of the fragment enacts a quasi-dialectical oscillation between wit and irony, that is, between the creative desire for synthesis and the destructive scepticism of diaeresis. It is essential to this oscillation that both moments of creation and destruction are maintained – recall that 'it is equally fatal to the spirit to have a system and not to have a system; it will simply have to decide to combine the two'. In terms of the aesthetic absolutism discussed above, romanticism is torn between – it *is* the tearing of this between – the desire for a complete work of art and the ironic abandonment of the work in a movement of parodic dissolution. We have seen that both poles of this alternation are (barely) held together by the genre of the fragment.

Lacoue-Labarthe and Nancy try to capture the sense of this alternation in the conclusion to *The Literary Absolute* with the notion of 'romantic equivocity' (AL 419–25/LA 121–27). How this equivocity works in relation to the fragment is discussed in a crucial earlier passage from the book. I quote at length:

> Romanticism's most specific gesture, the gesture that distinguishes it infinitesimally but all the more decisively from metaphysical idealism, is one by which, discreetly and without really wanting to, and at the very heart of the quest for or theory of the Work, it abandons or excises the Work itself – and thus is transformed in an almost imperceptible manner into the 'work of the absence of the work', as Blanchot has put it. It is the minimal but incisive particularity of this mutation that the motif (and not the form, the genre or idea) of the fragment has continually led us to perceive, without ever placing it before our eyes. . . .
>
> Within the romantic work, there is interruption and dissemination of the romantic work, and this in fact is not readable in the work itself, even and especially not when the fragment, *Witz* and chaos are privileged. Rather, according to another term of Blanchot, it is in the *unworking* (*désoeuvrement*), never named and still less thought, that insinuates itself throughout the interstices of the romantic work.
>
> (AL 80/LA 57)

What this passage seeks to make clear – and this is intended as praise rather than criticism – is the extent to which Lacoue-Labarthe and Nancy's understanding of the fragment, and indeed of Jena Romanticism as a whole, draws heavily on Blanchot's conception of literature, thereby also showing the extent of the debt that Blanchot's conception of literature owes to Jena Romanticism. Indeed, for all its careful exposition (and despite a rather precious and irritating prose style), it is difficult to see in what respect *The Literary Absolute* conceptually surpasses Blanchot's short and limpid 1964 essay 'The

Athenäum', which has been my clandestine companion throughout this lecture. Indeed, Lacoue-Labarthe and Nancy's notion of romantic equivocity would simply seem to be a redescription of Blanchot's notion of ambiguity, which, as I have shown in Lecture 1, is the truth of literature for Blanchot.[68]

For Blanchot, the ambiguity of romanticism – what he discusses elsewhere in terms of the two slopes of literature – is centred in both its revolutionary desire to write the great novel of the modern world, and the failure to bring this desire to completion, leaving romanticism littered with unfinished works, sketches, programmes and projects. As we have now seen in detail, what Jena Romanticism does manage to complete is the genre of the fragment, a form which embodies incompletion and discontinuity. This is why the fragment is 'the work of the absence of the work'. In Blanchot's terms, what this testifies to is the way in which the law of the Work is continually outstripped by a desire that is stronger than the Work, the Orphic desire for the origin of the artwork that scatters the Work in a movement of unworking or *désoeuvrement*, and sends Eurydice back down to Hades. After Jena Romanticism – and it is our naïveté *to* inhabit this 'after', this romantic modernity – literature will henceforth bear within itself

> this question of discontinuity or difference as a question of form – a question and a task German romanticism, and in particular that of *The Athenäum*, not only senses but already clearly proposed – before consigning them to Nietzsche and, beyond Nietzsche, to the future.
>
> (EI 527/IC 359)

The naïveté of romanticism is not that of a failed aesthetic absolutism which is ultimately tragic (Szondi) or ends up in a melancholy longing for absent reconciliation (Hegel). Rather, romanticism's naïveté is rooted in the self-consciousness of its unworking, the exploration of its lack of final synthesis in a continual process of self-creation and self-destruction, the quasi-dialectics of wit and irony, of *Wissen* and *skepsis*. The naïveté of romanticism is the faith in fragments as seeds of the future, in fragments as the possibility that the future might have a future, in fragments as the possibility of possibility. This is very little . . . this is almost nothing.

(d)
Cavell's 'romanticism'

I do not deny that truth can be used as a weapon; especially when it comes in fragments.

(CR 82)

(i)
The romanticization of everyday life

Romanticism is a persistent theme in Stanley Cavell's work, that has assumed increasing prominence in his later writings, in particular *In Quest of the Ordinary* (1988) and *This New Yet Unapproachable America* (1989). As one would expect from Cavell, the trajectory of his recovery of romanticism is singular: it leads from his abiding interest in the procedures of ordinary language philosophy, in particular Austin, back to the recovery of an American romantic tradition in Emerson and Thoreau, and forward into a strongly perfectionist reading of Wittgenstein and Heidegger, where these twin peaks of twentieth-century philosophy are seen 'as showing philosophy to be [possible] as a continuation of romanticism' (NYUA 5). Indeed, his intensification of interest in romanticism seems to be continuous with his perfectionist turn. The fascinating consequence of this linking of romanticism to perfectionism for the reading of Wittgenstein and Heidegger – that is, on Cavell's account, for the continuation of philosophy – is that their concern with the ordinary or the everyday cannot be assimilated to a defence of certain common-sense or common-room beliefs about the world, but rather that they are both engaged in a contestation of common sense in the name of a transfiguration of everyday life. Thus, the Wittgensteinian teaching that philosophy must become a practice of leading words from their metaphysical usage to their everyday usage becomes a *fantastic* practice (NYUA 66), insofar as Cavell claims that Wittgenstein views the *actual* everyday as a scene of illusion, best represented by a Spenglerian picture of culture as decline or a Nietzschean diagnosis of European civilization as nihilism (the time of dearth and darkness I spoke of above). On Cavell's reading, Wittgenstein is proposing a practice that would deliver us from the actual everyday to the *eventual* everyday (*eventual* might be considered speculatively here as both having an event character, an *Ereignis* in Heidegger's sense, and linking the eventual to the possible, in German *eventuell*), a deliverance which is not a Platonic ascent out of the cave and the public space of *doxa*, but is rather a descent – a downgoing – into the uncanniness of the ordinary, or, in Heideggerian terms, the enigma of the everyday (NYUA 46–47).[69] This would be what Cavell calls a *diurnalization* of philosophy's ambitions, looking beneath our feet rather than over our heads.

As I see it, Cavell's reading of Wittgenstein, particularly his biological interpretation of forms of life (NYUA 42–45), is a crucial advance upon the breathtaking cultural and political complacency of much that passes for Wittgensteinian philosophizing: the everyday is not a network of practices or forms of life to which we can return by leaving our colleges and taking a turn in the street or a job in Woolworths. Rather, the turn to the everyday demands that philosophy becomes *therapy* or, to use Cavell's words, 'the education of grownups'. That is, it becomes a way of addressing the crisis of late modernity where the everyday is concealed and ideologically repackaged as 'common sense', what the later Husserl rightly saw as *Lebensweltvergessenheit*. We do not, therefore, return to the ordinary, the everyday or the *Lebenswelt*, so much as turn to them for the first time, undergoing a turning around, a *conversion*. The ordinary is not a ground, but a goal. It is something we are in quest of, it is the object of an inquest, it is in question – hence Cavell's ambiguous title *In Quest of the Ordinary*. Of course, it is in relation to this sense of the ordinary as something extraordinary that we might begin to consider the relation between romanticism and everyday life:

> Romanticism's work here interprets itself, so I have suggested, as the task of bringing the world back, as to life. This may, in turn, present itself as the quest for a return to the ordinary, or of it, a new creation of our habitat; or as the quest, away from that, for the creation of a new inhabitation.
>
> (IQO 52–53)

The world must be romanticized, the quotidian must be made fantastic and the human made strange, 'attracting the human to the work of becoming human' (NYUA 10).

Although it is not dealt with at any length in *The Claim of Reason*, romanticism remains a persistent presence in that work. In the concluding pages of Part Two, after claiming that a serious bond between Wittgenstein and Heidegger can be found in the way in which they both acknowledge the question of the mystery of existence, Cavell adds gnomically, 'To be interested in such accounts . . . I suppose one will have to take an interest in certain preoccupations of romanticism' (CR 241). However, romanticism assumes more centrality in the extraordinary fourth part of *The Claim of Reason*. In addition to the allusions to romantic poets, especially Blake, in the multiple epigraphs to Part Four and the sporadic outbreaks of citations from romantic texts, Cavell writes:

> One can think of romanticism as the discovery that the everyday is an exceptional achievement. Call it the achievement of the human.
>
> (CR 463)

Thus, romanticism is the discovery of the exceptionality of the everyday, or, in terms discussed above, the uncanniness of the ordinary.

However, the discovery of the everyday as an exceptional achievement must be combined with the acknowledgement that this achievement is never achieved. That is to say, romanticism is that process of secularization (CR 470) or de-divinization that aims at the establishment of a community based on moral autonomy, but this ideal of community is never realized. Romanticism is, in my terms, a response to the problem of nihilism that aims at a de-theologized re-enchantment of the world. Happily, it fails. Which does not imply a rejection of romanticism, but an elaboration of its unworked, non-romantic essence. This is why Cavell concludes, 'So romantics dream revolution, and break their hearts' (CR 464).

(ii)
Emerson as the literary absolute

I will come back to this question of a broken-hearted romanticism below, but I first want to criticize a specific claim that Cavell makes about romanticism. It concerns Cavell's reading – or rather misreading – of *The Literary Absolute*. In the Preface to *In Quest of the Ordinary*, which is essentially a foreword to Cavell's 1983 Beckman lectures on romanticism, he notes:

> As I pack off the present material, a general misgiving is focused for me in my having just read *The Literary Absolute* . . . There I find features of my Beckman lectures preceded, generously and practically, in certain opening themes and strategies, from the other side of the philosophical mind – the German by way of France, opposed to the English by way of America – specifically, the theme of a romantic call for the unity of philosophy and poetry precipitated by the aftermath of Kant's revolution in philosophy.
>
> (IQO xi)

120

Cavell rightly sees the central demand of romanticism as the unification of philosophy and poetry, a demand that he places alongside another demand announced in the Foreword to *The Claim of Reason*, namely the unification of the two halves of the philosophical mind – the analytic and the Continental, of the English by way of America and the German by way of France. It presumably remains Cavell's philosophical ambition – or his ambition for philosophy – 'to define and date a place' of the overcoming of these opposed traditions; adding – with some justification, I think – that Part Four of *The Claim of Reason* is written 'as though these paths had never divided' (CR xiii). As Cavell has recently written, taking up a metaphor we discussed above, his thinking operates 'within the tear in the Western philosophical mind, represented, so I believe, by the distances between the English–American and the German–French dispensations'.[70]

However, this tear or rift in the Western philosophical mind reflects a third – and most important – aspect of division and demand for unification, which is the splitting within culture itself (CR xiii). This is a crisis at the level of everyday life, which calls for a mending of the world. The diagnosis of crisis emerges most strongly in a text like *This New Yet Unapproachable America*, where Wittgenstein is rightly read as a philosopher of culture, who opposes the nomadism and nihilism of contemporary life with a practice of philosophy which has in view the achievement of the everyday, the redemption or – Cavell's preferred word – *recovery* of culture. But rather than basing this claim in a reading of Wittgenstein's *Culture and Value* – a more obvious and highly illuminating para-text and successor to Schlegel's fragments – Cavell argues that it is the very form of the *Philosophical Investigations*, with its weave of voices, that provides a picture of a redeemed culture, *the imagined practice of an eventual everyday*. Of course, this makes Wittgenstein – and Cavell too – a prophet (NYUA 74).

Thus, the way in which Cavell's interpretation of romanticism is, as he says, 'preceded' by the concerns of *The Literary Absolute* permits us to focus three demands for unification in his work:

1 that of philosophy and poetry,
2 that of analytic and Continental philosophy,
3 that of culture with itself through the mediation of philosophy.

So far so good, we might say. This rehearses arguments set out above and shows that Cavell's work is continuous with the bewildering naïveté and failure of Jena Romanticism. However, continuing the above quote from *In Quest of the*

Ordinary, Cavell makes a crucial second claim that takes him well beyond the argument of *The Literary Absolute*. He writes:

> It would have been, it seems to me, of exactly no philosophical use for me to have sought to weigh the relative merits of these starting places [i.e. Cavell's own and Lacoue-Labarthe and Nancy's – SC] apart from establishing to my own satisfaction that, among other matters, *Emerson's writing bears up under the pressure of the call for philosophy, that he constitutes a fair realization of the bonding of philosophy and poetry that both Coleridge and Friedrich Schlegel had called for* [SC's emphasis].
>
> (IQO xii)

Thus, the romantic demand for the unification of philosophy and poetry is, Cavell claims, given a 'fair realization' in the writing of Emerson. A good deal turns here on what is meant by 'fair', and how this adjective modifies and softens the substantive 'realization'. If we let the adjective soften the substantive, then Cavell's claim would seem to be that Emerson is a 'fair realization' in the same way as one might speak of a fair likeness in portraiture, i.e. it is the best available under present conditions. However, Cavell makes the same claim in the opening pages of *This New Yet Unapproachable America*, entitled 'Work in Progress', the difference being that 'realization' is no longer qualified by 'fair', but stands alone. I quote at length:

> Accepting the thesis presented by Lacoue-Labarthe and Nancy (which they find anticipated in Walter Benjamin and in Maurice Blanchot) that the idea of literature becoming its own theory... is what constitutes romanticism (in its origin in the *Athenäum*), and beginning to see Emerson's responsiveness to that *Athenäum* material (or to its sources or its aftermath), my wonder at Emerson's achievement is given a new turn... So I should like to record my impression that, measured against, say, Friedrich Schlegel's aphoristic, or rather, fragmentary, call for or vision of the union of poetry and philosophy, Emerson's work presents itself as the *realization* [SC's emphasis] of that vision. I do not mean that Emerson's work is not 'fragmentary'. Indeed it seems to me that the puzzle of the Emersonian sentence must find a piece of its solution in a theory of the fragment: maintaining fragmentariness is part of Emerson's realization of romanticism.
>
> (NYUA 20–21)

Thus, Emerson's writing is no longer 'work in progress' – which, as Lacoue-Labarthe and Nancy remark and as we saw above, 'becomes the infinite truth of the work' (LA 48) or 'the work of the absence of the work' – but *the Work itself*, the realization of the ideality of romanticism. Measured against the fragmentary nature of Schlegel's call for the unification of philosophy and poetry, a call that results only in failure and unfinished works, Emerson is the realization of that call. Emersonian writing is the literary absolute, 'the transformation of genius into practical power', or again, 'the gradual domestication of the idea of Culture'.[71]

But what does this claim mean? How exactly is Emerson the realization of romanticism? This is obviously bound up with the enormously privileged status that Cavell attributes to Emersonian writing: that is, to the genre of the Emersonian essay, the Emersonian sentence and even the Emersonian word. First, and importantly, the Emersonian essay is not a renunciation of fragmentation in the name of wholeness – the great novel of secular modernity – rather Cavell claims that the essay is the realization of the fragment, the fulfilment of this genre. As Emerson writes of himself and the essay form in 'Experience', 'I am a fragment, and this is a fragment of me.'[72] Second, the Emersonian essay is not a realization of romanticism in the sense of a return to a pre-critical immediacy that allegedly characterized the art of antiquity. The essay as form is essentially self-conscious, self-critical and *modern*. In what sense is it therefore a realization? In his labyrinthine, and at times highly convoluted, discussion of Emerson's 'Experience', Cavell writes:

> I would like to say that Emerson's 'Experience' announces and provides the conditions under which an Emersonian essay can be experienced – the conditions of its own possibility.

> (NYUA 103)

Focusing on the phrase 'conditions of its own possibility', we might say that the Emersonian essay, like a miniature transcendental deduction – a hedgehog-sized version of the First Critique – self-consciously announces the conditions of possibility for its own intelligibility. The claim here is that each essay, each sentence and each word has a reflective self-awareness of the conditions of possibility for its own realization.

Now, the effect of this form of writing is *inertia* or what Stephen Mulhall calls 'lack of momentum'.[73] In *In Quest of the Ordinary*, Cavell quotes Thoreau, where the latter imagines that a philosophy book suitable for students would be written with next to no forward motion; it would be a book that culminates in each sentence, and for which we can find no reason to continue reading from one sentence to the next (IQO 18). For Cavell, the virtue of Emersonian (and, incidentally, Wittgensteinian) writing is that it knows when to stop, and this knowledge opens a certain relation to finitude. Indeed, reading an essay like Emerson's 'Experience', it is not difficult to see what Cavell means about Emersonian writing: the rhythms of Emerson's English are so strange to my English ears, the style has a staccato muscularity, where each sentence seems to be the culmination of the argument and an argument in itself, the sentences form a dense linguistic undergrowth, each sentence plant-like and damp with individual pathos, momentarily reflecting a light that seems to emanate from an unseen source.

Thus, Cavell presents Emerson (or, on Mulhall's account, presents himself)[74] as a realization of the Schlegelian demand for the unification of philosophy and poetry, and he presents the Emersonian essay – the sentence and the word – as the realization of the romantic fragment. That is to say, the 'hedgehog theory' of the fragment we discussed above, where the fragment is 'entirely isolated from the surrounding world' and 'complete in itself'.

However, and this is my critique, in terms of the reading of Jena Romanticism set out above, Cavell must be said to misread *The Literary Absolute* and misunderstand the theory of the romantic fragment. A misunderstanding that, I believe, is at least partially caused by the fact that Cavell overlooks the decisive influence of Blanchot's conception of literature upon Lacoue-Labarthe and Nancy. If, on my account, Jena Romanticism is rooted in the acute self-consciousness of its unworking or failure, the exploration of the lack of final synthesis in a continual process of self-creation and self-destruction and the quasi-dialectics of wit and irony, then Cavell's romanticism would seem to take us in a rather different direction. Jena Romanticism is rooted in essential ambiguity, which is the ambiguity of the genre of the fragment itself. The ambiguity of the fragment is continually directed and open to the future, a future underwritten by a lack of final synthesis. I would argue that it is the very futuricity of fragments that explains why we carry on reading them, and why their reading is not, as Cavell suggests, characterized by lack of momentum or inertia, but rather by a relentless and vertiginous forward motion without destination. The abrupt and discontinuous music of the fragments leaves the reader perpetually dissatisfied, perpetually craving more and perpetually frustrated by their seeming superficiality and evanescence. Now, Cavell's claim that Emerson represents a (fair) realization of the unification of philosophy and poetry, and an achievement of the theory of the fragment, misunderstands how the fragment works – or rather, unworks. *To speak of realization in relation to the fragment is to misunderstand the fragment.* It is to try and arrest the restless futural movement of worklessness; it is to try and close down the future opened by fragments; it is to put satisfaction in place of the dissatisfaction that haunts romanticism; it is to claim the coincidence of ideality and reality that characterizes the aesthetic absolutism discussed above, and whose pernicious political consequences we mentioned. Finally – and paradoxically, as we shall soon see – Cavell's claim for Emerson *disarms the threat of scepticism* by arresting the limping of irony; it permits us *not* to be disappointed with criteria; it leaves the romantic without a broken heart.

(e)
Digression II: Why Stanley loves America and why we should too

The name 'Emerson' has a privileged status in Cavell's discourse. But it has to be associated with another name, a name to which it is intimately linked, a name which functions like 'Germanien' for Heidegger, like 'Auschwitz' for Adorno and like 'Israel' for Levinas. That name is 'America'.

The place of Emerson in Cavell's work is profoundly related to America as a place for philosophy, as a response to the question 'Has America expressed itself philosophically?' (IQO 11). The singular trajectory of Cavell's thought, that takes him back from the philosophical present of Wittgenstein and Heidegger to Emerson and Thoreau, is driven by the fact that Emerson and Thoreau are *American* philosophers, part of an *American* formation, foundation and inheritance. As Cavell notes in *This New Yet Unapproachable America*, Emerson's writing is the 'provision of experience for America, for "these" shores' (NYUA 92). Again, in *In Quest of the Ordinary*:

> On the contrary, my wish to inherit Emerson and Thoreau as philosophers, my claim for them as founding American thinking, is a claim both that America contains an unacknowledged current of thinking, *and* that this thinking accomplishes itself by teaching the inheritance of European philosophy – an inheritance that should make me not the master of this European philosophy, but also not its slave.
>
> (IQO 181–82)

125

Neither master nor slave to the European tradition, but a distinct and distinctive voice – these are handsome republican sentiments that aspire to putting America on an *equal* philosophical footing with Europe. But I think Cavell goes slightly further than this. We saw above how Cavell claims that Emersonian writing realizes the romantic demand for the unification of philosophy and poetry, analytic and Continental philosophy and the division within culture itself. Now, the place where this *union* is most actively sought, where the gradual domestication of culture might take place, is *America*. Might we not hear this when Cavell writes:

> To claim Emerson and Thoreau as of the origin in America, not alone of what is called literature but of what may be called philosophy, is to claim that literature is neither the arbitrary embellishment nor the necessary other of philosophy. You can either say that in the New World, distinctive philosophy and literature do not exist in separation, or you can say that the American task is to create them from one another, as if the New World is still to remember, if not exactly to recapitulate, the cultural labors of the Old World.
>
> (IQO 182)

America is an origin or is of the origin in a way that precedes the bifurcation of philosophy and literature. America's founding texts ignore or sublate this bifurcation; they are, in a sense, both pre- and post-Platonic, both the union of philosophy and poetry seemingly sundered by the *Republic* and sought by romanticism and its heirs.

Although Cavell does not make this vast claim for actually existing America, but for a kind of perfectionist *Amerique à venir*, in Emerson's words, 'this new yet unapproachable America that I have found in the West',[75] *America is the romantic place par excellence*. It is the place which *promises* romanticism, it has romantic promise, it is the achievement of romanticism *as* a promise. What Cavell often refers to as America's *belatedness* is also the reason for its place as the destination of Europe, as both Europe's exhausted disappearance and its fulfilled completion. This is perhaps what Hart Crane meant by referring to the American condition as 'an improved infancy'.[76]

But shouldn't such views arouse a little suspicion? Looking again at the above quotes from *In Quest of the Ordinary*, one might begin to wonder what Cavell could mean by 'inheritance' and 'founding'. What is the relation between the inheritance of the European philosophical tradition and the founding of America, specifically an American philosophical tradition? In Cavell, the notion of 'founding' is often connected with 'finding', namely the alleged 'finding' of America by Europeans – the title of Cavell's piece on Emerson in *This New Yet Unapproachable America* is 'Finding as Founding' – and the founding of a nation. What, one might ask, is the relation between philosophy and the founding of a nation? What does it mean to claim Emerson and Thoreau as founders of American philosophy, that is, as the origin of America's self-consciousness as something – as a place – distinct from Europe?

One might begin by noting the connection between founding/finding and inheritance, where the founding of an American philosophical tradition, and of America *tout court* as something new, is articulated together with the question of the inheritance of the European tradition. America inherits: that is to say, it is the recognition of both the exhaustion of the European tradition upon the territory of Europe, and of America as the continuation and completion of that tradition in a new territory. American philosophy, for Cavell, seems rooted in the experience of immigration, in the migration of words and worlds from the Old to the New, an experience of uprooting, displacement and settlement.

The question of founding raises the vast issue about the relation of America as it is figured in Emersonian writing to both the past of America as a place already founded, i.e. native American culture, and also to cultural memory of extermination and slavery, which has produced the many counter-traditions and counter-inheritances that are found in late American modernity. To his credit, Cavell has persistently raised the question of slavery and oppression in relation to Emersonian writing, and one might note the following revealing passage from *Must We Mean What We Say?*:

> It is simply crazy that there should ever have come into being a world with such a sin in it, in which a man is set apart because of his color – *the superficial fact about a human being*. Who could *want* such a world? For an American, fighting for his love of country, that *the last hope of earth* [SC's emphasis] should from its beginning have swallowed slavery, is an irony so withering, a justice so intimate in its rebuke of pride, as to measure only with God.
>
> (MWM 141)[77]

It must be asked: What is the relation of Cavell's Emersonian perfectionism to the hybrid ensemble of traditions and inheritances which make up the great rhizome of American cultural identity?

Although it is doubtless banal to be reminded of this fact, the connection between philosophy and the founding of a nation or *polis* has decisive precedents in the philosophical tradition, whether one thinks of Plato's misadventure in Syracuse or Heidegger's repetition of Platonism in his National Socialist commitment. However, although it would be wrong to accuse Cavell of falling prey to the gross naïveté of philosophical nationalism, one can nonetheless note a continual *continentalism* in Cavell's writing that typifies a whole genre of philosophical and political discourse, a continental drift where the names 'America' and 'The United States' become synonyms, and where the name of the nation is inflated and identified with an entire continent. Cavell, like so many others, does not speak of the Americas, but of America in the singular, which means the United States. American philosophy is, at best, a national philosophy with pretensions of becoming a *continental* philosophy.

What does America mean as a philosophical event? What is the place of America in philosophical discourse? We might begin by considering a tradition of political philosophy that to my knowledge begins with Locke, where America is characterized as an infinite state of nature, and therefore the condition of possibility for the development of private property, mercantile capitalism and liberal government.[78] America is imagined as an infinite and empty space, as the wild, uncultivated, unpopulated resource for individual property and capital accumulation. Of course, America was not empty before European colonization and this myth of emptiness is as pernicious as Zionist claims that Palestine was empty prior to the establishment of the state of Israel.

What is the time of America? Philosophically and politically, America is the thought and the land of the *future*.[79] This is a trope that also recurs in political philosophy, for example in Tom Paine, where American revolutionary democracy is declared to be the future of Europe, an American future that begins in France in 1789 and will spread to all corners of Europe – even England.[80] In this way, for Paine, the New World regenerates and rejuvenates the Old World and the onward march into the future will be accompanied by the music of collapsing monarchies. For Europe, America is an idea, an idea of democracy as Tocqueville described, an idea in the Kantian sense, the promise of a better future and the expression of political hope. Within the United States, America is also an idea, it is the core of a political theology. It is something in which the citizen is obliged to believe either as an object of love or intellectual and cultural hatred (which is but another form of love).

America is the place for utopia, its locale. Which is to say that America is the romantic place par excellence, the place where, in Emersonian terms, genius might be transformed into practical power. This is particularly visible in Coleridge's plans for Pantisocracy alluded to above, but also in Blake's prophetic dreamscape where the ideas of revolution, liberty and passion are defended against the wrath of Albion.[81]

But what of America as a place? The idea of America as the place for utopia, as the place where ideality should be (but cannot be) realized, allows us to highlight what I would see as a 'founding' *disjunction* in the experience of America. What does one find in the West? Does one approach the unapproachable America? One anecdote amongst others comes to mind: driving from Death Valley to Las Vegas is a trip from the unearthly to the unreal. One traverses the desert and – lo! – the New Jerusalem rises out of the desert, shimmering with inexplicable, tacky splendour. Las Vegas is a shining beacon of nihilism, a place where European civilization evaporates into a series of casino complexes. Concrete, steel and glass accelerate into the desert scrub, a hallucinatory architecture adorns itself in a sub-mythology of imaginative travesty: Desert Sands, Excalibur, Treasure Island.

America is an experience of absolute disjunction. On the one hand, it is to be overwhelmed by the utter sublimity of nature, say the un-Alpine granite vastness of Yosemite. But on the other hand, America is the cheerful celebration of the disappearance of culture into kitsch: the Liberace Museum, Graceland. There are two Americas and perhaps they are equally unreal: the double unreality of nature and culture. I also think here of the appearance that American cities have for the European, the cinematically- induced conviction that this is what cities should look like – muscular, vast, inhuman spaces. But their effect exceeds reality, which is what Baudrillard, in his piece of romantic cultural metaphysics, means by hyperreality.[82] American culture, in its justified historical revolt against Europe, is perhaps the aspiration that culture might achieve the condition of nature, become nature. I think this is what Baudrillard means when he describes America as the last remaining primitive society on earth.[83] This might sound like faint praise, but praise it is.

Two Americas: both utopia and distopia. This much would seem to be clear in Cavell when he reads Wittgenstein as a philosopher of culture in the tradition of Nietzsche and Spengler, where culture is diagnosed as decline, as nihilism.[84] Cavell reads Wittgenstein as a philosopher of culture in order to read his own culture as this decline, as the acceleration of European nihilism. But, for Cavell, the experience of culture as decline in America and as America is always linked

129

to the perfectionist hope for a redemption of culture through a recovery of the everyday, the demand for a sky under which philosophy might be possible (NYUA 7). For Cavell, and this is the source of his disagreement with Rorty, the greatest danger is a culture without philosophy, that is, without that endless play of voices that Cavell finds at work in Wittgenstein's *Investigations*. It is the latter that provides Cavell with both the diagnosis of culture as decline – the actual everyday – and the image of a redeemed culture – the eventual everyday. In Cavell, this two-Americas problem is focused in his repeated invocation of Emerson's remark, 'I know the world I converse with in the city and in the farms is not the world I *think*'.[85]

But how is one to approach this new but unapproachable America? Is one to approach it? Cavell does not pretend to solve this dilemma, rather he recommends to us another Emersonian sentence, 'Patience, patience, we shall win at the last'.[86] What might Cavell mean by this? What I find here – and it is very little – is the offer of 'a passive practice', that is, a way of inhabiting the actual everyday with one eye on the eventual everyday, a passive power that Cavell explicitly links to Thoreau's notion of civil disobedience (NYUA 115). Such is perhaps Cavell's weak messianism.

However, Cavell's most revealing passage on America appears in his 1969 essay on *King Lear*, and it allows one to glimpse another America in Cavell, an America of unworked romanticism, a separated and tragic America. Cavell writes:

> Those who voice politically radical wishes for this country may forget the radical hopes it holds for itself, and not know that the hatred of America by its intellectuals is only their own version of patriotism.
>
> (MWM 345)

America, Cavell insists, needs to be loved. It needs love like no other nation, and like no other nation has it been the object of love. The union of love is what America has always wanted; it is what it tore itself apart in the Civil War trying to achieve. America has never been able to bear its separateness and therein lies its tragedy. In lines written at the height of the fateful involvement of the United States in Vietnam, Cavell writes of America, in an act of literary civil disobedience:

> *Union* is what it wanted. And it has never felt that union has been achieved. Hence its terror of dissent, which does not threaten its power but its

integrity. So it is killing itself and killing another country in order not to admit its helplessness in the face of suffering, in order not to acknowledge its separateness.

'America', Cavell goes on, 'is the anti-Marxist country', the nation where, as Baudrillard cheerfully notes, the nineteenth century did not happen.[87] But things could change. After all, it's a free country, 'but it will take a change of consciousness. So phenomenology becomes politics' (MWM 346).

'Has America happened?' (NYUA 114). Cavell grants that this is a romantic question, the romantic question par excellence, for it concerns the unification of philosophy and poetry as a unification of culture with itself and the possibility of a transformation of genius into practical power. Such a unification would be the moment when phenomenology becomes politics, the fantastic moment when Plato lives happily ever after in Syracuse and when Heidegger benevolently looks down from his hut on a Germany resolute in its collective Dasein. Now, although Cavell comes close to a form of cultural nationalism (or even cultural continentalism) that is both historically fallacious and politically pernicious, failing to take account of the deep hybridities of American memory; and although Cavell's names – 'Emerson' and 'America' – call for a careful critical dismantling, I would claim that nonetheless he avoids the deepest naïveté of romanticism, namely its aestheticization of politics. America, for him, is the tragic experience of separation I will return to below, it is an unworked America that hesitates in the tension between nihilism and its overcoming, between the actual everyday and the eventual everyday. America is a philosophical event that can never happen. All that remains is an approach and a series of hallucinatory clichés: the Manhattan skyline emerging from the mist to the accompaniment of Gershwin, the soiled pearl of Las Vegas shimmering in the baking desert heat, the sublimity of the night-time Chicago skyscape. We arrive and it is too late. There is only the approach.

(f)
Cavell's romanticism

What happens to us at the death of the body is what happens to the music when the music concludes. There is a period of reverberation, and then nothing.

(CR 410)

131

(i)
I live my scepticism

Cavell's 'romanticism' is, on the view I have presented, not romantic. His reading of *The Literary Absolute*, and particularly his claims for 'Emerson' and 'America', yield a version of romanticism that can be offered as an aesthetic absolutism ripe for Hegelian/Schmittian critique. However, and this is the positive thought that I would like to pursue in concluding, this does not mean that Cavell's thought is not ultimately romantic, despite itself, and despite its 'romanticism'.

The curious thing about Cavell's Emersonian 'romanticism', at least on my account, is that it is *un-Cavellian*. As is clear from the opening chapters of *The Claim of Reason*,[88] Cavell's thought is dominated by the insight that *criteria come to an end* (CR 412). The idea of a criterion, which is understood as the means by which the existence of something is established with certainty, thereby refuting the possibility of scepticism, fails to provide us with the certainty we desire. To take the famous Wittgensteinian example of whether I have criteria to decide whether another person is in pain, Cavell concludes that my criteria will always fall short. There is no epistemic assurance that my words will reach all the way into the other's interiority. Thus, rather than refuting scepticism, criteria – whose necessity only arises at that fateful moment when attunement or agreement (*Übereinstimmung*) is threatened or lost, when the social contract breaks down – reveal the truth of scepticism, that is, its irrefutability. Of course, to acknowledge the truth of scepticism is not the same as admitting that scepticism is true, for this would constitute a further escape into a new inverted metaphysics of certainty, namely relativism. Rather Cavell is seeking to draw us into a position where we are denied *both* the possibility of an epistemological guarantee for our beliefs and the possibility of a sceptical escape from those beliefs. Of course, this is hard for us to bear, but it is here that we must learn to, as Putnam puts it, 'wriggle'.[89]

The burden of much of Cavell's argument in *The Claim of Reason* is to show that this struggle with scepticism provides both the animating intention and dramatic tension of Wittgenstein's *Philosophical Investigations*. The deeply self-conscious and wilfully unsystematic rhetorical form of the *Investigations*, particularly its endless play of questioning and answering voices, is, according to Cavell, intended to show our continual exposure to the threat of scepticism. The *Investigations* is both paradigmatic of philosophy, insofar as criteria do not overcome scepticism but are disappointed and disappointing, and paradigmatic of what it means to be human as such, because the denial of scepticism would ultimately be the denial of what it is to be human.

To grasp this second claim, we have to understand that the problem of scepticism (particularly scepticism concerning other minds) is not first and foremost a theoretical problem. For Cavell, unlike Heidegger,[90] there is no everyday or common-sense alternative to scepticism (CR 431). To entertain sceptical doubt is an everyday occurrence, and there is nothing about other minds that satisfies me for all practical purposes. (Is this true? Does it not assume the activity of reflection at all stages of everyday life?) As Cavell puts it, to live without scepticism 'would be to fall in love with the world' (CR 431). Perhaps the desire that governs so much philosophy is this wish to fall in love with the world and to achieve what Cavell calls 'empathic projection' (CR 420) with the other, the identity of subject and object without remainder, slack or excess. Perhaps this goes some way to explaining what is going on in Heidegger's existential analytic of inauthenticity in Division I of *Being and Time* – but that's another story for another occasion. For Cavell, on the contrary, 'I live my scepticism' (CR 437). That is, scepticism is a praxis, it is a practice of the self conditioned by the acknowledgement of ignorance and limitation. As Cavell puts it, 'My ignorance of the existence of others is not the fate of my natural condition as a human knower, *but my way of inhabiting that condition*' (CR 432). Thus, the real problem with scepticism, according to Cavell, is that we attempt to convert the way we inhabit the human condition into a theoretical problem and this prevents an acknowledgement of the limitedness of the human glimpsed in scepticism.

However, it should be noted that the theoreticism of scepticism is only a problem for modern, epistemological scepticism and the same claim cannot simply be made for ancient scepticism, which was not merely theoretical doubt about the truth of certain metaphysical theses, but a practical doubt about the whole of one's life, a full existential *epoche*. In this light, Cavell's work might be viewed as a tacit recovery of the ethos of ancient scepticism.[91]

(ii)
Cavell's tragic wisdom

This brings me to what I see as the central insight of Cavell's work, what one might call its *tragic* wisdom, which, like a musical leitmotif, is rarely explicitly formulated but which constantly returns in different variations throughout his work: *the need for an acceptance of human finitude as that which cannot be overcome.* That is to say, an acceptance of the finiteness of the finite, of the limitedness of the human condition.

Contra Mulhall, this is why Cavell's work can be seen as neither Christian nor anti-Christian, i.e. crudely 'Nietzschean', insofar as both the Christian and the Nietzschean share the belief that the human condition is something that must be overcome whether in redemption through the person of Christ revealed through Scripture or through Zarathustra's teaching of the overman. To express this with a historical figure, I think Cavell rightly accepts Pascal's tragic vision of the limitedness of the human condition without his accompanying faith in the possibility of overcoming that condition through redemption. As Mulhall's use of Charles Taylor's *Sources of the Self* attempts to show, the roots of Cavell's philosophical preoccupations may well be religious, but I do not see why this entails that their consequences should be religious.[92] To make this move is to sidestep the problem of nihilism which has been the framing theme of this book. Philosophy cannot say sin, but neither can it say salvation. What philosophy can say is itself, an endless self-assertion, an endless arrogance and arrogation of the voice that is in conflict with the religious (i.e. Kierkegaardian–Weilian) vision of dying to the self that characterizes the awaiting for God.

However, such assertion is not the expression of the self's mastery, but the expression of its frailty, its separateness; a minimal but irreducible ipseity that returns reluctantly to itself in the absence of God, a self for whom at the moment of the body's death, 'there is a period of reverberation and then nothing'. In these *disappointing* circumstances – and it has been my claim that philosophical modernity is the attempt to live with(in) the disappointment of religion – the best that can be hoped for is an acknowledgement of this limitedness, whilst the worst is the failure to make this acknowledgement. Responding to the sceptical teaching of *King Lear* – ventriloquized through the character of Edgar – Cavell writes:

> What the sceptic opens my eyes to is the knowledge that *this is the best* – the occurrence of this tree, of that stone, at that distance, in this light, myself undrugged and unhampered, in the best of health.
>
> (CR 432–33)

'*This is the best*' – such is the maxim of the person who has survived scepticism, something that is doubtless true of a tragic figure like Edgar, but perhaps equally true of the comic hero: of Chaplin, Keaton (CR 452), or, as Cavell has recently said, Groucho Marx – for these are also survivors of scepticism. Perhaps the secret desire of this lecture is to replace Emerson with Groucho Marx as the hero of Cavell's philosophy and as a spokesman for this new yet unapproachable America.[93] The inanity and insanity of Groucho's words, these words in migration, these words of immigration, such is Cavell's *spectre de Marx*: Groucho rather than Karl-o.[94] Recalling the most Marxist moment in Cavell – 'It wasn't hurting, I was just calling my hamsters' (CR 89) – we can see how the whole problem of scepticism (was he really calling his hamsters?) also opens in the experience of the comic.

Moving from the comic to the tragic, the path from scepticism to tragedy becomes clear in Part Four of *The Claim of Reason, '*tragedy is the public form of the life of scepticism with respect to other minds' (CR 476). That is, in Cavell's terms, tragedy is the dramatization of the failure to acknowledge others. The sceptical teaching of tragedy – and the tragic teaching of scepticism – is the fact that I cannot know the other. In Part Four of *The Claim of Reason*, Cavell gives three examples of tragedy by looking at Shakespeare's *The Merchant of Venice*, *A Winter's Tale*, and a stunning, extended reading of *Othello*. The book closes with the image of Othello and Desdemona dead on their nuptial bed. For Cavell, this image constitutes an emblem for the truth of scepticism. Othello – like America – could not yield to what he knew, he could not accept the tragic wisdom of the limitedness of his knowledge of Desdemona and consequently he failed to acknowledge her separateness, her alterity. This is why Othello kills Desdemona.

For Cavell, intrinsic to any acceptance of the limitedness of the human condition, of the finiteness of the finite, is an acknowledgement of *separation*. In a retrospective remark, Cavell writes, 'I have argued for an understanding of the having of the self as an acceptance of the idea of being by oneself' (CR 367). Cavell is proposing here a conception of self in terms of 'aloneness', 'oneness', or what Thoreau calls 'holiness'.[95] In relation to the problem of scepticism, the claim here is that scepticism concerning other minds becomes a way of acknowledging the other's separateness from me and my separateness from the other. Of course, to say that I and the other are separated is to say something about the nature of our relationship, namely that it is a relationship across separation, a relation between separated terms, an absolute relation. Of course, this is what Levinas, and Derrida after him, call *justice*. As Cavell puts it:

Lecture 2

There is no assignable end to the depth of us that language reaches; that nevertheless there is no end to our separateness. We are endlessly separate, for *no* reason.

(CR 369)

'For *no* reason' – as Cavell puts it elsewhere, where the rationality of moral argumentation breaks down, we do not witness the collapse of morality but the beginning of moral relationship (CR 326). Both scepticism and tragedy conclude with the recognition of separation, with the anti-Hegelian recognition that intersubjective relations are not based on cognition or recognition, but on acknowledgement.[96]

But what is romantic about Cavell's tragic wisdom? Simply this: that the picture of philosophy (and picture of culture) that Cavell claims to find in Wittgenstein's *Investigations*, with its endless circulation and oscillation of voices and positions, is the very picture which I claimed above was the truth of romanticism, namely its non-romantic essence. The play or 'wriggling' between the demand for criteria and the sceptical disappointment of that demand – what Putnam sees as the necessity of learning to live with the double bind of acknowledgement and alienation (RP 178) – can be mapped directly onto the quasi-dialectics of wit and irony that I presented above in relation to Schlegel. The criterial demand for *Witz* and *Wissen*, the attempt to unify subject and object in a creative act of synthesis, is always subject to the destructive activity of irony, that 'höchste und reinste *skepsis*'. The naïveté of romanticism is rooted in the self-consciousness of its failure, of the fact that the demand for the *Work* – the aesthetic or literary absolute – like the demand for criteria, will always open itself to the sceptical movement of unworking, it will never achieve 'realization', not even a 'fair realization'. In terms of the problem of other minds, the empathic projection of the philosopher stumbles across a seam in human experience behind which the other withdraws. The general claim made above was that this oscillation between wit and irony, work and unworking, and criteria and scepticism is (barely) held together by the genre of the fragment itself. This is what I meant when I stated that Cavell's claim for Emerson was un-Cavellian and un-romantic. Namely, that it attempts to realize the ideal, thereby disarming the sceptic and freezing the movement of irony in the living present of aesthetic *Witz* and *Wissen*. The work is always in progress, which is to say that it opens the future, is the possibility that the future might have a future.

What is Cavellian and romantic, in my view, is the endless wriggling between

136

criteria and scepticism, a movement that is manifested in both romantic texts and the *Investigations* themselves, but equally in the fragmentary quality of Cavell's prose. Exemplary in this regard, I feel, is Part Four of *The Claim of Reason*, which might be read as an amnesial rewriting of the *Athenäum Fragments*. With its endless play of voices and sheer aphoristic force, Cavell's writing recalls the practice of romantic fragmentation. It is a writing that is rambling, deviatory, tendentious, obscure, but littered with moments of explosive brilliance. Cavell's style is Shandeyesque: it is marked by ellipses, circumlocutions, parentheses, occasionally agonizing formulations which are, turn and turn about, defensive and defenceless. I note his predilection for certain words, for an idiosyncratic and quasi-religious, quasi-legal language: settlement, dispensation, inheritance, entitlement, rescue, recovery, rebirth; and his taste for present participles: accounting, counting, acknowledging, founding, finding, declining. And yet, in reading Cavell there is the conviction that one is listening to a philosophical voice, that this voice, like no other I know currently writing in English, exemplifies philosophizing.

(iii)
Finiteness, limitedness

I have claimed that romantic oscillation – between wit and irony, work and unworking, criteria and scepticism – yields an insight into finitude, a tragic wisdom centred in an acceptance of the limitedness of thought, of the finiteness of the human condition as that which cannot be overcome. In the Lyceum Fragments, Schlegel notes in passing, before quickly dismissing the idea, that wit is the substitute for an impossible happiness (CR 59). For me, this remark captures well the mood of melancholy that is the ambience of the fragments, the night whose vast profile is briefly traced by those tiny explosions of wit and irony.

But what exactly is the link between the romantic fragment and the thinking of finitude? As I discussed in Lecture 1, for all systems of thought that take seriously the question of finitude and the problem of nihilism, the fundamental philosophical quest is that of finding a *meaning* to finitude. If death is not the gateway to another life, and if it is not just going to have the contingent character of a brute fact, then one's mortality is something that one has to project freely, as the product of a resolute decision. Death is therefore something to be achieved; it is a Work.

137

However, the interpretation of romanticism given here emphasizes its exploration of the lack of final synthesis, its inability to produce the aesthetic absolute, the great work, the work of death that would give meaning to life and overcome nihilism. The ceaseless quasi-dialectic within romanticism perpetually postpones the possibility of finding a meaning to finitude, thereby making death impossible, ungraspable and unworked. In their refusal of final synthesis, fragments provoke us into an acceptance of finitude as that which evades the grasp of my criteria, as that towards which I am certainly destined but without knowing the time and the manner of my arrival. Beneath their explosive brilliance, their substitution for an impossible happiness, romantic fragments quietly recall us to the unworking of the work, the ungraspability of the finite, the impossibility of death and the endless process of mourning. We are left unable, impotent and insomniac, trying to imagine what happens when the body dies, when the reverberation of life fades into silence. As Beckett writes, and this will be the topic of Lecture 3, 'No, life ends, and no, there is nothing elsewhere'.[97]

The future is faced with fragments, with fragments of an impossible future, a future that itself appears fragmentary. And *this is the best,* and *for no reason*. Out of the bonfire of our intellectual vanities come the ashes of compassion, of tenderness and generosity, and for no reason. After the unworking of human arrogance, we become 'the finally human natives of a dwindled sphere'.

Lecture 3

Know happiness – on Beckett

We *have* to talk, whether we have something to say or not; and the less we want to say and want to hear the more willfully we talk and are subjected to talk. How did Pascal put it? 'All the evil in the world comes from our inability to sit quietly in a room.' To keep still.

(Stanley Cavell)

(a)
Beckett and philosophical interpretation

The writings of Samuel Beckett seem to be particularly, perhaps uniquely, resistant to philosophical interpretation. To speak from the vantage point of a conceptual framework, an interpretative method or any form of metalanguage, is, at the best of times, a hazardous exercise with regard to those texts regarded as 'literary' – *traduttore, traditore*. However, the peculiar resistance of Beckett's work to philosophical interpretation lies, I think, in the fact that his texts continually seem to pull the rug from under the feet of the philosopher by showing themselves to be conscious of the possibility of such interpretations; or, better, such interpretations seem to lag behind the text which they are trying to interpret; or, better still, such interpretations seem to lag behind their object by saying too much: something essential to Beckett's language is lost by overshooting the text and ascending into the stratosphere of metalanguage.[1]

None of the once fashionable, but now rather stale, philosophical clichés in terms of which Beckett's work has been discussed seem vaguely adequate to their object, whether it is the sub-Cartesian interpretation where Beckett is allegedly concerned with 'the inexpressible nature of the self whose figurings people the landscape of post-Cartesian modernity', or the sub-Heideggerian interpretation where Beckett strives to attain 'the existential authenticity of being prior to language or of being *as* language', or the sub-Pascalian absurdist interpretation where Beckett expresses 'the quintessential and pessimistic tragic fate of modern man'; or whatever.[2] Even if it is granted that the inadequacy of such interpretations has the unintended merit of sending one back to the text in search of other meanings, it might well be that philosophically mediated meanings are precisely what we should *not* be in search of when thinking through Beckett's work. Indeed, there seems to be some sort of inverse or perverse relation between the resistance of Beckett's work to interpretation and the philosophical abstraction and assuredness of the interpretations offered in its name.

A possible explanation of the pitfalls of philosophical interpretation when faced with Beckett might begin by examining the network of philosophical allusions in a work like the so-called *Trilogy*,[3] particularly in its many semi-hidden references to Descartes.[4] For example, in the Third Part of the *Discourse on the Method*, Descartes writes:

> In this respect, I would be imitating a traveler who, upon finding himself lost in a forest, should not wander about turning this way and that, and still less stay in one place, but should keep walking as straight as he can . . . for in this way, even if he does not go exactly where he wishes, he will at least end in a place where he is likely to be better off than in the middle of a forest.[5]

To which Molloy, who thinks himself much better off in the middle of a forest than elsewhere, would seem to respond in the following way:

> And having heard, or probably read somewhere, in the days when I thought I would be well advised to educate myself, or amuse myself, or stupefy myself, or kill time, that when a man in a forest thinks he is going forward in a straight line, in reality he is going in a circle, I did my best to go in a circle, hoping in this way to go in a straight line.
>
> (T 78)[6]

Or again one might consider the parody of Cartesian rational method in *The Unnameable* (T 357–58), or when Molloy refers to himself as 'nothing more than a lump of melting wax' (T 45), or when Moran rehearses the movement of

Cartesian doubt, denying the existence of his messenger Gaber – all too obviously the Angel Gabriel – of his chief Youdi – all too inevitably Yahveh, interestingly glossed by Nussbaum as 'You die'[7] – and even himself:

> To keep nothing from you, this lucidity was so acute that at times I came even to doubt the existence of Gaber himself. And if I had not hastily sunk back into my darkness I might have gone to the extreme of conjuring away the chief too and regarding myself as solely responsible for my wretched existence . . . And having made away with Gaber and the chief (one Youdi), could I have denied myself the pleasure of – you know. But I was not made for the great light that devours, a dim lamp was all I had been given, and patience without end, to shine on in the empty shadows. I was a solid in the midst of solids.[8]

Beckett's work seems to offer itself generously to philosophical interpretation only to withdraw this offer by parodically reducing such interpretation to ridicule, 'They must consider me sufficiently stupefied, with all their balls about being and existing' (T 320). Or when Molloy sneers, 'Can it be we are not free? It might be worth looking into' (T 35). Beckett's response to philosophical interpretations of his work might well have been analogous to that offered in *Malone Dies*, where, after losing his stick, Malone offers himself the solace of contemplating the essence of the stick in a mini-pastiche of Platonic epistemology, 'the Stick, shorn of all its accidents, such as I had never dreamt of'. Malone concludes, 'what a broadening of the mind' (T 233).

Beckett's work contains innumerable philosophical red herrings. In *Malone Dies*, ten lines before we are introduced to a parrot being taught to quote Leibniz, we find the following cryptic reference to Spinoza, 'One day I took counsel of an Israelite on the subject of conation' (T 200). This is compounded by some unsubtle punning on marrano as 'merino', 'I could not help thinking that the notion of a wandering herd was better adapted to him than to me'. However, to propose one example, from amongst the myriad possible philosophical interpretations of Beckett, the protagonist in *The Unnameable*, at this point in the guise of Mahood, writes:

> *De nobis ipsis silemus*, decidedly that should have been my motto. Yes, they gave me some lessons in pigsty Latin too, it looks well sprinkled through the perjury.
>
> (T 302)

As most philosophically literate readers will realize, *de nobis ipsis silemus* is a quotation from the preface to Bacon's *Instauratio Magna*, which in turn is famously employed by Kant as the motto to the B edition of the *Kritik der reinen Vernunft*.[9] Of course, the motto is borrowed with heavy irony, as the protagonist in *The Unnameable* is unable to keep silent, least of all about itself.[10] Now, if one had the leisure, the competence and the intelligence, one could imagine a philosophical interpretation of Beckett that might begin from this connection, showing how he inherits a certain Kantian or post-Kantian philosophical world-view. The focus of such an interpretation would naturally be the problem of the subject in and after Kant and the whole question of the status of philosophy, the aesthetic and art after the Copernican turn, that is, after the critique of metaphysics and the turn to the subject as the ground of knowledge. Of course, the epistemological subject or transcendental unity of apperception in Kant is something that must be logically presupposed in the deduction of the categories – the 'I think' must accompany all my representations – but the subject is not itself an item of knowledge; that is, it is formal and insubstantial. As I said above, the Kantian subject is subject without substance.

Thus, when the voice in *The Unnameable* writes, at the beginning of its exhausting 112-page final paragraph, 'I, of whom I know nothing', one might well want to pursue the question of the 'I' in Beckett and the continuous negotiation that it maintains with the 'not I' in terms of the way the category of the subject is reduced from an ontological substance to a logical place-holder in Kant and how this question becomes the veritable *Brennpunkt* of post-Kantian idealism and romanticism – *What a broadening of the mind!*

Now, although such an interpretation would not be foolish or fallacious and might even offer an illuminating historical analogy between the discourses of modern philosophy and modernist literature, nonetheless one feels that even such a clever interpretation inevitably both lags behind the text that it is trying to interpret and overshoots it: saying too much and saying too little, saying too little by saying too much. In relation to Beckett, the philosophical hermeneut becomes a rather flat-footed puppet dancing to the author's tune. As the voice in *The Unnameable* says with sardonic compassion, 'So they build up hypotheses that collapse on top of one another, it's human, a lobster couldn't do it' (T 342).

(b)
The dredging machine (Derrida)

How is one therefore to avoid the platitudes of philosophical metalanguage with regard to Beckett? As Derrida remarks with distressing candour in a rare direct reference to Beckett, 'It is very hard'.[11] After confessing that Beckett is an author to whom Derrida feels very close, 'but also too close' (although, one might ask: how could one be *too* close to Beckett?), and that he has avoided writing on Beckett because of this proximity, Derrida adds:

> How could I write in French in the wake of or 'with' someone who does operations on this language which seem to me so strong and so necessary, but which must remain idiomatic? How could I write, sign, countersign performatively texts which 'respond' to Beckett? How could I avoid the platitude of a supposed academic metalanguage?

What Derrida seems to be suggesting is that because one cannot avoid the platitude of metalanguage and the inevitable lagging behind and overshooting of philosophical interpretation, Beckett has to be avoided. One cannot hope to be faithful to the *idiom* of Beckett's language because any interpretation assumes a generality that betrays that idiom, what Derrida will also call a text's *signature*. Derrida describes the hermeneutic problem raised by Beckett's writing in very direct terms:

> When I found myself, with students, reading some of Beckett's texts, I would take three lines, I would spend two hours on them, then I would give up because it would not have been possible, or honest, or even interesting, to extract a few 'significant' lines from a Beckett text. The composition, the rhetoric, the construction and the rhythm of his works, even the ones that seem the most 'decomposed', that's what 'remains' finally the most 'interesting', that's the work, that's the signature, this remainder which remains when the thematics are exhausted.[12]

I will come back to the question of the work achieved by Beckett's writing in connection with Adorno, but Derrida is suggesting that the work of Beckett's work, its work-character, is that which refuses meaning and remains after one has exhausted thematization. Such a remains (*reste*) would be the irreducible idiom of Beckett's work, its ineffaceable signature. It is this remainder that is both revealed through reading and resists reading.

145

These suggestive remarks can be illuminated with reference to Derrida's *Glas*. In the Genet column, Derrida finds what he calls 'the good metaphor' for describing his interpretative practice, that of a dredging machine:

No, I see rather... a sort of dredging machine. From the dissimulated, small, closed, glassed-in cabin of a crane, I manipulate some levers and, from afar, I saw that done at Saintes-Maries-de-la-Mer at Eastertime, I plunge a mouth of steel in the water. And I scrape the bottom, hook onto stones and algae there that I lift up in order to set them down on the ground while the water quickly falls back from the mouth.[13]

With this 'good metaphor', we can see that what Derrida is trying to avoid in reading is a relation of mastery over his object, the kind of dominating mastery that Sartre exerted over Genet in his *Saint Genet*, where the object of interpretation is imprisoned within the dialectical and emancipatory narrative of existential psychoanalysis. Rather, Derrida pictures the reader within the cabin of a rather clumsy dredging machine, manipulating a series of levers. A steel mouth scrapes the bottom of the sea with what Derrida calls a 'toothed matrix', picking up morsels here and there, but letting the water and silt pass between its teeth. The operator of the dredging machine can barely hear the sea from within his cabin.

What this metaphor shows, I think, is that however much the philosophical hermeneut may wish to elevate a particular literary text into an order of meaning or give a coherent interpretation, water and silt will inevitably slip through the teeth of the reading machine and *remain*. Derrida writes, in a formulation difficult to translate, 'la matrice transcendantale laisse toujours retomber le reste du texte'.[14] That is, whatever transcendental, metalinguistic or hermeneutic key is employed to unlock the text, such a matrix will always let the text fall back and remain as a remains. In this sense, we might say that the goal of Derrida's reading practice is to *let the remains remain*. You cannot catch the sea in your hands. And yet, this does not mean that reading can ever attain the goal of a pure remains and that we might be able to undergo some kind of experience of language as language outside of metalinguistic interpretation. Not at all. For Derrida, as he remarks elsewhere in *Glas*, 'the death agony of metalanguage is structurally interminable', and 'metalanguage is itself irreducible'.[15] Thus, with regard to Beckett, there is no way of circumventing the platitudes of philosophical metalanguage and giving immediate expression to the work-character of the work, to its idiom. Yet, although metalanguage is unavoidable, Derrida adds elsewhere in *Glas*:

> I do not cease to decapitate metalanguage, or rather to replunge its head into the text in order to extract it from the text, regularly, the interval of a respiration.[16]

Employing another aquatic metaphor, Derrida is seeking to submerge the reader's head in the language of the text, almost to the point of drowning, only to gulp the oxygen of metalanguage in a moment's respiration and plunge the reader once again into the text. This movement of immersion and respiration describes, I think, the *rhythm* of reading, a double bind which recognizes both the impossibility of a pure experience of language, and the inadequacy of all metalinguistic interpretation, 'a plurality of continuous jerks, of uninterrupted jolts – such would be the rhythm'.[17] For what it is worth, such would also be the rhythm of a deconstructive reading and, as Derek Attridge suggests, Beckett is a (perhaps, the) paradigm case of a self-deconstructive writer, and with respect to his work, 'there is not much left to do'.[18]

(c)
The meaning of meaninglessness and the paradoxical task of interpretation (Adorno I)

The philosopher who has come closest to describing the difficulties of interpreting Beckett and gone furthest in taking up the challenge that he poses to philosophy is, without doubt, Adorno. He writes of the challenge that Beckett's work presents to philosophy:

> One could almost [*fast* – in a sense everything hangs on this 'almost'. Why almost?, SC] say that the criterion of a philosophy whose hour has struck is that it prove equal to this challenge.

(NL 284/NTL 244)

These words are taken from Adorno's 1961 essay on *Endgame*, 'Versuch, das Endspiel zu verstehen', where we should hear the way in which *Versuch* qualifies the verb *verstehen*; any attempt at understanding must remain an attempt because understanding would betray the idiom of Beckett's writing. In addition to this essay, there are scattered remarks on Beckett in essays from the 1960s, notably 'Commitment' ('Engagement') from 1962, and 'Is Art Lighthearted?' ('Ist die

Kunst heiter?') from 1967, as well as the important references towards the end of *Negative Dialectics* discussed above.[19] Adorno also intended to dedicate his final, unfinished *Aesthetic Theory* to Beckett, and although there are only scattered, but fascinating, references to Beckett in the text, it is clear that his work provides the best literary (setting to one side the musical and the visual) model of the aesthetic modernism defended in that work.[20]

As other commentators have pointed out, Adorno reads *Endgame* as an *Endgeschichte des Subjekts*, a history of the subject's end or the end-history of the subject.[21] As Adorno writes in the closing chapter of *Aesthetic Theory*, 'Those childlike and bloody clowns' faces in Beckett, through which the subject disintegrates, are the historical truth about the subject' (AT 370/AST 354).[22] What this means for Adorno is that 'the catastrophes that inspire *Endgame*', notably the fact of Auschwitz which Beckett never calls by name, as if it were subject to a *Bilderverbot*, have shattered or disintegrated the conception of the individual still presupposed in the absurdist vision of existentialism.[23] That is, although Camus might begin *The Myth of Sisyphus* from the postulate of the world's absurdity — i.e. the absence of meaning in a world without God — this absurdity is viewed from the standpoint of the individual. The task of existentialism, on this reading, is a shoring up of the individual subject and its claims to freedom, radical choice and moral autonomy. The temptation of suicide that is opened by the situation of absurdity is overcome in an affirmation of the subject's freedom. For Adorno, Beckett's drama abandons this existentialist position 'like an outmoded bunker' (NL 291/NTL 249). Adopting a classical Marxist analysis — although we should note how these social categories take on the pathos of a pessimistic lyricism in Adorno's hands — Adorno notes that 'the individual is revealed to be a historical category, both the outcome of the capitalist process of alienation and a defiant protest against it' (NL 291/NTL 249). Adorno declares, 'what is left of the subject is its most abstract characteristic: merely existing (*da zu sein*) and thereby already committing an outrage' (NL 293/NTL 251). Beckett's characters are 'empty *personae*, truly mere masks through whom sound merely passes'.

In Adorno's hands, Beckett engages in a reversal of existential philosophy, 'which has been standing on its head, and puts it back on its feet' (NL 295/NTL 253). What this means is that Beckett accepts the postulate of absurdity and hence the meaninglessness of existence as a starting point. In Jaspers's and Heidegger's terms, he accepts the situatedness into which we are thrown. However, unlike existential philosophy, Beckett refuses to transfigure this initial meaninglessness into a meaning for existence, whether through an account of the subject's freedom surging up into this thrownness, or through the deduction of Heideggerian existentials, i.e. *Befindlichkeit* as the a priori meaning of thrownness. For Beckett, the absurd cannot be turned into a meaning for the meaninglessness of existence, for if it did so it would become something universal, an idea. This is why, in Adorno's terms, existential philosophy remains an idealism, for it assumes a meaning to existence and an identity between subject and object, even when the poles of that relation have been transposed into the relation of transcendence between *Dasein* and *Welt*. 'Instead', Adorno continues:

> the absurd turns into forlorn particulars that mock the conceptual, a layer composed of minimal utensils, refrigerators, lameness, blindness, and the distasteful bodily functions. Everything waits to be carted off to the dump.
>
> (NL 293/NTL 252)

Thus, the initial metaphysical absurdity of *Endgame* must not be viewed as some sort of Sartrean pretext for philosophical pronouncements, or even for a Brechtian political didacticism; rather 'meaning nothing becomes the only meaning' (*das nichts Bedeuten wird zur einzigen Bedeutung*) (NL 305/NTL 261). In this way, Beckett returns us to the condition of particular objects, to their materiality, their extraordinary ordinariness: the gaff, the handkerchief, the toy dog, the sheet, the pap, the pain-killer. In opposition to what Adorno would see as the residual idealism of existential philosophy, this would be Beckett's *materialism* 'Dragged out of the sphere of inwardness, Heidegger's *Befindlichkeiten* and Jaspers' situations become materialist' (NL 293/NTL 252). Beckett thus returns the existentialist concept of situation to 'its actual content' (NL 294/NTL 252) by refusing to transfigure it into a meaning. For Adorno, as we said above, this content is the shattering of the individual, or, in a key phrase, 'the dissociation of the unity of consciousness into disparate elements, into non-identity (*die Nichtidentität*)' (NL 294/NTL 252).

So, if Beckett's advance over existential philosophy lies in its refusal to translate the meaninglessness of absurdity into a meaning for existence by keeping our focus on the particular and the material — which is also a refusal of the conceptual order of philosophy — then is one to conclude that the meaning of Beckett's work is that there is no meaning? Is this the meaning of the phrase 'meaning nothing becomes the only meaning'? If so, what is the task of interpretation? Is there a task for interpretation at all?

Adorno notes that

> Interpretation . . . cannot pursue the chimerical aim of expressing the play's meaning in a form mediated by philosophy.
>
> (NL 283/NTL 243)

He goes on:

> Beckett shrugs his shoulders at the possibility of philosophy today, at theory in general.
>
> (NL 284/NTL 244)

Thus, Beckett's legendary refusal to interpret his own work is not merely the consequence of a subjective aversion on his part, rather it is the expression of the hermeneutic impropriety of any attempt to extract a philosophical meaning from an artwork. However, this does not entail that interpretation is redundant: it might well be impossible, but it is still *necessary*. As Adorno writes in *Aesthetic Theory*:

> The non-objective status of interpretation does not deliver us from it, as though there was nothing to interpret. Refraining from interpretation on this basis is the confusion that started all the talk about the absurd.
>
> (AT 48/AST 40)

Reading the above remark self-referentially, one might say that Adorno also 'shrugs his shoulders' at the possibility of philosophy today, where philosophy must subordinate itself to artistic praxis. Adorno writes, in a paratactic formula reminiscent of Friedrich Schlegel:

> This is why art needs philosophy to interpret it, in order to say what art cannot say, although it can only be said in art, insofar as it does not say it.
>
> (AT 113/AST 107)

Art and philosophy here move within a dialectic whose name is neither art nor philosophy, but *aesthetic theory*. Thus, the title *Aesthetic Theory* is a description of the content of Adorno's conceptual praxis, a praxis which is not philosophy, which is always complicit with abstraction and hence with domination and reification, and is not art. For Adorno, such is the paradox at the heart of aesthetics, a paradox that would be evaded if one believed either that the truth content of artworks could be fully conceptualized in philosophical interpretation, or if one sacrificed the necessity for interpretation — for conceptual communication. The paradox is well stated by Zuidevaart, 'Art needs a philosophy that needs art'.[24]

Unsurprisingly, given what has been said above, the interpretative task of aesthetic theory with regard to Beckett has a necessarily paradoxical form:

> Understanding it can only mean understanding its unintelligibility, concretely reconstructing the meaning of the fact that it has no meaning.
>
> (NL 283/NTL 243)

I would like to focus on the words 'concretely reconstructing the meaning of the fact that it has no meaning'. That is to say, it is a question of the concrete elucidation of the meaning of meaninglessness, a remark that I would want to put alongside Derrida's remark on the work-character of the work as a remainder that remains after the exhaustion of thematization. Adorno writes of Beckett:

> Thought becomes a means to produce something in the work, a meaning which cannot be rendered directly in tangible form, and a means to express the absence of meaning.
>
> (NL 282/NTL 242)

Thus, it is not true to say that Beckett's work is meaningless as if meaninglessness were a fact that did not need to be conceptually communicated; rather it is a question of establishing the *meaning of meaninglessness*, making a meaning out of the refusal of meaning that the work performs without that refusal of meaning becoming a meaning. It is a question of conceptualizing and communicating that which resists conceptualization and refuses communication — a necessary and impossible task. Adorno summarizes the problem in a passage from *Aesthetic Theory*:

> Beckett's *oeuvre* seems to presuppose this experience [i.e. of the negation of meaning, SC] as if it were self-evident, and yet it pushes further than the abstract negation of meaning. . . Beckett's plays are absurd not because of the absence of meaning — then they would be irrelevant — but because they debate meaning. They broach its history. His work is governed by the obsession with a positive nothingness, but also by an evolved and thereby equally deserved meaninglessness, and that's why this should not be allowed to be reclaimed as a positive meaning.
>
> (AT 230/AST 220–21)

151

In terms I will explain in more depth towards the end of this lecture in relation to Cavell, I think it is a question of meaninglessness becoming an *achievement* rather than a fact, meaninglessness becoming the work of Beckett's work. By debating the meaning of meaning, Beckett's work permits us to trace the history of the dissolution of meaning and to delineate some sort of genealogy of nihilism. Such a genealogy would permit neither the restoration of meaning in an ever-falsifiable and faded positivity, some version of the overcoming of nihilism, nor the irrelevant metaphysical comfort of meaninglessness.

Incidentally, and to dispel a common misunderstanding, the acknowledgement of a moment of non-identity in artworks that resists conceptualization or the order of meaning, by no means entails that when faced with a writing like Beckett's *there is nothing to say*, where keeping silent is the supposed touchstone of hermeneutic authenticity or even the goal of artistic activity. Not at all. The reading of Beckett demands a determinate and, indeed, laborious work of interpretation, where there is an endless amount of things to say. The point is, however, that such interpretation will not amount to a positive meaning, but rather the concrete reconstruction of the negation of meaning. The dredging machine continues its work even as the water and silt escape it and *because of this fact*. As we will see below, the inability to mean something in Beckett does not mean that we stop speaking, but rather that we are *unable* to stop — *pour finir encore*. Silence is not, as Nussbaum and so many commentators on Beckett assume, the goal of his work, rather writing is the necessary *desecration* and *desacralization* of silence: 'We have to talk'. Beckett's deeper truth is that given the absence of meaning, the story continues, the voice carries on speaking, 'Where do these words come from that pour out of my mouth, and what do they mean, no, saying nothing?' (T 340).[25]

In this connection, I would like to consider briefly Deleuze's powerful and refreshingly totalizing reading of Beckett that appeared as a long essay appended to a French edition of Beckett's pieces for television.[26] Beginning from the notion of exhaustion (*épuisement*) understood in distinction from fatigue as the emptying of all possibility, Deleuze advances and defends a developmental and quasi-dialectical reading hypothesis based on a tripartite interpretation of Beckett's use of language and media. For Deleuze, *Langue I* is the language of Beckett's novels, culminating in *Watt*, where Beckett is engaged in an *ars combinatoria* whose intention is to exhaust the possible through the elaborate extension of rationality into meaningless absurdity, something that is particularly clear in the celebrated sucking stones scene from *Molloy*, and *Watt*'s endless W(h)at(t) (K)not(t)s.

152

However, if *Langue I* attempts to exhaust words through the reasonable but finally absurd deployment of reason, then, according to Deleuze, this exhaustion requires a *Langue II*, which can be traced through Beckett's novels and dramatic works and 'éclate à la radio'.[27] *Langue II* is the language of nameless voices in Beckett, the flux of protagonists 'flayed alive by memory' (T 245), that speak against the possibility of speaking, that try to be done with words by voicing an almost inaudible murmur, something that is already evident in both *The Unnameable* and *How It Is*. But, Deleuze adds, in addition to the two previous categories, there is a *Langue III*, which attempts to exceed language by aspiring to a *pure* image, an image that is no longer part of the imagination of names and voices, of reason and memory, as in *Langue I* and *II*, but is image without imagination. This is how Deleuze reads Beckett's locution *Imagination Dead Imagine*.

Although *Langue III* can be found in the novels and dramatic works – Deleuze refers to *How It Is* and *Act Without Words* – it finds its true expression in Beckett's televisual works.[28] The hypothesis here is that the images, voices, space, silence and music of Beckett's televisual work – in Deleuze's taxonomy: *Quad* is space with silence, *Ghost Trio* is space with voice and music, *Only the clouds . . .* is image with voice and poem, and *Nacht und Träume* is image with silence, song and music – have less and less need of words. It is the medium of television that finally allows Beckett to surmount what Deleuze calls 'the inferiority of words'.[29] It is not only, Deleuze claims, that words are 'liars', but that they are too engraved with memory, significance, associations and habits – the sticky surface of words, 'Elle colle. Elle nous imprisonne et nous étouffe.' ('It sticks. It imprisons and stifles us.')[30] As such, words deny access to 'the void or the visible in itself, silence or the audible in itself' (*'le vide ou le visible en soi, le silence ou l'audible en soi'*).[31]

Despite the too easily teleological or developmental character of Deleuze's reading – a veritable conceptual juggernaut of philosophical interpretation – this is a compelling thesis which offers a much-needed interpretation of Beckett's televisual work. However, I would claim that Deleuze significantly underestimates the fateful necessity of language in Beckett. Although Beckett's protagonists desire to be done with words, to be finally silent, such silence is impossible, unattainable. However much the protagonists in Beckett want to transcend words, in the televisual works through musicality or visuality, the achievement of this transcendence is always denied. Although *le vide* and its positive vision of annihilation is what the protagonists in Beckett devoutly wish for, it is precisely this that they cannot have, and the words continue, 'I can't go on, I'll go on'. As I will explain presently, the double bind or negative dialectic within which Beckett's work moves is that between the inability to speak and the inability to be silent. If language is a medium that no longer satisfies us, then there is no resource outside of language to which we might turn for support. *Le vide* is only ever glimpsed in the ever-failing approximations at its articulation. Despite its conceptual power, Deleuze's reading of Beckett, like so many others, is what Christopher Ricks rightly calls 'An Academy of Lagado' reading of Beckett, referring to the passage in Book Three of *Gulliver's Travels* where Swift ridicules the plan to abolish words altogether.[32] The deeper truth is that Beckett's words are, in Ricks's locution, *dying* words, a 'syntax of weakness'[33] that cannot be transcended through the spatial or imagistic potential of television, a fading, fateful language – ill seen, ill said.

(d)
Hope against hope – the elevation of social criticism to the level of form (Adorno II)

The task of interpretation as the concrete elucidation of the meaning of meaninglessness, of the meaning of the work that negates meaning, raises the question of *form* in relation to Beckett and Adorno. In opposition to both Sartre's theatre, which employs a highly traditional dramatic form in order to put forward an engaged philosophical or political content, and Lukács's denunciation of Beckett's work as a decadent formalism devoid of the content required by socialist realism, in Beckett, 'form overtakes what is expressed and changes it' (NL 281/NTL 241). This explains Adorno's remarks about the 'organized meaninglessness' (*organisierte Sinnlosigkeit*) (NL 283/NTL 242) of Beckett's drama, where although the play negates the possibility of meaning, it still does this in a *form*, it is *organized* meaninglessness. The fact that traditional dramatic forms, like the Aristotelian unities, are employed parodically and that 'parody means the use of forms in the era of their impossibility' is simply to acknowledge the *crisis* of form within modernism, where the autonomy of modernist art is a problem because this autonomy, by definition, can no longer be governed by the constraints and conventions of tradition.

Within modernism it is no longer clear *what* counts as a work of art and *how* a work counts. In Adorno's account of aesthetic modernism, the negation of meaning in Beckett is achieved by way of *form*, even if it is, in the words of

Molloy, 'a form fading among fading forms' (T 17). This is a point well made by Zuidervaart:

> In general, *Aesthetic Theory* argues that negation of meaning becomes aesthetically meaningful when it is realized in the material with which the artist works. Because such a realization requires form, authentic negation requires formal emancipation, not emancipation from form . . . Beckett's absurdist plays are still plays. They do not lack all meaning. They put meaning on trial.[34]

In this way, Adorno's larger claim can be defended, namely that the best modernist artworks in their negation of meaning can be interpreted as determinate negations of contemporary society and can give an idea, a semblance – albeit a formal semblance – of what a society free from domination might be like, where individuals are not reduced to exchange equivalences in a totally commodified society:

> As society becomes more total, as it draws itself together into a more complete and unitary system, the works which store up the experience of this process become all the more the other to society.
>
> (AT 53/AST 45)

Although such remarks proceed from the contestable – indeed, dubious – thesis that we inhabit totally administered societies, where the *Lebenswelt* contains no uncolonized moral practices that might function as sites of resistance to instrumental rationality, it is clear that, for Adorno, Beckett's work successfully negotiates the dialectic between the necessary autonomy of the artwork and the function of social criticism. It achieves this not by raising its voice against society, in the manner of Brecht or Sartre – the critical content of art that is always recuperable by the society it attempts to negate – but rather *by the elevation of social criticism to the level of form*. Towards the end of *Aesthetic Theory*, Adorno writes:

> [Art's] most obligatory criterion today is to leave unreconciled all realistic deceit, no longer tolerating any harmlessness according to its own lights. If it is still possible, social criticism must be elevated to form, dimming down any manifest social content.
>
> (AT 371/AST 354)

This remark explains Adorno's otherwise rather shocking formulation in the

155

final paragraph of his critique of committed art, that 'This is not the time for political works of art; rather politics has migrated into the autonomous work of art, and it has penetrated most deeply into works that present themselves as politically dead' (NL 430/NTL2 94). Beckett is more committed than either Sartre or Brecht by being less committed, he is more realistic by being less realistic. To reiterate, in their achievement of form and their determinate negation of content and meaning, Beckett's works exhibit an aesthetic autonomy that, far from conspiring with apolitical decadence, gives indications of the transformative political praxis from which they abstain, namely 'the production of a right or just life' (NL 429/NTL2 93). The essential thing here is that such indications are only given through abstention, that is, by refusing to give indications at the level of content. It is by keeping this in mind, I think, that we can explain the apparently deeply pessimistic conclusion to Adorno's essay on *Endgame*:

> The last absurdity is that the peacefulness of the void and the peacefulness of reconciliation cannot be distinguished from one another. Hope skulks out of the world, which cannot conserve it any more than it can pap and pralines, and back to where it came from, death.
>
> (NL 321/NTL 274–75)

This seemingly hopeless conclusion must be qualified by recalling Adorno's criterion for authentic artworks, namely that they must 'efface any memory-trace of reconciliation – in the interest of reconciliation' (AT 348/AST 333). That is to say, reconciliation, the utopian or critical moment in artworks, the moment when they give an indication of the transformative political praxis from which they abstain, is only discernible in those artworks which have abandoned the traditional idea of reconciliation. Thus, it is because hope has been driven skulking out of the world by Beckett's *Endgame* that there is hope. Hope against hope. Such is Adorno's austere messianism, a messianicity without messianism in Derrida's formulation.[35] Art's *promesse de bonheur* is a promise that must always be broken (AT 26/AST 17). It is precisely by virtue of the impossibility of redemption that we must see things from this standpoint.[36]

> Is there then no hope? Good gracious, no heavens, what an idea! Just a faint one perhaps, but which will never serve.
>
> (T 336)

(e)
Nothing is funnier than unhappiness — Beckett's laughter
(Adorno III)

However, although Adorno goes further than any other interpreter of Beckett in his enormous sensitivity to the difficulties of interpretation, it is evident that the fact that interpretation inevitably lags behind Beckett does not stop Adorno interpreting Beckett with characteristic black *gusto*. Adorno inserts Beckett into his own contestable account of contemporary society as total reification and the domination of identity thinking: 'Beckett's trashcans are emblems of a culture rebuilt after Auschwitz' (NL 311/NTL 266–67); Beckett's language is a 'jargon of universal disrespect' (NL 309/NTL 264); Beckett's characters inhabit 'the preestablished harmony of despair' (NL 310/NTL 265), and are like 'flies twitching after the fly swatter has half squashed them' (NL 293/NTL 251). For all its many merits, one cannot help but feel that Adorno's hectoring — even bullying — hyperbole comes nowhere near to evoking the recoiling evasiveness and uncanny ordinariness of Beckett's language, something like its *idiom*, what Christopher Ricks (and I will come back to this below) not unproblematically names Beckett's 'Irish bull'.[37] In reading Adorno's essay on Beckett, one cannot help but feel that the latter's syntax of weakness is drowned out by the former's declamatory and slightly triumphalistic antitheses.

For me, this failure to evoke Beckett's idiom is particularly evident in Adorno's persistent underestimation of the subtle but devastating force of Beckett's humour. That is, humour does not, as Adorno suggests, *evaporate* in Beckett 'along with the meaning of the punchline' (NL 301/NTL 258); rather humour is this very experience of evaporation, which is the evaporation of a certain philosophical seriousness and interpretative earnestness. Humour does not evaporate in Beckett; rather laughter is the sound of language trying to commit suicide but being unable to do so, which is what is so tragically comic. It would be a question here of linking humour to idiom, because it is surely humour that is powerfully and irreducibly idiomatic in any natural language. It is humour that resists direct translation and can only be thematized humourlessly — *ergo* the mortal tedium of philosophical discussions of laughter.

To his credit, Adorno discusses Beckett's humour in a later piece, 'Is art lighthearted?', claiming that given (and it is no tiny premise after all) 'the complete disenchantment of the world' (NL 606/NTL2 253), art can neither be lighthearted nor serious, neither tragedy nor comedy, not even tragi-comedy, which was of course how Beckett described *Godot*. Adorno makes a similar remark in an appendix to *Aesthetic Theory*, noting with regard to *Godot* and *Endgame* that 'The spectator's laughter fades away in the face of the laughter on stage' (AT 505/AST 466). But is this really one's experience of Beckett on the stage or on the page? Adorno insists, in a formulation of which he is fond, and whose Beckettian source might well be in Dante's *Inferno*,[38] that 'A dried up, tearless weeping takes the place of laughter. Lamentation has become the mourning of hollow, empty eyes' (NL 605/NTL2 252–53). In the essay on Beckett, Adorno writes, 'the only face left is the one whose tears have dried up' (NL 290/NTL2 249). I can find no textual authority for tearless weeping in Beckett. On the contrary, both the protagonist in *The Unnameable* and Worm are described as crying without ceasing.[39] More importantly, I find Adorno's remarks on this point intuitively unconvincing and I would claim that Beckett's humour does not exhaust itself in the manner suggested. If we laugh until we cry, then this is because we are laughing so hard, not because we are unable to laugh. Admittedly, Beckett's humour is dark, very dark – 'Nothing is funnier than unhappiness, I grant you that'[40] – and his lightning traces of wit illuminate a moonless, starless night; but those traces also allow us to see the night as such. Some examples:

1   Clov to Hamm, 'Do you believe in the life to come?' Hamm to Clov, 'Mine was always that. Got him that time.'
2   Mahood to himself, 'The tumefaction of the penis! The penis, well now, that's a nice surprise, I'd forgotten I had one. What a pity I have no arms.'
3   Molloy on Lousse's parrot, 'Fuck the son of a bitch, fuck the son of a bitch. He must have belonged to an American sailor, before he belonged to Lousse. Pets often change masters. He didn't say much else. No, I'm wrong, he also said, Putain de merde! He must have belonged to a French sailor before he belonged to the American sailor. Putain de merde! Unless he had hit on it alone, it wouldn't surprise me. Lousse tried to make him say, Pretty Polly! I think it was too late. He listened, his head on one side, pondered, then said, Fuck the son of a bitch. It was clear he was doing his best.'
4   Moran hallucinating Youdi's words to Gaber, 'Gaber, Gaber, he said, life is a thing of beauty, Gaber, and a joy for ever. He brought his face nearer mine. A joy for ever, he said, a thing of beauty, Moran, and a joy for ever. He smiled. I closed my eyes. Smiles are all very nice in their own way, very heartening, but at a reasonable distance. I said, Do you think he meant human life?'

5 Molloy on the impermeability of the *Times Literary Supplement*, 'Even farts made no impression on it. I can't help it, gas escapes from my fundament on the least pretext, it's hard not to mention it now and then, however great my distaste. One day I counted them. Three hundred and fifteen farts in nineteen hours, or an average of over sixteen farts an hour. After all, it's not excessive. Four farts every fifteen minutes. It's nothing. Not even one fart every five minutes. It's unbelievable. Damn it, I hardly fart at all, I should never have mentioned it. Extraordinary how mathematics help you to know yourself.'[41]

Beckett's humour at its most powerful – and perhaps verbal humour as such, one thinks of the genius of Groucho Marx – is a paradoxical form of speech that defeats our expectations, producing laughter with its unexpected verbal inversions, contortions and explosions, a refusal of everyday speech that lights up the everyday: estranged, indigent and distorted, 'as it will appear one day in the messianic light'. Laughter is an acknowledgement of finitude, precisely not a manic affirmation of finitude in the solitary, neurotic laughter of the mountain tops (all too present in imitators of Nietzsche, although administered with liberal doses of irony by Nietzsche himself), but as an affirmation that finitude cannot be affirmed because it cannot be grasped. As Beckett quips in his *Proust*, '"Live dangerously", that victorious hiccough in vacuo, as the national anthem of the true ego exiled in habit.'[42] Laughter returns us to the limited condition of our finitude, the shabby and degenerating state of our upper and lower bodily strata, and it is here that the comic allows the windows to fly open onto our tragic condition. Ricks puts the issue extremely well:

> So that although it makes sense to read Beckett, as many do, as a writer who is oddly criss-crossed, a writer who manages to be excruciatingly funny despite possessing a deeply dispiriting apprehension of life, the opposite makes sense too: the conviction that Beckett's apprehension of death is not dispiriting, but is wise and fortifying, and therefore is unsurprisingly the lens of his translucent comedy.[43]

Pushing this a little further, I would even go so far as to claim that the sardonic laughter that resounds within the ribs of the reader or spectator of Beckett's work is a site of uncolonizable resistance to the alleged total administration of society, a node of non-identity in the idealizing rage of commodification that returns us not to a fully integrated and harmonious *Lebenswelt* but lights up the comic feebleness of our embodiment.[44]

159

To summarize, Adorno's piece on *Endgame* is, in my view, the philosophically most powerful and hermeneutically most nuanced piece of writing on Beckett. Nonetheless, one is perhaps obliged to conclude that ultimately it tells us more about Adorno's preoccupations than those of Beckett's text, and perhaps this is inevitable. But if it is provisionally granted that Beckett is able to make a philosopher as subtle and intelligent as Adorno appear slightly maladroit and flat-footed – and if this is perhaps essential to the discourse of aesthetic theory with respect to its privileged objects – then what is the philosophical hermeneut to do when faced with this work? What is one to do when faced with Beckett?

Nothing. That is, nothing that will be able to avoid the pitfalls into which other philosophical interpretations of Beckett have fallen and which my discussion of Derrida and Adorno has brought sharply into relief. If the platitudes of metalanguage are structurally interminable, and yet metalanguage is intrinsically incredible, standing in need of what Derrida called 'decapitation', then *allons-y*! I would like to offer a reading of Beckett's *Trilogy* and as a banister against which to steady myself as I try to climb, I will follow Maurice Blanchot's brief, but extremely suggestive, discussions of Beckett.

(f)
Storytime, time of death (*Molloy, Malone Dies*)

In the *Trilogy*, there is a relentless pursuit, across and by means of narrative, of that which narration cannot capture, namely the radical unrepresentability of death. Yet, and this is the paradox upon which, arguably, the entirety of Beckett's fiction turns, to convey this radical unrepresentability, the *Trilogy* must represent the unrepresentable. That is to say, it must construct a series of representations, a litany of voices, names and figures, 'a gallery of moribunds' (T 126), that revolve or, to use Beckett's word, 'wheel' (T 270) around a narrative voice or a protagonist, passing in succession. These wheeling figures, these 'delegates' (T 272), have names that have become familiar: Molloy (but also Dan (T 18)), Mellose and Mollose (T 103), Jacques Moran,[45] Malone, Mahood (but also 'Basil and his gang' (T 278 and 283), the billy-in-the-bowl) and Worm. But, in the *Trilogy* we also find earlier delegates recalled: Murphy (T 268) and the pseudo-couple Mercier-Camier (T 272), a mini-library of Anglo-Gallo-Hiberno-nyms, a series of 'M' names (forgetting Watt for a moment) which is completed by a 'W', an inverted 'M', where Worm 'is the first of his kind' (T 310).[46]

The dramatic tension of the *Trilogy*, to my mind, is found in the disjunction that opens up between the time of narrative, the chain of increasingly untellable and untenable stories, and the non-narratable time of the narrative voice, which I am choosing to see as the time of dying, what was described in Lecture 1 as the impossible temporality of *le mourir* in distinction from *la mort*, the time of the possible. The double bind within which the *Trilogy* wriggles, and out of which it is written, is that between the impossibility of narration or representation and its necessity. The development of the *Trilogy*, to speak provisionally in a quasi-teleological vocabulary, is one where the experience of disjunction between these two temporal orders becomes increasingly acute, where, in Blanchot's terms, the order of the work (of narrative, representation and storytelling) breaks down or opens into the experience of *désoeuvrement*, a worklessness which should not be confused with formlessness. Blanchot summarizes his reading of the *Trilogy*:

> Aesthetic sentiments are out of place here. Perhaps we are not in the presence of a book, but perhaps it is a question of much more than a book: the pure approach of a movement from whence all books come, from this original point where doubtless the work is lost, which always ruins the work, which restores endless worklessness in the work, but with which an ever more primal relationship has to be maintained, on pain of being nothing.
>
> (LV 313)

This disjunction between the time of narrative and the time of dying can be traced in *Molloy* by considering the symmetries and dissymmetries between the two parts of the novel. Initially at least, the figures of Molloy and Moran, the latter being the agent given the assignment of finding the former, an encounter which never takes place, seem to be completely opposed. Moran, with his authoritarian relationship to his son, also named Jacques, his dutiful relation to God, whether through the intermediary of Father Ambrose or the agency/archangelcy of Gaber, and his possessive relation to self and to nature, is sharply distinct from Molloy, 'the panting anti-self',[47] with his expropriative relation to nature. To employ a psychoanalytic register, which much in the novel seems to encourage and which, I think, must be refused because it is so encouraged – for an example of a psychoanalytic red herring, see Moran's anagrammatic gift to Freudian readers, where 'the Libido' becomes, somewhat clumsily, 'the Obidil', 'And with regard to the Obidil, of whom I have refrained from speaking until now, and whom I so longed to see face to face' (T 149) – the happily Oedipal Moran can be played off against the pre-Oedipal Molloy with his failed quest for identification with his mother and his consequent abjection.

However, there is a progressive and deepening symmetry between the two parts of the novel, where, if you like, the authoritarian Oedipal subject becomes the pre-Oedipal abject self, what Moran calls 'the disintegration of the father'. Moran loses his faith, telling Father Ambrose 'not to count on me any more' (T 161), and the virile bourgeois subject undergoes 'a crumbling, a frenzied collapsing' (T 137), through a syntax of weakness, through a poetics of increasing impotence, 'I grew gradually weaker and weaker and more and more content' (T 150), 'on me so changed from what I was' (T 136). On a more careful reading, the novel reveals what Molloy calls his 'mania for symmetry' (T 78),[48] where a chain of cumulating correspondences between Molloy and Moran can be detected: both hear a gong (T 82, 106), both ride bicycles and end up on crutches (T 60, 161) because of their painfully stiffening legs, both hear a strange voice offering succour (T 84) or giving orders (T 121, 156, 162), and both attain a point of stasis with Molloy in his ditch, 'Molloy could stay, where he happened to be' (T 84), and Moran in his shelter prior to the real or hallucinated arrival of Gaber, 'I was all right where I was' (T 151).

However, more profoundly, the symmetry resides in the narrative form of both parts of the novel, where each protagonist writes from a position outside the events described in the narrative. Molloy writes at the behest of a man who gives him money in exchange for his pages (T 9), Moran writes his 'report' under the orders of Youdi (T 84–85, 161). Indeed, they both seem to be writing for the agent Gaber, Moran explicitly, Molloy implicitly insofar as 'the queer one' who takes his pages, like Gaber, visits on Sunday and is always thirsty, usually for beer (T 9, 86, 161).

What underpins the symmetry is the disinterestedness and disaffection of the relation each of the protagonists maintain to their writing, and it is here that the disjunction between the time of narrative and the time of dying can most clearly be seen. Molloy, finally in his mother's room, wants nothing more than to be left alone, to 'finish dying' (T 9), but 'they do not want that'. He is thus under an obligation or 'remnants of a pensum' (T 31) to write stories, although the origin of this obligation is unknown and the stories are incredible, 'What I need now is stories, it took me a long time to know that, and I'm not certain of it'

(T 14). This situation produces a characteristically paradoxical formulation of Beckett's writerly credo:

> Not to want to say, not to know what you want to say, not to be able to say what you think you want to say, and never to stop saying, or hardly ever, that is the thing to keep in mind, even in the heat of composition.
>
> (T 27)

It is only when this is kept in mind that 'the pages fill with true ciphers at last' (T 60). Moran expresses a similarly disaffected attitude towards the writing of his 'report', calling it 'paltry scrivening' (T 121), and noting towards the end that 'it is not at this late stage of my relation that I intend to give way to literature' (T 139):

> What a rabble in my head, what a gallery of moribunds. Murphy, Watt, Yerk, Mercier and all the others. I would never have believed that – yes, I believe it willingly. Stories, stories. I have not been able to tell them. I shall not be able to tell this one.
>
> (T 126)

Moran tells untellable stories because he is following orders, although he admits that he is writing not out of fear, but rather out of the deadening force of habit, a habit whose implacable narrative drive opens onto the impossibility of that which the narrative voice cannot give itself, namely death.

In contradistinction to Moran's initial certainty about death, where he visits his little 'plot in perpetuity' with its gravestone already in place (T 124), Molloy writes:

> Death is a condition I have never been able to conceive to my satisfaction and which therefore cannot go down in the ledger of weal and woe.
>
> (T 63)

This inconceivability of death is explored at length in *Malone Dies*, where the space of narrative is reduced from *Molloy*'s landscape of forest, seashore and town – Turdy, Turdyba, Turdybaba, Bally, Ballyba, Ballybaba and Hole[49] – to a bed in a room where a figure, called Malone (who notes, without conviction, 'since this is what I am called now' (T 204), just as Moran noted, 'This is the name I am known by' (T 88)) lies dying. He is immobile except for a hand holding a pencil (a 'Venus', which is later associated with 'Cythera' (T 192, 217): morning star, evening star, source of venery)[50] that glides over the page of

a child's exercise book. The third person present indicative of the book's title —
Malone meurt — at the very least leaves it open as to whether Malone dies or not,
as Ricks rightly points out: '*Malone Dies*: does he? In a first person narrative, you
can never be sure.'[51] In Heideggerian terms, the voice gives itself the possibility
of death *as* possibility on the first page of the text, 'I could die today, if I wished,
merely by making a little effort', only to deny this possibility, 'But it is just as
well to let myself die, quietly, without rushing things ... I shall be neutral and
inert ... I shall die tepid, without enthusiasm' (T 165). A little later, the voice
runs through the same pattern of assertion and negation, articulating the whole
gravity of the body, the fact of being riveted to oneself:

> If I had the use of my body I would throw it out of the window. But
> perhaps it is the knowledge of my impotence that emboldens me to that
> thought. All hangs together, I am in chains.
>
> (T 201)

Thus *Malone Dies* takes place in the impossible time of dying, and it is into this
ungraspable temporal stretch that the voice gives itself the possibility of telling
stories, 'while waiting I shall tell myself stories, if I can' (T 115). Thus, Malone
is an identity minimally held together by a series of stories — of Saposcat or
Sapo, the Lamberts, Macmann, Moll, Hairy Mac, Sucky Moll, Quin, Lemuel
and Lady Pedal — but these stories are no longer credible. The tales are like the
teller, 'almost lifeless', 'all my stories are in vain' (T 214). Each of the stories
breaks down into tedium — 'this is awful' (T 175), the voice says, 'what tedium'
(T 174, 198, 201). The reader is continually referred back from the time of
narrative to the time of mortality, to 'mortal tedium' (T 200), the time of
dying. The time of narrative and possibility, where the voice is able to lay hold of
time and invent, continually breaks down into an unnarratable impossibility, a
pattern typified by Beckett's entire syntax of weakness that can be found in a
whole series of self-undoing phrases in the *Trilogy*: 'Live and invent. I have tried.
Invent. It is not the word. Neither is live. No matter. I have tried' (T 179).

A similar disjunction between the time of narrative and the time of dying can
be illustrated with a couple of examples from *Endgame*. First, Nagg is unable to
tell the rather hackneyed Jewish joke about the Englishman, the tailor and a pair
of trousers, and this inability is marked textually with a series of stage
directions, where Nagg moves between the voices of the Englishman, the tailor,
the raconteur and his normal voice, 'I never told it worse (*Pause. Gloomy*) I tell
this story worse and worse'.[52] However, this disjunction can be seen even more

164

clearly in the central speech of *Endgame*, Hamm's ham-fisted soliloquy where he tries to tell the story of how Clov came into Hamm's service, what Adorno neatly calls 'an interpolated aria without music' (NL 312/NTL 267). Once again, Beckett marks the disjunction in stage directions by calling for a shift between 'narrative tone' and 'normal tone':

> Enough of that, it's storytime, where was I? (*Pause. Narrative tone*) The man came crawling towards me, on his belly. Pale, wonderfully pale and thin, he seemed on the point of – (*Pause. Normal tone*) No, I've done that bit. (*Pause. Narrative tone*) I calmly filled my pipe – the meerschaum, lit it with . . . let us say a vesta, drew a few puffs. Aah! (*Pause*) Well, what is it *you* want? (*Pause*).[53]

Blanchot asks, 'Why these vain stories?' (LV 310), and responds that it is in order to people the emptiness of death into which Malone and the whole gallery of moribunds feel they are falling, 'through anxiety for this empty time that is going to become the infinite time of death'. Stories both try to conceal the failure of narrative identity by drawing the self together into some sort of unity whilst, at the same time, Malone's transcendent sarcasm – an example: 'A stream at long intervals bestrid – but to hell with all this fucking scenery' (T 254) – is directed towards trying to disengage the time of narrative from the time of dying. Malone tries to silence the emptiness by telling stories but only succeeds in letting the emptiness speak as the stories break down into mortal tedium. Thus, stories are a deception, but a necessary deception: we cannot face the emptiness of death with them or without them. They return us insistently to the passivity, ungraspability and impossibility of our dying, 'with practice I might be able to produce a groan before I die' (T 232). Beckett is often given to the phrase 'come and go' and it provided the title for a 1965 dramaticule.[54] Malone writes, 'Because in order not to die you must come and go, come and go' (T 213). Stories enable one to come and go, come and go, 'incessant comings and goings' (T 268), until one dies and 'the others go on, as if nothing had happened' (T 214). On.

(g)
My old aporetics – the syntax of weakness (*The Unnameable*)

This experience of disjunction between the time of narrative and the time of dying is pushed even further in *The Unnameable*, what Adorno describes as

Beckett's 'wahrhaft ungeheuerliche Roman' ('truly monstrous or genuinely colossal novel' – NL 426/NTL2 90), in comparison to which, and in opposition to both Sartre and Lukács, the 'official works of committed art look like children's games'. The opening pages of *The Unnameable* are the methodologically most self-conscious part of the *Trilogy*, where the narrative voice gives the faintest sketch of the method to be followed in the text: an *aporetics*.[55]

> What am I to do, what shall I do, what should I do, in my situation, how proceed? By aporia pure and simple? Or by affirmations and negations invalidated as uttered, or sooner or later. Generally speaking. There must be other shifts. Otherwise it would be quite hopeless. But it is quite hopeless. I should mention without going any further that I say aporia without knowing what it means. Can one be ephectic otherwise than unawares? I don't know.
>
> (T 267)

This echoes a line from early in *Malone Dies*:

> There I am back at my old aporetics. Is that the word? I don't know.
>
> (T 166)

Of course, these phrases are performative enactments of the very method being described. They are aporetic descriptions of aporia, suspensions of judgement (hence 'ephectic') on the possibility of a self-conscious suspension of judgement: 'I don't know'. We proceed by aporia, that is, the path to be followed is a pathless path, which means that we do not proceed, but stay on the same spot, even if we are not quite at a standstill, although this is the voice's desire: 'the bliss of coma' (T 298), 'the rapture, the letting go, the fall, the gulf, the relapse to darkness' (T 179). As a consequence, we wheel about as if with one foot nailed to the floor.

Although *The Unnameable* is hardly a discourse on method, the word reappears at several key moments in the text,[56] and Beckett's aporetics are a performative and quasi-methodological expression of what we saw above as the impossibility and necessity of narration: we have to go on and yet we can't go on (and yet we can't not go on). This technique – and it is a question of technique here, of a quite rigorous rhetorical technique at work in Beckett's writing – might be characterized in terms of what Adorno rightly calls, once again with reference to *Endgame*, a technique of reversal. He writes:

Where they come closest to the truth, they sense, with double comedy, that their consciousness is false; that is how a situation that can no longer be reached by reflection is reflected. But the whole play is constructed by this technique of reversal.

(NL 320/NTL 274)

It is in terms of this technique of reversal that I would understand the above remark about 'affirmations and negations invalidated as uttered'. As Stanley Cavell points out, this can be seen as an almost spiritual exercise in logic, where statements are made, inferences derived, negations of inferences produced and these negations are, in turn, negated (MWM 126). The language of *The Unnameable* is an endlessly elaborating series of antitheses, of imploding oxymorons, paradoxes and contradictions, a 'frenzy of utterance' (T 275), where a coherent and perhaps even formalizable technique of repetition is employed to give the appearance of randomness and chaos.[57] Some examples: 'I, say I. Unbelieving... It, say it, not knowing what... So I have no cause for anxiety. And yet I am anxious... Perhaps it's springtime, violets, no, that's autumn... Perhaps it's all a dream, all a dream, that would surprise me' (T 267, 276, 376, 381). Or a longer passage:

These things I say, and shall say, if I can, are no longer, or are not yet, or never were, or never will be, or if they were, if they are, if they will be, were not here, are not here, will not be here, but elsewhere. But I am here. So I am obliged to add this. I who am here, who cannot speak, cannot think, and who must speak, and therefore perhaps think a little, cannot in relation only to me who am here, to here where I am, but can a little, sufficiently, I don't know how, unimportant, in relation to me who was elsewhere, who shall be elsewhere, and to those places when I was, where I shall be.

(T 276)

It is a question here of an uneasy and solitary inhabitation of the aporia between the inability to speak and the inability to be silent (T 365). We cannot speak of that which we would like to speak – on my reading, the unrepresentability of death – and yet we cannot not speak, blissful though this might seem: 'you must go on, I can't go on, I'll go on'. There is only this voice, this meaningless voice 'which prevents you from being nothing' (T 341) and all it has are words 'and not many of them' (T 381). And even when Malone writes 'I am lost, not a

167

word' (T 241) or Krapp – a later delegate – says 'Nothing to say, not a squeak',[58] this is not yet silence, it is yet a word, yet a squeak.

To return to my epigraph, Beckett's work, and – to generalize suddenly and rather violently – literature as such *is a long sin against silence* (T 345) *that arises from our inability to sit quietly in a room.* The origin of the sin being unknown, we still sit in our thousand furnished rooms to read and even write books, which, of course, only produces inconstancy, boredom, anxiety and the desire for movement – to come and go, to come and go.

The radicality of *The Unnameable* with respect to the earlier parts of the *Trilogy* is that the disjunction between the time of narrative and the time of dying takes place within the unit of the sentence itself, where each series of words seems to offer and deny 'the resorts of fable' (T 283). Of course, there are fables in *The Unnameable*, the quite hilarious story of Basil, arbitrarily renamed Mahood (T 283), the billy-in-the-bowl, who completes the dwindling physicality of the 'M' names, and Worm. What is one to say of Worm? First of his kind, 'who hasn't the wit to make himself plain' (T 310). Worm is unborn, unperceiving, unspeaking, uncreated, 'nothing but a shapeless heap' (T 328), a 'tiny blur in the depths of the pit' (T 329). And in this heap, a wild and equine eye cries without ceasing. He makes no noise apart from a whining, the noise of life 'trying to get in' (T 335, a terrifying remark). With this last in the series of 'bran-dips' (T 359), the stakes have been raised once again: for if Mahood, like Malone, craved for that which he could not give himself, i.e. death, then Worm is not even born, 'Come into the world unborn, abiding there unliving, with no hope of death' (T 318). Worm is that which somehow *remains*, he is a remainder, what Blanchot calls 'une survivance' (LV 312) outside of life and the possibility of death. Although he is the first of his kind, it is difficult to imagine how this series might continue and perhaps Worm is the end of the line.[59]

However, despite such fables, which have to be tempered with the by now familiar comments on the inadequacy of narrative – 'this hell of stories' (T 349)[60] – *The Unnameable* is made up of an endlessly proliferating and self-undoing series of sayings and unsayings, what I called above Beckett's syntax of weakness.[61] Some examples:

> But my good-will at certain moments is such, and my longing to have floundered however briefly, however feebly, in the great life torrent

streaming from the earliest protozoa to the very latest humans, that I, no, parenthesis unfinished. I'll begin again. My family.

(T 295)

And again:

And would it not suffice, without any change in the structure of the thing as it now stands, as it always stood, without a mouth being opened at the place which even pain could never line, would it not suffice to, to what, the thread is lost, no matter, here's another.

(T 353)

And again:

I resume, so long as, so long as, let me see, so long as one, so long as he, ah fuck all that, so long as this, then that, agreed, that's good enough, I nearly got stuck.

(T 367)

As Ricks rightly points out, this is a syntax of weakness not because the syntax is weak, but rather because it presses on, 'unable to relinquish its preservance and to arrive at severance'.[62] As I claimed in my Preamble, Beckett's sentences are a series of weak intensities, antithetical inabilities: unable to go on and unable not to go on. It is this double inability which describes, I think, the weakness of our relation to finitude, the articulation of a physical feebleness, a dwindling, stiffening corporeality, which is a recipe not for despair but for a kind of *rapture*: 'There is rapture, or there should be, in the motion crutches give' (T 60).

In the final and most interesting chapter of Ricks's brilliant (but at times exasperatingly eclectic, allusively hyperactive and a little too self-consciously witty) book on Beckett, which is the closest he gets to some sort of discourse on method, this syntax of weakness is described as 'the Irish bull'. Ricks defines bull with Coleridge as the bringing together of two incompatible thoughts, with the *sensation*, but not the *sense*, of their connection. In this sense, the bull is a counter-concept to wit, which recalls my discussion in Lecture 2, and Ricks quotes Sydney Smith, 'for as wit discovers real relations that are not apparent, bulls admit of apparent relations that are not real'.[63] In this sense, the best of Beckett's bulls would be his favourite Democritean fragment, 'Nothing is more real than nothing'.[64] The bull is a self-contradictory language of oxymorons, antitheses, paradoxes and reasoned absurdities. In this sense, for Ricks, Beckett's

169

syntax of weakness is a load of bull, a series of studied contradictions that constitute acts of resistance, a chain of small syntactical insurrections. Ricks writes:

> The bull is the resource of a pressed, suppressed, oppressed people, a people on occasion pretending to be self-subordinated by foolishness so as the better to keep alive a secret of self-respect and to be insubordinate and even safely provocative.[65]

For Ricks, as becomes clear in the final pages of his book, literature is a load of bull; that is to say, it is a site of resistance to the society that fosters its progressive marginalization. Such is the double bind of aesthetic autonomy which permits art its own sphere of judgement and jurisdiction whilst exiling that sphere from the core of rationality.

However, this compelling thesis – close to Adorno's outlined above, although Ricks makes no mention of the latter – has to be tempered both by Ricks's slightly whimsical noises about the Irishness and catholicity of Beckett's bull ('He is a catholic writer'),[66] and his rather ritualized potshots at 'the institutionalizing of deconstruction'.[67] As a veteran of theory wars, Ricks wants to claim Beckett as a realist, against the alleged linguistic idealism of deconstruction. This is part of a wider argument that would see the practice of criticism as serving the autonomy of literature and exhibiting the relations that literature maintains to, in the words of Eliot cited approvingly in the final pages of Ricks's book, 'all the other activities, which, together with literature, are the components of life'.[68] However, such sentiments, from which I do not necessarily dissent insofar as Ricks is attacking the complacent scepticism of certain philosophically challenged tendencies within contemporary debate, would not exist in such stark opposition to a more generous understanding of Derrida's work, as I have tried to indicate above.

Rather, my disagreement with Ricks is more philosophical insofar as his claims are advanced on the unargued assumption and availability of such items as reality and life. First, on reality, I think it is rather pointless and sterile to want to claim Beckett as some sort of straightforward, common-sense empirical realist in opposition to the alleged linguistic idealism of deconstruction. Such a gesture is, in Nietzsche's sense, reactive and risks rehearsing rather stale and philosophically antiquated debates between idealism and realism. There are many senses of the real, not all of them opposed to idealism: Kant's transcendental idealism and Heidegger's fundamental ontology offer two notable examples. If one accepts, as I do, that there is an outside to language for Beckett, which one might call reality (although other names would serve), the problem that his fiction explores, surely, is the difficult necessity of negotiating that real linguistically: how does one say *how* it is, *as* it is?

Second, on life, is this something simply available to us as an item to which we can turn or be returned by literature? If one accepts, as Ricks seems to, the diagnosis of aesthetic modernity in terms of autonomy – i.e. that autonomy is an ambiguous advance insofar as art is both liberated because it is given its own sphere of justification and is a practice no longer underwritten by the constraints of tradition, and exiled insofar as it becomes unclear what counts as a work of art and how it counts, where autonomous works become increasingly marginalized from society – *then* doesn't Ricks precisely overlook the enormous problem of the relation that autonomous art might maintain with life? What exactly is life, under conditions of modernity? What is the relation of art to life? *Is* life life?

Returning to the specifics of Ricks's argument, shouldn't his claim that Beckett's Irish bull is a site of resistance both to the alleged pyrrhonic and pyrrhic complacencies of 'deconstruction' and to the contemporary society that fosters literature's progressive marginalization, entail a *critical history* of the relations of literature to life in modernity? If aesthetic modernism can be defined in terms of the difficulties of knowing what counts as art and how it counts, then doesn't this situation find its analogue in the life-world we inhabit, where it is deeply unclear what counts as life and how it counts? In short, does not Ricks's reactive critique of the alleged linguistic idealism of deconstruction continually risk the positing of a radically de-historicized and – paradoxically – *idealized* concreteness with regard to such items as reality and life? As the consequence of a critical history of the relations of literature to life (and only as the consequence of such a history), such an idealized concreteness is not, I think, simply to be dismissed as an illusion, but is rather to be maintained through a *utopian* conception of the life-world. The undoubted felicities of Beckett's bull do not return us to life as it is allegedly lived, but rather engage in a massive and unrelenting critique and dismantling of the illusoriness of what passes for life, through which we can detect the faintest glimmer of a world transfigured by a messianic light.

(h)
Who speaks? Not I (Blanchot)

Who speaks in the work of Samuel Beckett? Who is the indefatigable 'I' who always seems to say the same thing? It is with these seemingly innocent questions that Blanchot begins both of his pieces on Beckett.[69] Yet with this question we brush against an (perhaps, *the*) enigma.

The obvious response to the question, 'Who speaks?', is to tie the 'I' to the narrative voice of the text and to identify that voice with the controlling intentionality of the author. Who speaks? Samuel Beckett speaks. Well, yes, this is doubtless correct, there existed a writer whose name was Samuel Barclay Beckett, who wrote the books we have read, who played first-class cricket for Trinity College Dublin, who received the Croix de Guerre in 1945 and the Nobel Prize for literature in 1969, who had terrible boils on his neck ('bristling with boils ever since I was a brat' – T 75), etc., etc., etc. There is an irreducible existential residuum of authorial experience in the creation of any text that we might call 'literary'.[70] But, to ascribe the voice that speaks in the work with the author Samuel Beckett, or to identify the narrative voice with a controlling consciousness that looks down upon the drama of Beckett's work like a transcendent spectator, is to fail to acknowledge the strangeness of the work under consideration and to read the work as an oblique confession or, worse still, a series of case studies in a reductive psycho-biography. After remarking, 'For if I am Mahood, I am Worm too, plop',[71] the voice in *The Unnameable* continues:

> Or is one to postulate a *tertius gaudens*, meaning myself, responsible for the double failure [i.e. of Mahood and Worm, SC]? Shall I come upon my true countenance at last, bathing in a smile? I have the feeling I shall be spared this spectacle. At no moment do I know what I'm talking about, nor of whom.
>
> (T 310–11)

If one is to be capable of listening to the voices that speak from the pages of the *Trilogy*, then it is at the very least necessary to suspend the hypothesis identifying the narrative voice of Beckett's work with the smiling third party of a controlling pure consciousness and ascribing the latter to Samuel Beckett. As Blanchot writes, rightly, 'il n'y a pas de parole directe en littérature' ('in literature there is no direct speech' – EI 479/IC 327). That is – and this is Blanchot's hypothesis

– in Beckett's work we approach an experience, a *literary* experience, that speaks to us in a voice that can be described as impersonal, neutral or indifferent: an incessant, interminable and indeterminable voice that reverberates outside of all intimacy, dispossessing the 'I' and delivering it over to a nameless outside. Beckett's work draws the reader into a space – the space of literature – where a voice intones obscurely, drawn on by a speaking that does not begin and does not finish, which cannot speak and cannot but speak, that leads language towards what Blanchot calls with reference to *Comment c'est* 'an unqualifiable murmur',[72] what I will describe presently as a buzzing, the tinnitus of existence. As Blanchot writes, this is 'étrange, étrange' (EI 484/IC 330).

Blanchot's point about the narrative voice can be restated by following a crucial feature of Beckett's prose in the *Trilogy*. On three occasions in the second part of *Molloy* (T 115, 128, 152), we come across the words 'Not I', employed in a seemingly innocent way during Moran's monologue. However, this phrase comes to pervade *The Unnameable* in a number of crucial passages, not all of which can be cited, and which begin to be repeated with ever-increasing frequency – mania even – towards the end of the text.[73] About a third of the way into *The Unnameable*, the voice writes:

> But enough of this cursed first person, it is really too red a herring, I'll get out of my depth if I'm not careful. But what then is the subject? Mahood? No, not yet. Worm? Even less.
>
> (T 315)

Slightly further on, we read:

> I shall not say I again, ever again, it's too farcical. I shall put in its place, whenever I hear it, the third person, if I think of it.

Unsurprisingly enough, and in accord with the aporetic method sketched above, the voice does not always 'think of it' and persistently falls back into the first person. However, the point here is that the voice is attempting to move from the first person to the third person, from 'I' to 's/he/it' (a Beckettesque pun of questionable taste offers itself here, but I will resist). The voice insists that 'it's not I speaking', but another, a more impersonal and neutral voice. In this way we can begin to make sense of the first line of *The Unnameable*, 'I, say I. Unbelieving' (T 267) and the almost mantric phrase that is repeated obsessively towards the end of the text, 'It's not I, that's all I know' (T 380). But the crucial passage in this regard is the following; I quote in full:

It's always he who speaks, Mercier never spoke, Moran never spoke, I never spoke, I seem to speak, that's because he says I as if he were I, I nearly believed him, do you hear him, as if he were I, I am far, who can't move, can't be found, but neither can he, he can only talk, if that much, perhaps it's not he, perhaps it's a multitude, one after another, what confusion, someone mentions confusion, is it a sin, all here is a sin, you don't know why, you don't know whose, you don't know against whom, someone says you, it's the fault of the pronouns, there is no name, for me, no pronoun for me, all the trouble comes from that, it's a kind of pronoun too, it isn't that either, I'm not that either, let us leave all that, forget about all that, it's not difficult.

(T 371–72)

There is no name for the voice that speaks in *The Unnameable*. Whoever speaks in Beckett's work, it is not 'I', it is rather 'he' (although this is still a pronoun, and that's the trouble), the third person or the impersonal neutrality of language. The neutral character of the third person is what Blanchot refers to as 'the narrative voice', and, for him (thinking of Kafka rather than Beckett),[74] to write is to pass from the 'I' to the 'he' (EI 558/IC 380). In literature – and this is the defining quality of the literary for Blanchot – I do not speak, it speaks. In relation to Beckett, Blanchot writes of 'a soft specter of speech' (EI 485/IC 331), the unqualifiable murmur at the back of our words. The narrative voice is like some spectre that lingers in the background of our everyday identity, disturbing the persistent 'I' of our monologues and dialogues, denying the 'daydream gratification of fiction'[75] and reappearing at nightfall, a kind of void that opens up in the work and into which the work evaporates in a movement of worklessness. There is an irreducible logic of spectrality at work in literature, the night of ghosts, that denies us the sleep of the just in the name of justice. This is perhaps why Blanchot defines the writer as 'the insomniac of the day'.[76]

Who speaks? Not I. On this point an interesting connection can be made between *The Unnameable* and the extraordinary 1973 dramatic piece *Not I*,[77] a piece that I would want to see as a distilled redrafting of *The Unnameable*, and which employs a very similar, apparently manic, pattern of repetition and breathless phrasing as in the final pages of the latter.[78] On five occasions in a ten-minute dramaticule, the Mouth cries 'what? . . . who? . . . no! . . . she!'. As Beckett laconically points out in the only note to *Not I*, the Mouth is engaged in 'vehement refusal to relinquish the third person'. Although it should be noted

174

that this third person is 'she' rather than 'he', and it is here that one might want to raise the question of gender and challenge the alleged neutrality of the narrative voice.

On several occasions, the Mouth speaks of a buzzing in the ears, 'for she could still hear the buzzing... so-called... in the ears... the buzzing?... yes... all the time the buzzing... so-called... in the ears'. This buzzing is described as 'a dull roar in the skull... dull roar like falls', which can be linked both to what was said above about murmuring and with references to 'the noise' in the *Trilogy*.[79] For example, Malone notes:

> What I mean is possibly this, that the noises of the world, so various in themselves and which I used to be so clever at distinguishing from one another, had been dinning at me for so long, always the same old noises, as gradually to have merged into a single noise, so that all I heard was one vast continuous buzzing.
>
> (T 190)

Who speaks in the work of Samuel Beckett? It is not the 'I' of the author or a controlling consciousness, but rather the 'Not I' of the insomniac narrative voice that opens like a void in the experience of literature, *as* that experience towards which literature approaches, what I described in Lecture 1 in terms of the *il y a*. Beckett's work leaves us 'open to the void' (T 377), and this void is not the ultramarine blue of Yves Klein or Derek Jarman, but a more sombre monochrome; not the Mediterranean, but the Black Sea:

> These creatures have never been, only I and this black void have ever been. And the sounds? No, all is silent. And the lights, on which I had set such store, must they too go out? Yes, out with them, there is no light. No grey either, black is what I should have said. Nothing then but me, of which I know nothing, and this black, of which I know nothing except that it is black and empty. That then is what, since I have to speak, I shall speak of, until I need speak no more.
>
> (T 278)

The narrative voice approaches a void that speaks as one vast, continuous buzzing, a dull roar in the skull like falls, an unqualifiable murmur, an impersonal whining, the vibration of the tympanum (T 352). This is what I mean by the tinnitus of existence. It is, I believe, this condition that the voice in Beckett's work is trying to approach. It is this truth with which Beckett's frenzy

175

of utterance is concerned (T 275). Of course, there is *only* the approach, because the voice cannot grant itself the possibility of its own disappearance into the void – death is impossible. Thus, we resort to fables, 'To tell the truth – no, first the story' (T 300). That is just how it is; and that is how I read a phrase towards the end of the 1981 text *Ill Seen Ill Said*, 'Absence supreme good and yet'.[80] It is this 'and yet' that is so determinate for Beckett's art, this holding back from the bliss of absence, this qualification of the rapture of annihilation in a syntax of weakness.

(i)
No happiness? (Cavell)

The stalest of all the stale philosophical clichés in terms of which Beckett's work has been interpreted is the claim that it celebrates the meaninglessness of existence and is therefore nihilistic. As Stanley Cavell points out in his characteristically associative, occasionally flaky, often maddening, needlessly gratuitous, but genuinely insightful essay on *Endgame*, such a claim comes close to the truth but not for the reasons it imagines. He writes:

> The discovery of *Endgame*, both in topic and technique is not the failure of meaning (if that means the lack of meaning), but its total, even totalitarian success – our inability not to mean what we are given to mean.
>
> (MWM 116)

Using the Biblical clue of the name Hamm, Cavell speculatively links *Endgame* to the story of Noah, interpreting the shelter that houses the characters in the play as the Ark, the family as Noah's and the time of the play as taking place sometime after the Flood. In contrast to Adorno, *Endgame* takes place after the Flood rather than after Auschwitz, although Adorno acknowledges in passing the possible link of the name of Hamm to Noah's son (NL 312/NTL 267), and Cavell contextualizes his interpretation with reference to the threat of nuclear catastrophe, as his rather tangential analysis of *Dr Strangelove* indicates (MWM 134–37). As the Bible tells us, Hamm is cursed by God because he looked upon his father naked after he had engaged in a bout of serious drinking, when he should have averted his eyes and simply covered him up, as did the good sons Shem and Japheth. Hamm's response to this curse, according to Cavell, is to try and end the dependence of the world upon God and to break the covenant that binds creatures to their creator. The world must therefore be *un-created*

176

(MWM 140), not because it is without meaning but because it is *too full of meaning*. The total, even totalitarian, success of meaning is evidenced by the fact that God can be posited as its source, filling the empty space at the heart of human endeavour. Cavell goes on:

> Only a life without hope, meaning, justification, waiting, solution – as we
> have been shaped for these things – is free from the curse of God.
>
> (MWM 149)

Hamm's attempted de-creation of the universe is an attempt to lift the curse of God and end the rule of meaning.

Before going on to show what I think can be retained from Cavell's essay, I would like to pause and briefly consider its relation to the rather stringent qualifications on interpretation I outlined above with reference to Adorno. Although the motif of de-creation can be found in Adorno's remarks on Beckett, it is clear that there are problems with Cavell's reading from an Adornian perspective, and not just from that perspective. From the first lines of Cavell's essay, he is concerned with establishing the *meaning* of Endgame (MWM 115). In the second paragraph of the essay, two candidates for explaining the meaning of *Endgame* are discussed and rejected: both the socialist realist critique and the absurdist realist eulogy share the common assumption that the merits or demerits of an autonomous artwork can be judged with reference to a reality which that work either reflects or fails to reflect. Cavell's claim against both these interpretations is that they fail to acknowledge the *problem* of modernist art, namely that 'in modernist arts the achievement of the autonomy of the object is a *problem* – the artistic problem' (MWM 116). In modernism, as we have already seen, autonomy is a problem because it is no longer underwritten or legitimated by tradition, 'by the conventions of an art'. Thus, the modernist artist 'has continually to question the conventions upon which his art has depended'. From an Adornian perspective, the problem initially raised by Cavell's essay – although it disappointingly disappears after the opening couple of pages – is the right one: modernist artworks put meaning on the agenda.

However, two questions can be raised here: first, are modernist artworks items for which one might or should try and find a meaning? Second, does Cavell's interpretation provide such a meaning? As I see it, the Adornian response to the first question disqualifies Cavell's response to the second question. That is to say, the Adornian claim that aesthetic modernism engages in a determinate negation of social meaning through the form or work-character of autonomous artworks means that to look for a meaning in relation to modernist art is, to turn Cavell's words back upon him, to fail to see the problem.

On the second question as to the felicity of Cavell's interpretation, we might briefly consider Jay Bernstein's Adornian critique of Cavell, where he rightly claims that Cavell continually *overshoots* the object of his interpretation. That is, Cavell overshoots the refusal or negation of meaning in Beckett by interpreting the shelter *as* the Ark, and identifying Hamm *with* his Biblical precursor, and locating the time of the play *after* the Flood. However, Bernstein runs this argument together with a less persuasive claim, connected to Cavell's conception of the ordinary discussed at length in Lecture 2. Bernstein suggests that Cavell's insistence on the ordinariness of the events and characters described in *Endgame* (MWM 117 and 119) is premised upon a belief in the ordinary as that to which we can turn when we have learned, with Wittgenstein, to stop philosophizing. Bernstein writes, 'it would nonetheless be false to claim that *we* could ever be in a position to just acknowledge the facts of life', adding that this belief 'dehistoricizes our predicament, and Beckett's, too much'.[81]

I grant that there is a constant risk of de-historicization in Cavell (as there was in Ricks) which perhaps devolves from the socio-historical impoverishment of the ordinary language philosophy that influenced him so greatly. Yet, nonetheless, I feel that Bernstein wilfully misreads Cavell on this point insofar as the latter embraces an explicitly perfectionist conception of the everyday discussed in Lecture 2, where the ordinary is the object of a quest, a task, something to be achieved and *not* an available fact. Bernstein misreads the quotation from Cavell cited above as the epigraph to this lecture (MWM 161): the point is not, as Bernstein seems to suggest, that 'we could just sit still, just stop theorizing',[82] but rather the deeper Pascalian or Beckettian truth that we *have* to talk, whether we have something to say or not, we *cannot* keep still and sit quietly in a room. As I read Cavell, this inability to be silent is evidence of our tragically limited condition, and testimony to the flawed humanity that arises out of such limitedness – such is the truth of scepticism, the acknowledgement of separateness. Although in Bernstein's defence one might say that Cavell's perfectionist conception of the everyday is nowhere near as evident in the essays in *Must We Mean What We Say* as in the later books, *In Quest of the Ordinary, This New Yet Unapproachable America* and *Conditions Handsome and Unhandsome*, I would nonetheless claim that it is embedded in the subordinate clauses of the following sentence, itself quoted by Bernstein, 'then, *if ever*, the fullness of time; then, *if ever*, the achievement of the ordinary, the faith to be plain, or not to be' (MWM 156, SC's emphasis).[83] So, *contra* Bernstein, I would claim that Cavell's perfectionist conception of the everyday is not a case of 'misplaced concreteness',[84] but a utopian moment of ever-deferred reconciliation glimpsed in art and philosophy and arising from a philosophy of history analogous to Adorno's, although a good deal less sociologically and historically nuanced. In Cavell's Emersonian register, the relation to 'This New America' is only discovered in the approach. America itself remains unapproachable.

Returning to the claim with which I began this section, namely that Beckett is celebrating the meaninglessness of existence, we are now in a position to see that this is indeed true but not at all in the intended sense. That is:

> Solitude, emptiness, nothingness, meaninglessness, silence – these are not the *givens* of Beckett's characters, but their goal, their new heroic undertaking.
>
> (MWM 156)

On Cavell's reading, Beckett is not telling us that the universe *is* meaningless, rather meaninglessness is a task, an achievement, the achievement of the ordinary or the everyday. If meaninglessness were a fact, then the theological solution to this situation would make sense, it would be the very making of sense, the redemption of meaning in a meaningless world. As Beckett puts it:

> We'd end up by needing God, we have lost all sense of decency admittedly, but there are still certain depths we prefer not to sink to.
>
> (T 344–45)

However, the situation would seem to be precisely the opposite: the world is overfull with meaning and we suffocate under the combined weight of the various narratives of redemption – whether they are religious, socio-economic, political, aesthetic or philosophical. What passes for the ordinary is cluttered with illusory narratives of redemption that conceal the very extraordinariness of the ordinary and the nature of its decay under conditions of nihilism. What Beckett's work offers us, then, is a radical de-creation of these salvific narratives, a paring down or stripping away of the resorts of fable, the determinate negation of social meaning through the elevation of form, a syntax of weakness, an approach to meaninglessness as an achievement of the ordinary without the rose-tinted glasses of redemption, an acknowledgement of the finiteness of the finite and the limitedness of the human condition. Returning to the opening theme of this lecture, might not the very extraordinary ordinariness, the uncanny everydayness, of Beckett's work be the source of its resistance to philosophical interpretation?

But what remains after we have been saved from salvation, redeemed from redemption?[85]

What remains?

Nothing?

Almost.

Only the vast profile of the night and the buzzing that recalls us to the infinite time of our dying, our breath panting on in the darkness, 'Dying on. No more no less. No. Less. Less to die. Ever less'.[86] And yet, into this night comes a voice, an injunction that resounds through Beckett's texts: *Imagine!*[87] For, like Hamm, we *are* cursed, cursed by the need for narrative, by the resorts of fable, flayed alive by memory. Hence we must attempt to people the void, to presume to be saved, 'For why be discouraged, one of the thieves was saved, that is a generous percentage'(T 233). Because we cannot sit quietly in a room, because we have to live and invent, knowing that invention is the wrong word, as indeed is life. We go on. This is very little . . . almost nothing. But perhaps that's just human, 'You're on earth, there's no cure for that'.[88] Imagine. After all, a lobster couldn't do it.

Beckett ends *Ill Seen Ill Said* with the following words:

Decision no sooner reached or rather long after than what is the wrong word? For the last time at last for to end yet again what the wrong word? Than revoked. No but slowly dispelled a little very little like the last wisps of day when the curtain closes. Of itself by slow millimetres or drawn by a phantom hand. Farewell to farewell. Then in that perfect dark foreknell darling sound pip for end begun. First last moment. Grant only enough remain to devour all. Moment by glutton moment. Sky earth the whole kit and boodle. Not another crumb of carrion left. Lick chops and basta. No. One moment more. One last. Grace to breath that void. Know happiness.[89]

No happiness? No? No. Know.

Notes

Preamble: Travels in Nihilon

1 See *The Ethics of Deconstruction: Derrida and Levinas* (Blackwell, Oxford, 1992). The line of argument initiated in this book has been extended and modified in a number of papers, in particular: (i) 'Deconstruction and Pragmatism: Is Derrida a Private Ironist or a Public Liberal?', *Deconstruction and Pragmatism*, ed. Chantal Mouffe (Routledge, London and New York, 1996), pp. 19–40; (ii) 'Habermas und Derrida werden verheiratet: Antwort auf Axel Honneth', *Deutsche Zeitschrift für Philosophie*, Vol. 42, No. 6 (1994), pp. 981–92; (iii) 'On *Specters de Marx*', *Philosophy and Social Criticism*, Vol. 21, No. 3 (May 1995), pp. 1–30.

2 Heidegger, *The History of the Concept of Time*, trans. T. Kisiel (Indiana University Press, Bloomington, 1985), p. 80.

3 See Stanley Cavell, 'Philosophy and the Arrogation of Voice', *A Pitch of Philosophy* (Harvard University Press, Cambridge MA, 1994), pp. 3–51.

4 On the pre-Nietzschean history of nihilism, see the immensely informative monograph by Stephen Wagner Cho, 'Nihilism before Nietzsche: On the Historical Origins of the Term' (unpublished typescript), where he shows that, in its pre-Nietzschean phase, nihilism does not have any stable or single meaning, but rather follows a subtle and variegated history where the concept is periodically reinvented and redescribed. For an extremely provocative and impressive challenge to the habitual history of nihilism, see Michael Allen Gillespie's *Nihilism Before Nietzsche* (University of Chicago Press, Chicago and London, 1995). Gillespie claims that the entire diagnosis of the death of God arises from the weakening of an overly omnipotent concept of 'God of will' whose origins lie in the *deus absconditus* of mediaeval nominalism. Gillespie impressively retells the history of modernity in terms of a misunderstanding of the notions of divine and human will, a misunderstanding inherited unconsciously by Nietzsche and continued by his contemporary inheritors. The key figure in this history is Fichte, and Gillespie

interprets Nietzsche's rejection of Schopenhauer's pessimistic and resigned understanding of the will as an unknowing return to a Fichtean position. Gillespie's general
thesis, which shares much with Heidegger despite the former's protestations (see pp.
xxi–xxii), is that the source of nihilism lies in an overly Promethean conception of
the will. Hence, the solution to nihilism will be in a step back from willing, a view
which – and here lies the obvious and massive difference with Heidegger – leads not
to *Gelassenheit*, but to an uncoupling of the identification of nihilism and liberalism.
Underlying Gillespie's account is an implicit *apologia* for a liberal conception of the
human being whose essence lies not in some Promethean will, but in a frail
imperfection that somehow muddles through. For although such a conception of the
human being may result in moral relativism and produce 'banality and boredom, it
does not produce a politics of terror and destruction'(p. xxiii).

5 Max Stirner, *The Ego and Its Own*, ed. D. Leopold (Cambridge University Press,
1995), p. 7.

6 Sartre, *Being and Nothingness*, trans. H. E. Barnes (Philosophical Library, New York,
1956), p. 784.

7 Dostoevsky, *The Devils*, trans. D. Magurshak (Penguin, Harmondsworth, 1971),
p. 126.

8 Dostoevsky, *The Diary of a Writer*, trans. B. Brasol (George Braziller, New York,
1954), p. 541.

9 *The Gay Science*, trans. W. Kaufmann (Vintage, New York, 1974), p. 289.

10 For a very useful discussion of the aesthetic and political context for Russian nihilism,
see Gillespie's 'The Demons Unbound. Russian Nihilism and the Pursuit of the
Promethean', in *Nihilism Before Nietzsche*, op. cit., pp. 135–73.

11 Turgenev, *Fathers and Sons*, trans. R. Edmonds (Penguin, Harmondsworth, 1965),
p. 123.

12 Ibid., p. 295.

13 On the sources of Nietzsche's concept of nihilism, see Elisabeth Kuhn, 'Nietzsches
Quelle des Nihilismus-Begriffs', *Nietzsche-Studien*, Vol. 13 (1984), pp. 253–78. See
also Gillespie, *Nihilism Before Nietzsche*, op. cit., pp. 178–81.

14 *The Birth of Tragedy*, trans. W. Kaufmann (Vintage, New York, 1967), p. 76.

15 The latter position is elegantly and persuasively discussed in Stephen Mulhall's *Faith
and Reason* (Duckworth, London, 1994). By contrast, for a rather turgid, reactionary
and depressingly limited religious response to nihilism, see Michael Novak's
'Awakening from Nihilism: Why Truth Matters' (Institute of Economic Affairs,
London, 1995).

16 Vaneigem, *The Revolution of Everyday Life*, trans. D. Nicholson-Smith (Rebel Press,
London, 1994), p. 178. This passive nihilist position is, I believe, most persuasively
represented by Richard Rorty's ironical liberalism, which I discuss in detail
elsewhere (see Note 1). See Rorty's *Contingency, Irony, Solidarity* (Cambridge
University Press, Cambridge, 1989).

17 Ibid., p. 260.

Notes

18 To my knowledge, the first significant discussion of the concept of nihilism in Heidegger, where it is also associated with the name of Nietzsche, appears in his infamous 1935 lecture course, *Introduction to Metaphysics*, trans. Ralph Mannheim (Yale University Press, New Haven and London, 1959), p. 203. Heidegger writes:

> But where is authentic nihilism at work? There, where they cling to familiar beings and believe that it is enough, as heretofore, to take beings as beings, since that is after all what they are. But with this they reject the question of Being and treat Being like a nothing (*nihil*), which in a certain way it 'is' insofar as it essences (*west*). To cultivate only beings in the forgetfulness of Being – that is nihilism. Nihilism thus understood is the *ground* for that nihilism that Nietzsche exposed in the first book of *The Will to Power*.
>
> *Against* this, to go expressly in the *question* of Being unto the limits of the Nothing, and to include the latter in the question of Being, is the first and only fruitful step toward a true overcoming of nihilism.

What is clear (and symptomatic) in this passage is that Heidegger understands nihilism in terms of the difference between Being and beings, and that the ontological difference provides the *ground* for Nietzsche's conception of nihilism in *The Will to Power*. Thus, nihilism is understood in terms of the forgetting of Being, and the first step that must be taken in any true overcoming of nihilism is to raise the *question* of Being. Although it is by no means certain, these remarks do permit one to speculate as to whether, in 1935 (hardly a neutral date), Heidegger still envisages the possibility of an overcoming of nihilism, a possibility that will be heavily qualified in his later work. A further speculation: might not Heidegger's guarded but unmistakable later criticisms of active nihilism in Nietzsche and Ernst Jünger be understood self-critically as a comment upon his own active nihilism of 1933, when he believed, however briefly, in an overcoming of nihilism through National Socialist revolution?

19 'Überwindung der Metaphysik', in *Vorträge und Aufsätze* (Neske, Pfullingen, 1954), p. 67.

20 The text was retitled 'Zur Seinsfrage' when it appeared in *Wegmarken*, 2nd edition (Klostermann, Frankfurt am Main 1978), pp. 379–419. An English version of the text is available in a parallel edition, with a rather poor translation and bizarre introduction, as *The Question of Being*, trans. W. Kluback and J. T. Wilde (Twayne, New York, 1958), Heidegger's original title was a direct response to Jünger's 1950 contribution to Heidegger's *Festschrift* on his sixtieth birthday, 'Über die Linie' in *Betrachtungen zur Zeit* (Schöningh, Paderborn, 1963), pp. 58–100. For a very persuasive account of Jünger's influence on Heidegger in the late 1920s and early 1930s, see Michael E. Zimmerman's *Heidegger's Confrontation with Modernity* (Indiana University Press, Bloomington, 1990), especially chapters 3–6, pp. 49–65. Zimmerman shows how Jünger's account of technology, and particularly his rhetoric of hardness, resoluteness, work and *Gestalt*, was decisive for Heidegger's political thinking in the early 1930s. Zimmerman usefully documents Heidegger's distancing

183

of his own work from Jünger's active nihilism and his turn towards Hölderlin's poetry, which is perhaps not so much the covert expression of political culpability as the admission of naïveté.

21 *Being and Time*, trans. J. MacQuarrie and E. Robinson (Blackwell, Oxford, 1962), p. 220.

22 Derrida, *Of Grammatology*, trans. G. Spivak (Johns Hopkins University Press, Baltimore, 1976), p. 23.

23 *Minima Moralia, Gesammelte Schriften*, Band 4 (Suhrkamp, Frankfurt am Main, 1980), p. 281; trans. E. F. N. Jephcott (Verso, London, 1974), p. 247.

24 For a reading of Adorno that emphasizes his relation to the problem of nihilism, see Jay Bernstein's 'Critical Theory – The Very Idea. Reflections on Nihilism and Domination', in *Recovering Ethical Life* (Routledge, London and New York, 1994), pp. 10–34.

25 All passages from this rather unfortunate translation have been checked and, where necessary, revised.

26 The final line from Benjamin's 'Goethes Wahlverwandtschaften', *Illuminationen* (Surhkamp, Frankfurt am Main, 1955), p. 135. Cited in *Negative Dialectics* (ND 369/ NDS 378).

27 Montaigne, *Essays*, Vol.1, trans. John Florio (Dent, London, 1910), p. 73.

28 A key text here is Heidegger's utterly distasteful eulogy to Albert Leo Schlageter, delivered on 26 May 1933 (in 'Martin Heidegger and Politics: A Dossier', ed. Richard Wolin, *New German Critique*, No. 45, 1988, pp. 96–97). Schlageter's 'hardness of will' allowed him to endure the 'most difficult' and 'greatest' death of all:

As he stood defenceless facing the rifles, the hero's inner gaze soared above the muzzles to the daylight and mountains of his home that he might die for the German people and its Reich with the Alemannic countryside before his eyes.

29 'The moment of my death henceforth always pending', *L'instant de ma mort* (Fata Morgana, Montpellier, 1994), p. 20.

30 Freud, 'Mourning and Melancholia', *On Metapsychology: The Theory of Psychoanalysis*, Vol. 11, Penguin Freud Library (Penguin, Harmondsworth, 1984), p. 253.

31 See *Being and Time*, op. cit., p. 437.

32 Beckett, *Endgame* (Faber, London, 1958), p. 20.

Lecture 1: *Il y a*

1 Cf. Philippe Lacoue-Labarthe and Jean-Luc Nancy, *L'absolu littéraire* (AL 79–80/LA 57–58).

2 On the difficult question of the development of Blanchot's work, see Michael Holland, 'Towards a method', in *SubStance*, No. 14 (1976), pp. 7–17. Holland has given a richly detailed and decisive account of Blanchot's development in his Introduction and editorial commentaries in *The Blanchot Reader* (Blackwell, Oxford,

1995), which appeared after this lecture had been written. On this question, see Foucault's remark in 'La pensée du dehors', *Critique*, No. 229 (June 1966), p. 530; trans. J. Mehlman, in *Foucault/Blanchot* (Zone Books, New York, 1990), p. 26: 'the distinction between "novels", "narratives", and "criticism" is progressively weakened in Blanchot until, in *L'attente, l'oubli*, language alone is allowed to speak'.

3 Bonaventura, *Nachtwachen* (Reclam, Stuttgart, 1964).

4 Levinas, 'Maurice Blanchot et le regard du poète', *Sur Maurice Blanchot* (Fata Morgana, Montpellier, 1975), p. 20.

5 Hélène Cixous, 'Blanchot, the writing of disaster: nothing is what there is', in *Readings* (Harvester, Hemel Hempstead, 1992), pp. 19–27.

6 Susan Hanson also makes the connection between this passage and the double plus and minus sign in the Foreword to her excellent translation of *L'entretien infini* (IC xxviii and xxxii, note 3).

7 For a reading of Blanchot's 'Literature and the Right to Death', that does not exploit the connection to the *il y a*, see Rodolphe Gasché's 'The felicities of paradox. Blanchot on the null-space of literature', in *Blanchot*, ed. C. Gill (Routledge, London and New York, 1996), pp. 34–69.

8 *Phenomenology of Spirit*, trans. A.V. Miller (Oxford University Press, Oxford, 1977), p. 360.

9 'Le Terrorisme, méthode de salut public', *Combat*, No.7 (July 1936), p. 147. The texts, contexts and issues relating to Blanchot's politics since the 1930s have now been discussed, with particular emphasis on the contested memory of Vichy France, by Steven Ungar in *Scandal and Aftereffect. Blanchot and France Since 1930* (University of Minnesota Press, Minneapolis, 1995). Ungar discusses 'Literature and the Right to Death' on pp. 121–24. For an illuminating discussion of the context for political engagement in France in the 1930s – using the figure of Georges Bataille as an emblem – see Jean-Michel Besnier's *La politique de l'impossible* (La découverte, Paris, 1988).

10 On this question of the relation between solitude and perversion, I refer to Sara Arrhenius and Cecilia Sjöholm, *Ensam och Pervers* (Bonnier Alba, Stockholm, 1995).

11 *Saint Genet,* trans. B. Frechtman (Heinemann, London, 1988), p. 448.

12 *Phenomenology of Spirit*, op. cit., p. 19.

13 Ibid., p. 26. Interestingly, this quotation from Hegel also appears, approvingly it would seem, as the epigraph to Bataille's *Madame Edwarda* (*Oeuvres Complètes*, Vol. III (Gallimard, Paris, 1971), p. 9), a text that would be fascinating to read on both of Blanchot's slopes of literature, for its evocation of the relation of transgressive sexuality to God, and also for its presentiment of horror in sexual ecstasy (cf. Bataille's 'Preface', p. 11).

14 'Crise de vers' in *Igitur, Divagations, Un coup de dès* (Paris, Gallimard, 1976), p. 251.

15 Blanchot discusses Ponge in PF 336–37/GO 52–53.

16 'A linear narrative? Blanchot with Heidegger in the work of Levinas', in *Philosophers' Poets*, ed. David Wood (Routledge, London and New York, 1990), p. 42.

17 *Writing and Difference*, trans. A. Bass (Routledge & Kegan Paul, London and New York, 1978), p. 103.

18 *Time and Being*, trans. J. Stambaugh (Harper and Row, New York, 1972), pp. 38–40.

19 It would be extremely interesting to compare Levinas's account of horror and its relation to literature with that of Julia Kristeva in *Powers of Horror. An Essay on Abjection* (trans. L. S. Roudiez (Columbia University Press, New York, 1982)), where horror is analysed in terms of abjection understood as that condition of the disintegration of the relation between self and other.

20 The passage is also cited by Blanchot in EI 29/IC 22.

21 Cited in Christopher Ricks's *Beckett's Dying Words* (Oxford University Press, Oxford, 1993), p. 93.

22 In *Les temps modernes*, No.38 (1948), p. 786; trans. A. Lingis in *Collected Philosophical Papers* (Martinus Nijhoff, Dordrecht, 1987), p. 11.

23 'The Facts in the Case of M. Valdemar' in *The Fall of the House of Usher and Other Writings* (Penguin, Harmondsworth, 1986), pp. 350–59.

24 The English translation here, 'literature has two slopes', is misleading.

25 I have attempted to discuss the question of community in Nancy in 'Re-tracing the political: politics and community in the work of Philippe Lacoue-Labarthe and Jean-Luc Nancy', in *The Political Subject of Violence*, eds. D. Campbell and M. Dillon (Manchester University Press, Manchester, 1993), pp. 73–93. See especially pp. 87–89.

26 On fatigue as an access to the neuter, see the opening untitled dialogue to *L'entretien infini* (EI xxii/IC xx–xxi).

27 See also ED 176–79 and 191–96. This passage is the focus for several interesting discussions of Blanchot, notably J. Hillis Miller, 'Death mask: Blanchot's *L'arrêt de mort*', in *Versions of Pygmalion* (Harvard University Press, Cambridge MA, 1990), pp. 179–210 (see especially pp. 179–80); Françoise Collin, 'La peur. Emmanuel Levinas et Maurice Blanchot', *Emmanuel Levinas, Cahier de l'Herne* (Editions de l'Herne, Paris, 1991), pp. 313–27 (see especially p. 320); and Hélène Cixous, 'Blanchot, The Writing of Disaster: Nothing Is What There Is', op. cit., see especially p. 19.

28 Of course, a lot more needs to be said here about the relation of the *il y a*, as the origin of the artwork, to the primal scene of childhood. In particular, and in addition to my cursory remarks on the above passage, it would be necessary to put Blanchot's primitive scene in the context of his comments on Serge Leclaire's book *On tue un enfant* (Seuil, Paris, 1975), which is interestingly discussed in the pages immediately prior to the above passage (*L'écriture du désastre*, pp. 110–17). Leclaire identifies the practice of psychoanalysis with the death of the child, 'Sa majesté l'enfant', the terrifying, all-powerful *infans* who Leclaire understands as the representant of primary narcissism.

29 Blanchot, *L'instant de ma mort* (Fata Morgana, Montpellier, 1994); see especially pp. 10, 11, 20.

30 I am freely borrowing here from Derrida's 'Remarks on deconstruction and pragmatism', trans. S. Critchley, in *Deconstruction and Pragmatism*, op. cit., pp.77–88.

31 Dostoevsky, *The Devils*, trans. D. Magurshak (Penguin, Harmondsworth, 1971), p. 126.

32 Dostoevsky, *The Diary of a Writer*, trans. B. Brasol (George Braziller, New York, 1954), pp. 538–42.

33 *Le Spleen de Paris* (Armand Collin, Paris, 1958), p. 110.

34 Nietzsche, *Nachgelassene Fragmente, Sämtliche Werke*, Kritische Studienausgabe, Vol. 13 (de Gruyter, Berlin, 1988), p. 146, note 11. Cited as the epigraph to Jill Marsden's *Ecstasy and Annihilation in Nietzsche's Philosophy of Eternal Return* (PhD thesis, University of Essex, 1992).

35 Chaucer, *The Pardoner's Tale*, in *The Complete Works of Geoffrey Chaucer*, ed. F. N. Robinson, 2nd edition (Oxford University Press, Oxford, 1957), p. 152; Donne, 'Holy Sonnets', in *Selected Poems*, ed. J. Hayward (Penguin, Harmondsworth, 1950), p. 170.

36 In *Critique*, No. 229 (June 1966), pp. 547–60; the English version of this essay appeared with added introductory paragraphs under the title 'Impersonality in the criticism of Maurice Blanchot', in *Blindness and Insight*, 2nd edition (Methuen, London, 1983), pp. 60–78.

37 I owe my title here to Gerald Bruns, whose extremely thoughtful remarks greatly aided the revision of this lecture. I also owe a great deal to Donna Brody, former research student at the University of Essex, who first brought the radicality of the *il y a* to my attention and whose work has been invaluable in thinking through these issues.

38 In this regard, see Elisabeth Bronfen's and Sarah Webster Goodwin's interesting introduction to *Death and Representation* (Johns Hopkins University Press, Baltimore, 1993), pp. 3–25, see especially pp. 7 and 20.

39 This idea is borrowed from J. Hillis Miller's *Versions of Pygmalion* (Harvard University Press, Cambridge MA, 1990).

40 *The Birth of Tragedy*, trans. W. Kaufmann (Vintage, New York, 1967), p. 42.

41 *Being and Time*, trans. J. MacQuarrie and E. Robinson (Blackwell, Oxford, 1962), p. 284. For Levinas's most sustained critique of Heidegger on death, see 'La mort et le temps', in *Emmanuel Levinas. Cahier de l'Herne* (Editions de l' Herne, Paris, 1991), pp. 21–75. My opposition between death as possibility and impossibility as a way of organizing the difference between Heidegger, on the one hand, and Levinas and Blanchot, on the other, does not tell the whole story and matters are rarely univocal in relation to Heidegger, particularly on the question of death and the entire thematic of authenticity and inauthenticity. For a more nuanced account of Heidegger on death, see Christopher Fynsk, *Thought and Historicity* (Cornell University Press, Ithaca, 1986), and Françoise Dastur, *La mort. Essai sur la finitude* (Hatier, Paris, 1994).

42 'Prolegomena to any Post-Deconstructive Subjectivity', in *Deconstructive Subjectivities*, eds S. Critchley and P. Dews (State University of New York Press, Albany, 1996), pp. 13–45.

43 'Paix et Proximité', *Les cahiers de la nuit surveillée*, No. 3 (Verdier, Lagrasse, 1984), p. 344.

44 *The Community of Those Who Have Nothing in Common* (Indiana University Press, Bloomington, 1994), p. 12. A question left unresolved here concerns the relation of death to femininity in Levinas, particularly in *Time and the Other*, that is, between the *mystery* of death and the *mystery* of the feminine, and whether, in the light of Elizabeth Bronfen's work, this repeats a persistent masculinist trope (see *Over Her Dead Body: Death, Femininity and the Aesthetic* (Manchester University Press, Manchester, 1992)). This also entails the related point as to what extent the Levinasian account of plurality is dependent upon his notion of fecundity and hence upon his account of the child, that is to say, the son, and therefore entails a male lineage of community that fails to acknowledge mother–daughter relations.

45 I borrow this formulation from Paul Davies. In this regard, see the following passage from 'Meaning and Sense':

> To renounce being the contemporary of the triumph of one's work is to envisage this triumph in a *time without me*, to aim at this world below without me, to aim at a time beyond the horizon of my time, in an eschatology without hope for oneself, or in a liberation from my time.
>
> To be *for* a time that would be without me, *for* a time after my time, over and beyond the celebrated 'being for death', is not a banal thought which is extrapolating from my own duration; it is the passage to the time of the other.
>
> (HAH 45/CPP 92)

46 In this connection, see Luce Irigaray, 'Questions to Emmanuel Levinas. On the divinity of love', in *The Irigaray Reader*, ed. M. Whitford (Blackwell, Oxford, 1991), pp. 178–89. Irigaray rightly questions Levinas as to whether the alterity of the child as the future for the father that is not the father's future, does not still remain within the sphere of the *pour soi*, where the child is *for* the father, a project beyond his powers of projection, but still *his* project (see especially p. 181).

47 Paul Davies, 'A linear narrative? Blanchot with Heidegger in the work of Levinas', in *Philosophers' Poets*, ed. David Wood (Routledge, London and New York, 1990), pp. 37–69.

48 A point of clarification here: in lectures given on Levinas at Essex University in November 1994, Rudi Visker spoke of an 'ethicization of the *il y a*' in Levinas's work. The claim here is that the overcoming or surmounting of the *il y a* in the move to the hypostasis of the subject that characterized Levinas's earlier analyses is abandoned in the later work, where the *il y a* is accorded an ethical significance previously denied to it. Now, there is some truth to this claim, and it would be a question of giving (which we cannot give here) a detailed periodization of the *il y a* across Levinas's work, noting differences of nuance in different texts written at different periods. It is certainly true to say, as Levinas says himself in *Ethique et infini*, that in his later work, although he scarcely speaks of the *il y a* as a theme, 'the shadow of the *il y a* and non-sense still appeared to me necessary as the very ordeal of

dis-inter-estedness' (EeI 42). The *il y a* is the shadow or spectre of nonsense that haunts ethical sense *but* – and this is crucial – for Levinas ethical sense cannot, in the final instance, be confused or conflated with an-ethical nonsense. The *il y a* is a threat, but it is a threat that must and can be repelled. This would seem to be confirmed by the 1978 Preface to *De l'existence à l'existent*, where, after writing that the *il y a* is the 'morceau de résistance' of the book, he goes on to describe the *il y a* in terms of 'inhuman neutrality' and 'a neutrality to be surmounted' (DEE 10–11). Thus, Levinas's basic philosophical *intention* does not alter, but whether his *text* is saying something at odds with his intention is another matter.

49 DQVI 115/CPP 165–66: 'And this implies that God is not simply the "first other", the "other par excellence", or the "absolutely other", other than the other (*autrui*), other otherwise, other with an alterity prior to the alterity of the other (*autrui*), prior to the ethical bond with the other (*autrui*) and different from every neighbour, transcendent to the point of absence, to the point of a possible confusion with the stirring of the *il y a*.'

50 *Transcendence et intelligibilité* (Labor et Fides, Geneva, 1984), p. 29; trans. S. Critchley and T. Wright in *Emmanuel Levinas: Basic Philosophical Writings* (Indiana University Press, Bloomington, 1996), p. 159, 'But perhaps this theology already announces itself in the very wakefulness of insomnia, in the vigil and troubled vigilance of the psyche before the moment when the finitude of being, wounded by the infinite, is prompted to gather itself into the hegemonic and atheist Ego of knowledge.'

51 Levinas goes some way to discussing this question in 'Transcendence and Evil' (DQVI 189–207/CPP 175–86), where, although Levinas recognizes the 'non-integrat-ability' or excess of evil, the horror of evil is understood by Levinas as the horror of evil in the other man and, hence, as the breakthrough of the Good and the 'approach of the infinite God' (DQVI 207/CPP 186).

52 Guy de Maupassant, *Contes et nouvelles*, ed. L. Forestier (Gallimard, Paris, 1979), pp. 913–38 (see especially p. 938); *Selected Short Stories*, trans R. Colet (Penguin, Harmondsworth, 1971), pp. 313–44, see especially p. 344.

53 Several years ago, I corresponded with Michel Haar after some discussions we had at the *Collegium Phaenomenologicum* in Perugia, where I had tried to explain my fascination with Levinas. He wrote, and I recall from a memory long troubled by his words, 'je ne vois pas qu'il y a éthique dès qu'il y a altérité' ('I don't see why there is ethics since there is alterity'). For Haar's powerful critique of Levinas, see 'L'obsession de l'autre. L'éthique comme traumatisme', *Emmanuel Levinas. Cahier de l'Herne* (Editions de l'Herne, Paris, 1991), pp. 444–53.

54 I owe this analogy to a conversation with Jay Bernstein.

55 In this context I will have to pass over the interesting and difficult question of whether Blanchot's relation to Levinas alters in the later book, *L'écriture du désastre*, which might justifiably be approached as a deeply sympathetic but subtly reconstructive reading of Levinas's *Otherwise than Being*.

56 Although it should be noted that when Blanchot edited the texts on Levinas that appeared in *La Nouvelle Revue Française* for republication in *L'entretien infini*, he moved

some pages dealing with the question of the *autrui*, devoted to a discussion of Robert Antelme's *L'espèce humaine*, into the essay 'The indestructible' (EI 191–200/IC 130–35). These pages, where the *autrui* is approached as the indestructible who is nonetheless destroyed in the Holocaust, might be read as offering some critical qualifications to Levinas's account of the relation to the *autrui*. Is this why they were moved when Blanchot was editing *L'entretien infini*? Michael Holland has pursued this hypothesis in 'Let's leave God out of this', a paper presented at The Institute for Romance Studies, University College London, May 1995. A brief discussion of the issues surrounding Blanchot's editing and rewriting of his pieces on Levinas in *L'entretien infini* can be found in Holland's *The Blanchot Reader*, op. cit., pp. 191–94.

57 Cf. *Ordnung in Zwielicht* (Suhrkamp, Frankfurt am Main, 1987).

58 After the thoughts contained in the final section of this lecture were already formulated, I made the happy discovery that many of my claims are similar to those proposed by John D. Caputo in his attempt to think obligation without reference to any substantive ethics. See his *Against Ethics* (Indiana University Press, Bloomington, 1993).

Lecture 2: Unworking romanticism

1 For ease of reference, Schlegel fragments will be referred to by their number as this is identical in the German and English editions.

2 From an earlier version of AF 116, to be found in KA 182.

3 Benjamin, *Der Begriff der Kunstkritik in der deutschen Romantik* (Suhrkamp, Frankfurt am Main, 1973), p. 9.

4 More speculatively, it might be asked: Does George Eliot's *Middlemarch* count as a romantic novel? I am following an interesting, if untestable, hypothesis offered by Ken Newton ('Historical Prototypes in *Middlemarch*', *English Studies*, Vol. 56, No. 5, October 1975, pp. 403–8), where he claims that Eliot's hero and heroine, Dorothea Brooke and Will Ladislaw, are based on the prototypes of Dorothea Veit and Friedrich Schlegel.

5 Nietzsche, *The Birth of Tragedy*, trans. W. Kaufmann (Vintage, New York, 1967), p. 91.

6 A reliable English translation can be found as an appendix to Andrew Bowie's *Aesthetics and Subjectivity* (Manchester University Press, Manchester, 1990), pp. 265–67.

7 See Part One of Benjamin's *Der Begriff der Kunstkritik in der deutschen Romantik*, op. cit., especially pp. 14–35.

8 Kant, *Critique of Pure Reason*, B.135.

9 Kant, *Critique of Practical Reason*, trans. L. W. Beck (Bobbs Merrill, Indianapolis, 1956), p. 31.

10 *Aesthetics and Subjectivity*, op. cit., p. 49; the question of Kant's Jewishness is discussed by Derrida in his commentary on Hegel in *Glas*, trans. J. P. Leavey and R. Rand (University of Nebraska Press, Lincoln and London, 1986), pp. 33–77.

11 'On Derrida's *Specters of Marx*', *Philosophy and Social Criticism*, Vol. 21, No. 3 (1995), pp. 1–30.

12 I do not discuss the dissonant presence of the sublime in the Third Critique, although this would obviously complicate the picture I am presenting here.

13 *Aesthetics and Subjectivity*, op. cit., p. 266.

14 Schelling, *System of Transcendental Idealism*, in *Philosophies of Art and Beauty*, eds A. Hofstadter and R. Kuhns (University of Chicago Press, Chicago, 1964), p. 355.

15 Coleridge, *Poems*, ed. J. Beer (Dent, London, 1963), p. 324.

16 This slippage from the beauty of nature to that of art is powerfully analysed by Adorno in *Aesthetic Theory* in the chapter on the 'Beauty of Nature', where Adorno writes, against the subordination of nature to spirit in Hegel's *Aesthetics*, that natural beauty is 'the trace of non-identity in things' (AT 114/AST 108).

17 Bernhard Lypp, *Ästhetischer Absolutismus und politische Vernunft* (Suhrkamp, Frankfurt am Main, 1972).

18 *Aesthetics and Subjectivity*, op. cit., p. 266.

19 Hegel, *Aesthetics*, trans. T. M. Knox (Oxford University Press, Oxford, 1975), p. 2.

20 *Aesthetics and Subjectivity*, op. cit., p. 266.

21 Ibid., p. 266.

22 Paul de Man, *Aesthetic Ideology* (Minnesota University Press, Minneapolis, forthcoming); and see Lypp, *Ästhetisher Absolutismus und politische Vernunft*, op. cit., p. 20.

23 *Poems*, op. cit., p. 18. For an excellent discussion of Pantisocracy, see Richard Holmes *Coleridge. Early Visions* (Penguin, Harmondsworth, 1990), pp. 59–88.

24 *Aesthetics and Subjectivity*, op. cit., p. 265.

25 Lukács, 'On the Romantic Philosophy of Life', in *Soul and Form* (Merlin Press, London, 1974), p. 42.

26 Carl Schmitt, *Political Romanticism*, trans. G. Oakes (MIT, Cambridge MA, 1986).

27 Ibid., p. 160

28 Ibid., p. 20.

29 Walt Whitman, *Leaves of Grass*, the first (1855) edition, ed. M. Cowley (Penguin, Harmondsworth, 1959), pp. 8 and 22.

30 *Political Romanticism*, op. cit., p. 15.

31 The poetic possibilities of the Schlegel-Hegel conflict were whimsically and wittily explored by August Wilhelm Schlegel in 1827, in a poem entitled 'Friedrich Schlegel und Hegel':

> Schlegel predigt gegen Hegel,
> Für den Teufel schieb' er Kegel.
> Hegel spottet über Schlegel
> Sagt, er schwatzt' ohn' alle Regel
> Schlegel spannt der Mystik Segel;
> Hegel faßt der Logik Flegel.
> Kommt, ihr Deutschen, Kind und Kegel,

Von der Saar bis an den Pregel!
Schaut, wie Schlegel kämpft mit Hegel!
Schaut, wie Hegel kämpft mit Schlegel!

A rough paraphrase might run: 'Schlegel preaches against Hegel/He plays skittles for the devil./Hegel pokes fun at Schlegel/Saying that he chatters without any rules./ Schlegel sets the mystic's sail/Hegel grasps the uncouth logic./Come, you Germans, with the whole family,/From the Saar to the Pregel!/See how Schlegel fights with Hegel!/See how Hegel fights with Schlegel!' Quoted in Ernst Behler's *Friedrich Schlegel* (Rowohlt, Hamburg, 1966), p. 173.

32 See *Aesthetics*, op. cit., pp. 64–69; and *Phenomenology of Spirit*, op. cit., pp. 5, 42, 43. These latter allusions to Schlegel are suggested by the editors of the Meiner edition of the *Phänomenologie des Geistes,* eds H. F. Wessels and H. Clairmont (Meiner, Hamburg, 1988), p. 630.

33 *Phenomenology of Spirit*, op. cit., p. 42.

34 Ibid., p. 43.

35 On the relation of melancholy and fragmentation, I am thinking of M. A. Screech's *Montaigne and Melancholy* (Penguin, Harmondsworth, 1983).

36 Hegel, *Aesthetics*, op. cit., p. 68.

37 On the self-consciousness of romantic naïveté, see Geoffrey Hartman's 'Romanticism and anti-self-consciousness', in *Romanticism*, ed. Cynthia Chase (Longman, London and New York, 1993), p. 45.

38 Cited in Cynthia Chase's helpful introduction to *Romanticism*, op. cit., p. 1.

39 Of course, such general statements obviously risk border conflicts between genres. For example, how would romanticism be distinguished from modernism on my account? Would it be distinguished? Would modernism simply be a rightfully impoverished continuation of romanticism? I return to this topic in Lecture 3.

40 Stevens, 'Adagia' in *Opus Posthumous*, revised edition (Faber, London, 1989), p. 185.

41 The importance of women to Jena Romanticism – in particular Rahel Levin, Caroline Schlegel and Dorothea Veit – is worthy of careful and extensive discussion as one of the privileged places where the construction of a philosophical or theoretical project can be seen in negotiation with the problem of sexual difference. In relation to this, see 'Die Frau', in *Der romantische Aufbruch. Die Früromantiker in Jena* (Romanikerhaus, Jena), pp. 19–23; Kurt Luethi, *Feminismus und Romantik* (Boehlaus, Vienna, 1985). The representation of women in the 'Athenäum Fragments', although by no means free from prevalent preconceptions, is surprisingly progressive for its time and a considerable advance on the overwhelming misogyny of classical German philosophy (Kant, Schopenhauer, Nietzsche). See, for example, the critique of marriage as legal concubinage and the possibility of plural marriages (AF 34); the critique of the dominant representation of femininity (AF 49); the association of women with philosophy (AF 102); the need for matronyms and matrilinear succession (AF 134); and an interestingly anti-Rousseauist view of women (AF 420).

42 Heidegger, 'What are poets for?', in *Poetry, Language, Thought*, trans. A. Hofstadter (Harper and Row, New York, 1971), pp. 91–142; Wittgenstein, *Philosophical Investigations*, trans. G. E. M. Anscombe (Blackwell, Oxford, 1958), p. viii.

43 On this connection between situationism and punk, see Jon Savage, *England's Dreaming* (Faber, London, 1991).

44 Raoul Vaneigem, *The Revolution of Everyday Life*, trans. D. Nicholson-Smith (Rebel Press, London, 1994), p. 202.

45 Ibid., p. 202.

46 On the legacy of situationism, see Sadie Plant, 'The situationist international: a case of spectacular neglect', *Radical Philosophy*, No. 55, Summer 1990, pp. 3–10. See also Plant's *The Most Radical Gesture. The Situationist International in a Postmodern Age* (Routledge, London, 1992).

47 Emerson, 'The American scholar', in *Selected Essays*, ed. L. Ziff (Penguin, Harmondsworth, 1982), p. 100.

48 Whitman, *Leaves of Grass* (Penguin, Harmondsworth, 1959), p. 6. This marriage between romanticism and liberalism, what Schmitt criticizes as the establishment of the private priesthood, obviously also raises the question of religion. If romanticism is the American religion (or if American religion is romantic), then this is perhaps because of its dependence upon protestantism and the specific affirmation of the ordinary or the everyday that can be found within protestant religion. In this connection, see 'The affirmation of ordinary life', in Charles Taylor's *The Sources of the Self* (Cambridge University Press, Cambridge, 1989), pp. 211–302. But is the American religion protestant? Is it even recognizably Christian? I refer here to Harold Bloom's provocative diagnosis of American religion as post-Christian and gnostic, whose central affirmation is that of the self in its apartness from community – which, I think, makes good sense of Whitman's poetics. If, as Bloom contends, religious ecstasy is collective in European protestantism, then in American 'protestantism' it is solitary. See Bloom, *The American Religion* (Simon and Schuster, New York, 1992).

49 Merleau-Ponty, *The Visible and the Invisible*, trans. A. Lingis (Northwestern University Press, Evanston, 1968), pp. 3–49.

50 Rilke, *Sämtliche Werke*, Vol. 1 (Insel, Frankfurt am Main, 1955), pp. 717–20. *Selected Poems*, trans. J. B. Leishman (Penguin, Harmondsworth, 1964), pp. 63–65.

51 See 'A mythology reflects its region . . .' and 'Connecticut composed', both from 1955, in *Opus Posthumous*, op. cit., pp. 141 and 302–4.

52 Merleau-Ponty, *In Praise of Philosophy* (Northwestern University Press, Evanston, 1963), p. 61. Although this is the topic for another lecture, I would like to show how Merleau-Ponty's work, particularly his later writings, is continuous with the romantic modernity I spoke of above and aims at a certain romantic re-enchantment of the world. Three motifs linking Merleau-Ponty to Jena Romanticism can be sketched here:

  1 The emphasis on irony and ambiguity in philosophy, and the interpretation of Socrates as a good ironist echoes Schlegel's interpretation of Socrates, discussed

below. Not only did Socrates know that he did not know, i.e. that 'there is no absolute knowledge', he knew also 'that it is by this absence that we are open to the truth' (ibid., p. 39). We might also note Merleau-Ponty's emphasis on the limping of philosophy, the *indirection* of language necessary to ontology, and the fact that brute or savage being cannot be approached frontally but only approximated to in a form of philosophical writing that he calls interrogation, and that Schlegel would call irony.

2 The form of the fragment found in the working notes to *The Visible and the Invisible*, which is usually – and justifiably from a biographical perspective – treated as contingent, but might be located within a broader tradition of fragmentary writing stretching back to Jena Romanticism.

3 The notions of hyper-reflection and hyper-dialectic – that is, a reflection without end and a dialectic without synthesis – are the very core of Jena Romanticism. Hyper-reflection is not an abandonment of the standpoint of reflection, but a reflection that knows itself *as* reflection, a reflection that recognizes itself as limited in its scope but limitless in its operation. The very limitedness of thought is the precondition for its limitlessness.

53 On what disastrous events might have ensued, had Coleridge and Southey actually emigrated to Pennsylvania, see Paul Muldoon's brilliantly imaginative reworking of the theme of Pantisocracy (and, modestly enough, the entire history of philosophy) in *Madoc. A Mystery* (Faber, London, 1990).

54 *La communauté désoeuvrée* (Christian Bourgois, Paris, 1986).

55 *Leaves of Grass*, op. cit., pp. 5 and 143.

56 Ibid., p. 5.

57 See Gasché's 'Ideality in Fragmentation', a foreword to Schlegel's *Philosophical Fragments*, op. cit., p. xiii.

58 *Der Begriff der Kunstkritik in der deutschen Romantik*, op. cit., p. 14.

59 I am thinking of Pascal's 'Two excesses: to exclude reason, to admit nothing but reason', *Pensées*, trans. A. J. Krailsheimer (Penguin, Harmondsworth, 1966), p. 85.

60 Schlegel remarks elsewhere that 'even the greatest, most universal works of isolated poetry and philosophy seem to lack this final synthesis' (AF 451).

61 To move a little quickly here, it might be noted that there are significant parallels between the model of romanticism that I offer here and Deleuze and Guattari's rhizomatic conception of writing. One might note that Deleuze and Guattari's conception of writing draws upon a certain 'romanticism', that of Kleist rather than Schlegel. As they write, it is a case of 'Kleist and Kafka against Goethe', *A Thousand Plateaus*, trans. B. Massumi (Athlone, London, 1992), p. 24. What I am claiming here for the fragment and for an unworked romanticism could well be related to Deleuze and Guattari's opposition to *major* literature (of the Work, of totality) in terms of a *minor* literature and a generalized rhizomatics. See *Kafka. Towards a Minor Literature*, trans. D. Polan (University of Minnesota, Minneapolis, 1986).

62 Peter Szondi, 'Friedrich Schlegel and romantic irony, with some remarks on Tieck's Comedies', in *On Textual Understanding and Other Essays*, trans. H. Mendelsohn (University of Minnesota Press, Minneapolis, 1986), p. 68.

63 Paul de Man, 'The rhetoric of temporality', in *Blindness and Insight*, Second Edition (University of Minnesota Press, Minneapolis, 1983), pp. 219–20.

64 Cited by Ernst Behler in his Introduction to Schlegel's *Dialogue on Poetry and Literary Aphorisms* (Pennsylvania State Press, University Park, 1968), p. 38.

65 *Der Begriff der Kunstkritik in der deutschen Romantik*, op. cit., p. 17.

66 *Ästhetischer Absolutismus und politische Vernunft*, op. cit., p. 34.

67 In this context, I can do no more than mention the vast question of the relation between Jena Romanticism and Kierkegaard, both to consider the extremely critical – and deeply Hegelian – account of Jena Romanticism in Kierkegaard's *The Concept of Irony*, and also to contest the function of irony in Kierkegaard's later work, where it is that which permits the transition from the aesthetic to the ethical. However, we should note the proximity between Kierkegaard and Jena Romanticism with regard to the thematics (if not the practice) of the fragment, the necessity for indirect communication and the question of the future, which opens, for Kierkegaard, in the thought of *repetition*.

68 For confirmation of Blanchot's influence on the notion of romantic equivocity, see AL 421–22/LA 123–24.

69 *Being and Time*, op. cit., p. 423.

70 *A Pitch of Philosophy. Autobiographical Exercises*, op. cit., p. 4.

71 Emerson, 'Experience' and 'The American Scholar', *Selected Essays*, op. cit., pp. 311 and 99.

72 Ibid., p. 309.

73 See Stephen Mulhall's extremely helpful book, *Stanley Cavell. Philosophy's Recounting of the Ordinary* (Oxford University Press, Oxford, 1994), p. xii.

74 In *Ecce Homo*, Nietzsche remarks, against his earlier Wagnerian incarnation, that every time one sees the name 'Wagner' in his work one should erase it and insert the name 'Nietzsche' (trans. R. J. Hollingdale, Penguin, Harmondsworth, 1979, p. 82). I wonder whether this remark might be applied to Cavell, and that every time one sees the name 'Emerson' one should strike it out and write 'Cavell'. This question of nomination and the proper name would seem to resonate with Cavell's recent autobiographical exercises in his Jerusalem Harvard Lectures and with the history of his own name: Goldstein–Cavalier–Cavalerskii–Cavaleriiskii–Cavell (*A Pitch of Philosophy*, op. cit., pp. 25–30). Cavell is therefore not so much a name as an alias. What interests me is why Cavell decides to tell us this fact. Why does he need to confess? After all, what's in a name? Interestingly, he shares this obsessional and confessional relation to the proper name with Derrida in his recent text *Circonfession*, where the young Jackie changes his name to Jacques when he publishes his first book (*Jacques Derrida*, Geoffrey Bennington and Jacques Derrida, University of Chicago Press, Chicago, 1993, p. 41). What is the difference between Jackie Derrida and

Jacques Derrida, or between Stanley Goldstein and Stanley Cavell? And to what extent is this question separable from the issue of Cavell's or Derrida's Jewishness?

75 Emerson, *Selected Essays*, op. cit., p. 302.

76 Cited in Harold Bloom's *The American Religion*, op. cit., p. 31.

77 This would be the place to begin a reading of Emerson's 'Emancipation Address' from 1844, which discusses at length the question of slavery in the British West Indies and the United States, in *Essays. Second Series* (Harrap, London, no date), pp. 191–229.

78 'Thus in the beginning all the world was *America* . . .', *Two Treatises of Government*, ed. P. Laslett (Cambridge University Press, Cambridge, 1988 (1960)), p. 301.

79 See Hegel's famous remark in the *Philosophy of History* (Dover, New York, 1956), pp. 86–87: 'America is therefore the land of the future'.

80 Paine, *Rights of Man* (Penguin, Harmondsworth, 1969).

81 Blake, *America: A Prophecy* (1793), in *The Prophetic Writing of William Blake*, eds D. J. Sloss and J. P. R. Wallis (Oxford University Press, Oxford, 1956), pp. 47–62.

82 Baudrillard, *America*, trans. C. Turner (Verso, London, 1988).

83 Ibid., p. 7.

84 See 'Declining decline. Wittgenstein as a philosopher of culture', in NYUA 29–75.

85 Emerson, *Selected Essays*, op. cit., p. 310.

86 Ibid., p. 310.

87 Baudrillard, *America*, op. cit., p. 90.

88 Cavell's arguments are impressively documented in Part Two of Mulhall's *Stanley Cavell. Philosophy's Recounting of the Ordinary*, op. cit., pp. 77–181. For an excellent account of scepticism in Cavell, see Gerald Bruns, 'Stanley Cavell's Shakespeare', *Critical Inquiry*, Vol. 16 (Spring 1990), pp. 612–32.

89 Hilary Putnam, *Renewing Philosophy* (Harvard University Press, Cambridge MA, 1992), p. 177.

90 *Being and Time*, op. cit., p. 229. Heidegger restates, in his fashion, the classical refutation of scepticism, 'A sceptic can no more be refuted that the Being of truth can be "proved". And if any sceptic of the kind who denies the truth, factically *is*, he does *not* even *need* to be refuted. Insofar as he *is*, and has understood himself in his Being, he has obliterated Dasein in the desperation of suicide; and in so doing, he has also obliterated truth. It has no more been demonstrated that there ever has "been" an "actual" sceptic . . . than it has been demonstrated that there are any "eternal truths"'.

91 For a discussion of ancient scepticism, see *The Modes of Scepticism,* J. Annas and J. Barnes (Cambridge University Press, Cambridge, 1985).

92 Mulhall, *Philosophy's Recounting of the Ordinary*, op. cit., pp. 301–2. I return to a similar question around religion in Lecture 3, where I criticize Martha Nussbaum's interpretation of Beckett.

93 See 'Nothing goes without saying', *London Review of Books*, Vol. 16, No. 1 (1994), pp. 3–5.

94 As Cavell speculates at the end of his review of the Marx Brothers scripts, such would be the gift of American culture to Derrida.

95 Incidentally, it is in terms of aloneness and separateness that Harold Bloom describes the American religion, the post-Christian, gnostic tradition that he traces back to Whitman's 'Song of Myself'. Bloom writes, with his characteristic penchant for provocation:

The American Orphic ecstasy never has been Dionysiac, for the Bacchic freedom is the freedom to merge into others. American ecstasy is solitary, even when it requires the presence of others as audience for the self's glory. Our father Walt Whitman, despite his self-advertisements and the dogmatic insistences of our contemporary gays, seems to have embraced only himself.

(*The American Religion*, op. cit., p. 264)

96 The elements of Cavell's work that I have chosen to emphasize have certain distinct resonances with the work of Levinas as interpreted in Lecture 1. Cavell's proximity to Levinas can be seen in the way in which the problem of scepticism (which is also extensively discussed by Levinas) opens a non-cognitive relation to the other as a distinctively *ethical* insight. The Cavellian need to accept the limitedness of human cognition, the need for acknowledgement of the other's separateness from me and my own irreducible separation can be placed alongside Levinas's account of the ethical relation to the other exceeding the bounds of knowledge. Might not such a view have the perverse consequence of viewing Levinas as a romantic thinker? For a brief but suggestive comparison of Levinas and Cavell, see Gerald Bruns's 'Stanley Cavell's Shakespeare', op. cit., pp. 619–20.

97 Beckett, *Six Residua* (Calder, London, 1978), p. 38.

Lecture 3: Know happiness – on Beckett

1 On interpretation overshooting that which it seeks to interpret, see Jay Bernstein, 'Philosophy's refuge: Adorno in Beckett', in *Philosophers' Poets*, ed. D. Wood (Routledge, London, 1990), pp. 183–85.

2 I have borrowed this somewhat caricatural list from Leslie Hill's excellent study, *Beckett's Fiction* (Cambridge University Press, Cambridge, 1990), p. 8. For the classic statement of the Cartesian reading of Beckett, which makes interesting remarks on the undeniable importance of Geulincx on Beckett, particularly *Murphy*, see Hugh Kenner's *Samuel Beckett. A Critical Study* (University of California Press, Berkeley, 1968, new edition), see especially Chapter 3, pp. 117–32. For an extraordinary 'philosophical' reading of Beckett that seems to read him as some sort of pre-Kantian metaphysical realist, claiming that Beckett's work functions like a series of ontological parables for the 'deepest, ontological reality', see Lance St John Butler's *Samuel Beckett and the Meaning of Being* (Macmillan, London, 1984). As will hopefully be shown below, it is precisely the possibility of such a 'philosophical' reading that

Beckett's work places in question. For a sub-Pascalian account of Beckett, see Martin Esslin's 'Samuel Beckett: The Search for the Self', in *The Theatre of the Absurd* (Doubleday, New York, 1961), pp. 27–39.

3 It is, at the very least, unclear whether the *Trilogy* can and should be viewed as a traditional trilogy, a trinitarian, unified – and consequently both theological and dialectical – work, in three discrete but interdependent parts (one-in-three and three-in-one). Such a view helps sustain the questionable belief that the titles of the novels that make up the *Trilogy* refer simply to the narrative voices in the various books or that the *Trilogy* can be read teleologically as a narrative of progressive disintegration and purification, a sort of phenomenological reduction to a pure authorial voice. (We can now add a sub-Husserlian philosophical interpretation to the list given in Note 2 above.) On this point, see Hill, *Beckett's Fiction*, op. cit., pp. 54–58.

4 For a useful account of the philosophical influences on Beckett, with particular emphasis on the influence of Spinoza on *Murphy* and the importance of Kant for *Watt*, see P. J. Murphy, 'Beckett and the Philosophers', in *The Cambridge Companion to Beckett*, ed. John Pilling (Cambridge University Press, Cambridge, 1994), pp. 222–40. Although I am not in a position to contest Murphy's statement that '*Watt* is perhaps the decisive work for reappraising Beckett's relationship to the philosophical tradition' (p. 229), I find some of the alleged parallels between Kant and Beckett, particularly on the question of synthetic a priori judgements and the transcendental imagination (pp. 235–36), slightly impressionistic and less than convincing.

5 Descartes, *Discourse on the Method, The Philosophical Writings of Descartes*, Vol. 1, trans. J. Cottingham, R. Stoothoff and D. Murdoch (Cambridge University Press, Cambridge, 1985), p. 123.

6 On other circles in the *Trilogy*, see T 83 and T 226. Indeed, the figure of the circle might be linked to Beckett's preoccupation with geometry and mathematics. Early in *Molloy*, the protagonist notes, 'Extraordinary how mathematics help you to know yourself' (T 30).

7 'Narrative Emotions: Beckett's Genealogy of Love', in *Love's Knowledge* (Oxford University Press, New York, 1990), p. 298.

8 Reference should also be made to the figure of Descartes as it appears in the early poem *Whoroscope* (in *Collected Poems in English and French,* Calder, London, 1977, pp. 1–6).

9 See *The Works of Francis Bacon*, eds Spedding, Ellis and Heath (Longman, London, 1858, reprinted Fromann Verlag, Stuttgart, 1963), Vol. 1, pp. 132–33. I owe the connection between Beckett and Kant to a suggestion by Gordon Finlayson.

10 A point also made by P. J. Murphy in 'Beckett and the Philosophers', op. cit., p. 233.

11 ' "This strange institution called literature": an interview with Jacques Derrida', in *Acts of Literature*, ed. D. Attridge (Routledge, London and New York, 1992), p. 60. For a reading of Derrida's references to Beckett in this interview, see Nicholas Royle's *After Derrida* (Manchester University Press, Manchester, 1995), pp. 159–74.

12 Ibid., p. 61.

13 Derrida, *Glas*, trans. J. P. Leavey Jr and R. Rand (Nebraska University Press, Lincoln and London, 1986), p. 204.

14 Ibid., p. 205.

15 Ibid., pp. 130 and 165.

16 Ibid., p. 115.

17 Ibid., p. 105.

18 *Acts of Literature*, op. cit., p. 61.

19 For 'Commitment' and 'Is Art Lighthearted?', see NL 409–30 and 599–606/NTL2 76–94 and 247–53.

20 For the source of the book's dedication to Beckett, see the 'Editors' Epilogue', AT 544/AST 498; for references to Beckett, see the translator's index.

21 See, in particular, Lambert Zuidevaart's account of Adorno's reading of Beckett, 'Paradoxical modernism', in *Adorno's Aesthetic Theory* (MIT Press, Cambridge MA and London, 1991), pp. 150–77.

22 I have modified this and all subsequent quotations from the English translation of *Aesthetic Theory*.

23 For the sake of argument alone, I will accept the extraordinary violence of Adorno's interpretation of what he calls 'existential philosophy', which treats Sartre, Camus, Jaspers and Heidegger as if they were saying the same, which is, of course, massively incorrect.

24 Zuidevaart, *Adorno's Aesthetic Theory*, op. cit., p. 213. However, some initial speculative questions arise here: if, as we saw above, Adorno's claim for Beckett is that he goes beyond existential philosophy by refusing the idealist core of the individual and by materializing the situation of existence, then what is the relation of Adorno's conceptual praxis of aesthetic theory to this materiality? Does it not also by necessity remain a residual idealism, still too philosophical in its refusal of philosophy? Also, might we not perhaps also approach Beckett's work as a conceptual praxis that we could call aesthetic theory, that is, a discourse that is neither art nor philosophy but somehow both at once? If so, then in what might the difference between Adorno's and Beckett's discourse consist?

25 In the light of an extremely interesting and intelligent interpretation of the garden scene at the end of *Molloy* with reference to Epicurus and Voltaire's *Candide*, Nussbaum claims that the goal of Beckett's fiction is *therapeutic*, it is a therapy of desire which tries to cure us of our religious (i.e. Christian) desire for redemption (p. 304). So far, so good. However, Nussbaum then goes on to claim that what lies on the other side of the desire for redemption, for Beckett, is silence (p. 306). Nussbaum puts Beckett in the same therapeutic camp as Lucretius and Nietzsche, the difference being that Beckett's 'pessimism [a word presumably employed in its non-Nietzschean sense, which is rather odd given the context, SC] ... denies a possibility that they hold open' (p. 308). This possibility is presumably that of an aesthetic overcoming of nihilism in the writing of a work, *Zarathustra* say. However, on the reading I am trying to develop here, the status of the work is precisely what Beckett achieves through a conception of form or worklessness, but a work which is a

determinate negation of meaning, a narrative against narrative. The consequence of Nussbaum's reading of Beckett is depressingly familiar (not to mention being pre-Nietzschean), namely, that Beckett's 'search for silence' is a 'nihilism' (p. 308). I will take up the question of Beckett's alleged nihilism in the final section of this lecture.

26 See Deleuze, 'L'épuisé', in *Quad et autres pièces pour la télévision* (Minuit, Paris, 1992), pp. 57–106. There is also a short text on Beckett's *Film* entitled 'Le plus grand film Irlandais' in *Critique et clinique* (Minuit, Paris, 1993), pp. 36–39.

27 Ibid., p. 74.

28 The televisual pieces are *Quad, Ghost Trio, Only the clouds...* and *Nacht und Träume* and can be found in Beckett's *Collected Dramatic Works* (Faber, London, 1986).

29 Deleuze, 'L'épuisé', op. cit., p. 104.

30 Ibid., p. 103.

31 Ibid., p. 103.

32 Ricks, *Beckett's Dying Words* (Oxford University Press, Oxford, 1993), p. 110.

33 This phrase, attributed to Beckett, can be found in Lawrence Harvey's *Samuel Beckett. Poet and Critic* (Princeton University Press, Princeton, 1970), p. 249. The phrase is interestingly deployed in Ricks's *Beckett's Dying Words*, op. cit., p. 82.

34 Zuidervaart, *Adorno's Aesthetic Theory*, op. cit., p. 175.

35 Derrida, *Spectres de Marx* (Galilee, Paris, 1993), p. 96.

36 *Minima Moralia, Gesammelte Schriften*, Band 4, op. cit., p. 281; trans. E. F. N. Jephcott, op. cit., p. 247.

37 Christopher Ricks, *Beckett's Dying Words*, op. cit., see especially chapter IV, pp. 153–203.

In Canto XXXII, those who have committed the sin of treachery are forbidden to cry because the freezing pit of hell turns their tears to ice as soon as they leave their eyes. See *The Divine Comedy. Inferno*, trans. C. S. Singleton (Princeton University Press, Princeton, 1970), p. 340. I owe this reference to Jason Gaiger.

39 For example, 'I know my eyes are open because of the tears that pour from them unceasingly' (T 279); and 'Tears gush from it practically without ceasing, why is not known' (T 331).

40 *Endgame* (Faber, London, 1958), p. 20.

41 *Endgame*, op. cit., p. 35, T 305, T 36; T 152, T 30.

42 Beckett, *Proust and Three Dialogues* (Calder, London, 1949), pp. 8–9.

43 Ricks, *Beckett's Dying Words*, op. cit., p. 20.

44 One might also want to explore a questionable etymological link here between *humour* and the *human*, because it could be claimed that Adorno's interpretation of Beckett in terms of the disintegration of the subject and the liquidation of the individual leaves no place for the *pathos* of a piece like *Endgame*, the way in which the play *moves* us. Two examples:

1 When Hamm asks Clov what his father Nagg is doing, and Clov replies simply 'He's crying' (p. 41);

2 When Clov tells Hamm that 'You know what she died of, Mother Pegg? Of darkness' (p. 48).

These moments of intense and sudden emotion punctuate Beckett – other examples could be given – often coinciding with humour, and move the reader or spectator in a highly pathetic and perhaps all too human way. It is difficult to see what place Adorno might have found for such moments in his analysis. It should be clear that my reading of Beckett on emotion diverges with that given by Nussbaum on the question of emotion ('Narrative Emotions: Beckett's Genealogy of Love', op. cit.). Nussbaum rightly, I think, claims that emotions for Beckett are not natural facts, but social constructs, and they are taught through stories. She also justifiably goes on to assert that Beckett's radical undermining of traditional patterns of narrative entails a critique of the emotions correlated to storytelling. However, she is wrong, I think, to infer from this that Beckett is attempting to divest his readers of their emotionality, 'if stories are learned they can be unlearned. If emotions are constructs, they can be dismantled' (p. 287). First, as I will show in my reading of the *Trilogy*, stories are ineliminable for Beckett. Although the protagonists in Beckett's fiction repeatedly express their dissatisfaction with narrative form, telling stories is their ineluctable fate. Second, the critique of the emotions that is allied to the dissatisfaction with narrative does not, I think, proceed towards an elimination of the emotions, but rather towards a less communally authorized and ritualized sense of pathos, that of the self in its separation from the other and its ever-failing desire for union, for love.

45 And how does one pronounce these names? Are they to be spoken *à la française*, in British English or Irish English? To take the example of Moran, is this to be pronounced with the stress on the first syllable, as in Irish English, on the second syllable, as in British English, or with equal stress on both syllables, as in French?

46 On 'M' and 'W' as names in Beckett, see the following passage from the beautiful late prose piece *Company*, 'Is there anything to add to this esquisse? His unnamability. Even M must go. So W reminds himself of his creature as so far created. W? But W too is a creature. Figment.' (*Nohow On*, Calder, London, 1992, p. 37.)

47 See Declan Kiberd, 'Beckett and the Life to Come', in *Beckett in Dublin* (Lilliput Press, Dublin, 1992), pp. 75–84, see especially p. 82. Incidentally, this lively essay argues the thesis that 'Three hundred years from now, he [i.e. Beckett] will be remembered more for his prose than his plays, and not only because he wrote some of the most beautiful prose of our century, but, more precisely, because he was in such texts a supremely religious artist' (p. 75). Although, given the nature of this claim, there is no way it can be refuted until the year 2292, I think that despite Kiberd's insightful remarks on the possible link between Beckett's drama, the conflict of puritan conscience and what we might call the protestantism of Beckett's theatre (pp. 76, 80, 81), Kiberd remains interestingly wrong, for reasons I will try to spell out in the final section of this lecture.

48 On the figure of symmetry in Beckett, see J. M. Coetzee's 'The Manuscript Revisions of Beckett's *Watt*', in *Doubling the Point. Essays and Interviews*, ed. D. Attwell (Harvard University Press, Cambridge MA, 1992), pp. 39–42.

49 On this nomenclature, Nussbaum claims (swallowing Beckett's psychoanalytic red herrings whole and with some sauce) that Moran's failure to get to Bally or to Hole 'may suggest that he [i.e. Moran] is impotent as well as guilty', 'Narrative Emotions: Beckett's Genealogy of Love', op. cit., p. 301. Despite the undoubted felicities offered by a psychoanalytic interpretation of *Molloy*, I find Nussbaum's use of psychoanalytic categories a little too easy and fluent (the object of guilt is 'parental sexual act' (p. 298), the object of disgust is 'above all the female body' (p. 299)). What does it mean to employ such interpretative categories in relation to a literary text of such theoretical self-consciousness as Beckett's? There is, I feel, the danger of a *hermeneutic literalism* here, which is also revealed when Nussbaum claims, mysteriously, that Beckett identifies Moran as the writer of all the novels in the *Trilogy* – 'he [i.e. Moran] identifies himself as the author of this entire novel and of Beckett's other novels' (p. 303). The claim is repeated on p. 308, a claim that can be refuted with reference to T 299: 'I am neither, I needn't say, Murphy, nor Watt, nor Mercier, nor – no, I can't even bring myself to name them'.

50 This might be connected with the opening lines of the late prose piece *Ill Seen Ill Said* (*Nohow On*, op. cit., p. 7), 'From where she lies she sees Venus rise'. A possible source for the reference to Cythera might be Baudelaire's distopic vision in 'Un Voyage à Cythère', *Les Fleurs du mal*, *Oeuvres Complètes*, Vol. 1 (Gallimard, Paris, 1975), pp. 117–19.

51 Christopher Ricks, *Beckett's Dying Words*, op. cit., p. 115.

52 *Endgame*, op. cit., p. 21.

53 Ibid., p. 35.

54 Beckett, *Collected Dramatic Works*, op. cit., pp. 351–57. The phrase can be found in T 168, 170, 176, 178, 201, 213, 214, 218, 226, 229, 254, 268, 353.

55 On the figure of aporia, see Hill, op. cit., pp. 63–64.

56 Cf. T 274, 278, 318, 321, 334, 338.

57 On repetition in the *Trilogy*, see the wonderfully detailed essay by Rubin Rabinowitz, 'Repetition and Underlying Meanings in Samuel Beckett's *Trilogy*', in *Rethinking Beckett*, eds L. St John Butler and R. J. Davis (Macmillan, London, 1990), pp. 31–67. See also Rabinowitz's *The Development of Samuel Beckett's Fiction* (University of Illinois Press, Chicago, 1984); Steven Connor, *Samuel Beckett: Repetition, Theory and Text* (Blackwell, Oxford, 1988); Hill, op. cit., pp. 66–68. Repetition is obviously also central to Beckett's later fictions, in a text like *Lessness* (1969), which contains 1,538 words, where words 770–1,538 repeat, in a different variation, words 1–769. On precisely this point see J. M. Coetzee's 'Samuel Beckett and the Temptations of Style', *Doubling the Point*, op. cit., pp. 45 and 49.

58 *Krapp's Last Tape* (Faber, London, 1959), p. 18.

59 Perhaps. For nothing is the end of the line in Beckett, the line of writing stretches on interminably – *pour finir encore*. On this question of ending and beginning, it would

be a question of reading *The Unnameable* together with Beckett's final novel, *Comment c'est* (Gallimard, Paris, 1961), a title which, in French, is at least a possible quadruple pun on the verb 'to begin' – *comment c'est* (how it is), the infinitive (*commencer*), the imperative (*commencez!*) and past participle (*commencé*). Thus, even at the end of *The Unnameable*, one re-commences with a further dissolution of narrative form in the punctuationless prose blocks of *Comment c'est*, where a crouched figure murmurs in the mud, its tongue lolling out.

60 For other remarks on storytelling in *The Unnameable*, see T 299, 354, 374, 381–82.

61 Although, to qualify the implied teleology of my reading of Beckett here, I am not claiming that the syntax of weakness is absent from other parts of the *Trilogy*, only that it is presented in *The Unnameable* in a more extreme fashion. Indeed, if one re-reads the opening pages of *Molloy* in the light of the quasi-method of aporetics, it becomes increasingly difficult to sustain a simple teleological reading of the *Trilogy*. For example, the opening paragraph of *Molloy* contains four uses of 'perhaps', five uses of 'apparently' and six uses of 'I don't know'! On the problems involved in teleological readings of Beckett, see my remarks on Deleuze and Nussbaum.

62 Ricks, *Beckett's Dying Words*, op. cit., p. 83.

63 Ibid., pp. 190–91.

64 Ibid., pp. 202–3 and T 177.

65 Ibid., p. 193.

66 Ibid., p. 8.

67 Ibid., p. 199.

68 Ibid., p. 201.

69 'Où maintenant? Qui maintenant?', essentially a review of the *Trilogy*, first appeared in *La Nouvelle Revue Française*, No. 10 (1953), pp. 678–86 and was reprinted in *Le Livre à venir* (LV 308–13) with some significant but minor changes, mainly deletions. An English translation by Sacha Rabinowitch, under the title 'Where Now? Who Now?', appeared in *The Sirens' Song: Selected Essays by Maurice Blanchot*, ed. G. Josipovici (Harvester, Brighton, 1982). 'Les paroles doivent cheminer longtemps', an *entretien* on Beckett's *Comment c'est*, first appeared under the title 'Notre épopée', in *La Nouvelle Revue Française*, No. 100 (1961), pp. 690–98 and was reprinted with very minor alterations in *L'entretien infini* (EI 478–86).

70 Obviously, in Beckett's case, this residuum has been extensively documented by Deirdre Bair in *Samuel Beckett: A Biography* (Jonathan Cape, London, 1978).

71 On the possible significance of terms such as 'plop' and 'ping' in Beckett, see J. M. Coetzee's 'Samuel Beckett and the Temptations of Style', in *Doubling the Point*, op. cit., pp. 43–49. Coetzee reads these terms as an 'editorial metalanguage . . . that repeatedly fractures the surface of the fiction', and which has 'evacuated itself of lexical content' (p. 45). This partially confirms his contestable thesis that, in his later fictions such as *Ping* and *Lessness*, Beckett marches 'with eyes open into the prison of style' (p. 49). But why should style be a prison? If style is redescribed in terms of form or worklessness, then might it not, on the contrary, be some kind of liberation, however formal or workless?

72 Although the main reference is to 'the murmur in the mud' in *Comment c'est*, references to murmuring can already be found in *The Unnameable*, initially to describe the voiceless noise emitted by Worm (T 310, 323, 351, 375, 376, 381).

73 See T 292, 315, 319, 326, 355, 369, 370, 371–72, 373, 374, 375, 380, 381.

74 There is an almost amusing moment in Blanchot's obituary for Beckett in *Critique* ('Oh tout finir', in Vol. XLVI, No. 519–20, August/September 1990, pp. 635–37; trans. L. Hill in *The Blanchot Reader*, op. cit., pp. 298–300), when he writes, 'In the eulogies that have been respectfully delivered in order to mark his (i.e. Beckett's) passing, the great works of the age have been evoked, Proust, Joyce, Musil and even Kafka'. For readers of Blanchot, it is this 'and even Kafka' that is so revealing.

75 Cf. J. M. Coetzee, 'Samuel Beckett and the Temptations of Style', in *Doubling the Point. Essays and Interviews*, op. cit., p. 49.

76 ED 185. On the themes of insomnia, sleep and the night in Beckett and Blanchot, see Deleuze's reading of Beckett; he writes, 'In the insomniac dream, it is not a question of realizing the impossible, but of exhausting the possible'. *'L'épuisé'*, op. cit., pp. 100–1.

77 Faber, London, 1973.

78 Possible precursors for the two characters in the cast of *Not I* – 'Auditor' and 'Mouth' – might be found in *Malone Dies*, 'the raising of the arms and going down, without further splash, even though it may annoy the bathers' (T 254); and in *The Unnameable*:

> Evoke at painful junctures, when discouragement threatens to raise its head, the image of a vast mouth, red, blubber and slobbering, in solitary confinement, extruding indefatigably, with a noise of wet kisses the washing in a tub, the words that obstruct it.
>
> (T 359)

On the connection between *Not I* and *The Unnameable*, see James Knowlson and John Pilling, *Frescoes of the Skull* (Calder, London, 1979), p. 197.

79 See T 189, 190, 325, 332, 345, 357.

80 Op. cit., p. 58.

81 J. M. Bernstein, 'Philosophy's Refuge: Adorno in Beckett', in *Philosophers' Poets*, op. cit., p. 184.

82 Ibid., p. 185.

83 Cited by Bernstein, p. 184.

84 Ibid., p. 185.

85 A similar formulation, although employed with precisely the opposite intention to my own, can be found in Nussbaum's essay on Beckett, 'We can be redeemed only by ending the demand for redemption, by ceasing to use the concepts of redemption' ('Narrative emotions: Beckett's genealogy of love', op. cit., p. 305). Nussbaum detects 'a deeply religious sensibility' at work in Beckett, a claim with which I do not disagree because it is what gives gravity to his engagement with nihilism. However, Nussbaum goes on from this to claim, completely counter-intuitively to my mind,

'the complete absence in this writing (i.e. Beckett's) of any joy in the limited and finite indicates to us that the narrative as a whole is an expression of a religious view of life' (p. 309). I trust that my discussion above of Beckett's laughter at the very least complicates Nussbaum's view. The cruel power of Beckett's humour exhibits a *joyous* relation to finitude, a celebration of human limitedness that is replete with sardonic, side-splittingly anti-depressant comedy. J. M. Coetzee gets this just about right in a remark on Beckett given in an interview:

> Beckett's prose, up to and including *The Unnameable*, has given me a *sensuous delight* that hasn't dimmed over the years. The critical work I did on Beckett originated in that sensuous response, and was a grasping after ways in which to talk about it: to talk about delight.
>
> (*Doubling the Point*, op. cit., p. 20)

On Nussbaum's interpretation, Beckett's alleged religiosity is also anti-social and anti-political: his religious 'despair' (p. 310) is trapped by the 'longing for the pure soul, hard as a diamond' (p. 310). Doubtless, from the purportedly factual (but actually idealized) perspective of Nussbaum's neo-Aristotelianism, where 'literary form and human content are inseparable' (p. 289 – How, I ask, is aesthetic modernity understandable on the basis of such inseparability?), Beckett's relentless negations of meaning appear anti-social and anti-political. But, recalling arguments stated above with reference to Adorno, I would claim that it is precisely in their abstention from political engagement that Beckett's work points towards 'the creation of a just life'. In a passage from *Aesthetic Theory*, whose Hellenistic irony would not be lost on Nussbaum, Adorno writes, 'The Greek military junta knew why it banned Beckett's plays, in which there is not one political word. Asociality becomes the social legitimation of art' (AT 348/AST 333).

86 'A Piece of Monologue', in *Three Occasional Pieces* (Faber, London, 1982), p. 12.

87 I am thinking of the way in which the word 'imagine' is employed as a refrain in *Not I*, but also as the first line and leitmotif of Beckett's *Company*: 'A voice comes to one in the dark. Imagine' (*Nohow On*, op. cit., p. 5).

88 *Endgame*, op. cit., p. 44.

89 *Ill Seen Ill Said*, in *Nohow On*, op. cit., pp. 96–97.

Acknowledgements

Although the use of the lecture format in this book is something of an organizing fiction, all of the texts have an occasional and oral origin.

Lecture 1 began as a paper for a conference on Blanchot at the Architectural Association, London, in January 1993, and Section (g) was given as a paper at a conference on Levinas at Loyola University, Chicago, in May 1993. The whole lecture was subsequently presented in three sessions at the Philosophy Faculty, University of Nijmegen, in February 1995. Section (e) was presented as a paper at a Doctoral Seminar in Philosophy at the Université de Paris XII (Créteil) in March 1995 and at the Nordic Summer School in Comparative Literature in Helsingør in June 1995. Thanks to Carolyn Gill, Adriaan Peperzak, Philippe Van Haute, Michel Haar and Arne Melberg.

Lecture 2 began in a conference organized around Stanley Cavell's visit to the University of Essex in February 1994. It was subsequently extended and presented as the 1994 Philosophy and Literature Lectures at Notre Dame University. Parts of the lecture were subsequently presented at the Universities of Stirling, Stockholm, Penn State, Vanderbilt and Brigham Young. Thanks to Stephen Mulhall, Gerald Bruns and the English faculty at Notre Dame, Nicholas Royle, Hans Ruin, Charles Scott, John Sallis and James Faulconer.

Lecture 3 was initially presented to a conference on the twentieth anniversary of the Comparative Literature Department at the University of Bergen in January 1995, and subsequently at the Slade School for Fine Art, and the University of Stockholm in 1995. Thanks to Atle Kittang, Per Buvik, Michael Newman and Roland Lyssel.

The argument of the Preamble was sketched in a presentation to the Research

School in Philosophy, Tilburg University, in February 1995. It was developed at a conference on nihilism at the University of Warwick in November 1995, and at the Architectural Association and the Critical Theory Seminar, University of Nottingham, in 1996. Thanks to Gido Berns, Keith Ansell-Pearson, Mark Cousins and Jon Simons.

However, these lectures began as teaching in graduate courses and reading groups in the Philosophy Department, University of Essex. Of particular importance was a research seminar on Beckett, Adorno and nihilism in Summer Term 1995, and I would like to thank Iain MacDonald, Jason Gaiger, Coryn Smethurst, Pat Upton and Tim Diggins for their participation. I would also like to thank Stephen Mulhall for introducing me to Stanley Cavell's work, and Jay Bernstein, who alone will be able to recognize the extent of my debt to our many discussions over the years.

The writing of the Preamble and Lecture 3, as well as the organization of the entire text, was undertaken during stays in Stockholm and I would like to thank the Kungliga Biblioteket for the use of their facilities. Something much more than gratitude is due to Cecilia Sjöholm.

Thanks to Jamie Thompson and Shizuka Yokomizo, former MA students in Fine Art at Goldsmiths College London, for their collaboration and for allowing me to use their images. Thanks to Andrew Benjamin for his constant enthusiasm and helpful encouragement for this project. Finally, thanks to Tony Bruce, Adrian Driscoll and Olivia Eccleshall at Routledge for their patience, care and diligence in the production of this book.

An earlier version of Lecture 1 was published under the title 'Il y a: A dying stronger than death (Blanchot with Levinas)', Oxford Literary Review, Vol. 15, 1993, pp. 81–131. The final section of this lecture (g) appeared as 'Il y a: Putting Levinas's hand to Blanchot's fire', in Maurice Blanchot: The Demand of Writing, Carolyn Gill (ed.), (Routledge, London and New York, 1996), pp. 108–22.

Index

redemption: Adorno on 18–24
religion: romanticism and 193n
religious disappointment: death of God *see*
  God; and problem of meaning 2, 3, 24
revolution: nihilism and 11–12, 51, 52,
  61; as realization of absolute freedom
  50–1; writing and 47, 50–2, *see also*
  French Revolution; terrorism
Ricks, Christopher: on Beckett 154, 157,
  159, 164, 169–71, 178, 186n
Rilke, Rainer Maria 41, 103–4
Rimbaud, Arthur 37, 41, 57
romanticism: Cavell and 117–38, *see also*
  Cavell, Stanley; of punk 99; religion
  and 193n; unworked 28, 97, *see also*
  Jena Romanticism
romantic modernity 96–7
Rorty, Richard 12, 98, 130
Rosenzweig, Franz 92
Rousseauism 91
Royle, Nicholas 199n
Russian anarchism 5, 8
Russian nihilism 5–6; Nietzsche on 8, *see*
  also nihilism

sacrifice of the artwork 38–9, 44, 45
Sade, Marquis de: Blanchot on 51–2, 54,
  61, 92; on God 67; rape fantasy in 52
sadism: dialectics and 53, 60; writing and
  51–2
Sartre, Jean-Paul 5; *Saint Genet* 146
Savage, Jon 99, *see also* punk
scepticism: Cavell on 132–7; Heidegger
  on 133; Wittgenstein on 132–3
Schelling, Friedrich von 87, 89
Schlageter, Albert Leo 184n
Schlegel, August Wilhelm 94, 191n
Schlegel, Caroline 192n
Schlegel, Friedrich 33, 85, 94;
  community 108; definition of a project
  110; fragments 97, 106, 108, 109,
  110–11; on French Revolution 113;
  Hegel on 95–6; infinite reflection

86–7; on irony 114–15, 136; on Kant
113; on the novel 33, 87, 105; on
poetry 86, 87, 110–11; on suicide 69;
unification of poetry and philosophy
123, 124; on wit 112–13, 136, 137, *see*
  also Jena Romanticism
Schleiermacher, Friedrich 89
Schmitt, Carl: on romanticism 92–4,
  95–6
Screech, M. A. 192n
Sex Pistols: Situationism of 99, *see also*
  McLaren, Malcolm; punk
silence: Becket and 152–4; of solitude 37
Situationists 91; punk and 11, 99;
  recuperation 98; Sex Pistols 99;
  Situationist International 11, 99
Sjöholm, Cecilia 185n
solitude: Blanchot on 37, 41; dread and
  37, *see also* dread; essential 41; silence
  of 37
Stevens, Wallace 28; definition of poetry
  99–100; on imagination 98–105; the
  necessary angel 103; plain sense of
  things 101; the pressure of reality 98;
  the task of the poetry 101–2
Stirner, Max 4–5
St John Butler, Lance 197n, 202n
suicide 25; aim of 70; bad faith of 71–2;
  Blanchot on 32, 68–70, 74;
  Dostoevsky on 5, 25; impossibility of
  74; logical 5, 6, 25, 69, *see also* death
surrealism: Blanchot and 36, 39
Swift, Jonathan 60
Szondi, Peter 112, 117

Taylor, Charles 134, 193n
terrorism 11; literary 51, 52, 61, *see also*
  revolution
Thatcherism: as bastard progeny of
  nihilism 99
Thoreau, Henry David 123–4, 125, 126,
  130, 135
Turgenev, Ivan: *Fathers and Sons* 5–6